SHOOTING
from the HIP

THE
PAT SPILLANE
STORY

PAT SPILLANE
and SEAN McGOLDRICK

Published in Ireland by
Storm Books
(a division of Sportcom Ltd.)
28 Windsor Park,
Monkstown
Co. Dublin

Copyright Storm Books 1998
ISBN 1 901055 01 9

Printed by Colorprint Ltd, Dublin, Ireland.

All rights reserved. No part of this publication may be copied,
reproduced or transmitted in any form without permission of the
publishers.

For my brothers Mike and Tommy, my sister Margaret and especially, my mother Maura, for helping me realise all my football dreams.
For my wife Rosarii, daughters Cara and Shóna, son
Pat (junior) for proving there is an even better life after football.

CONTENTS

Acknowledgements.. vii

1. End Game.. 1

2. A Born Footballer............................... 13

3. The Early Years................................. 21

4. Dreams Fulfilled................................ 31

5. Double Trouble.................................. 41

6. Back on the Summit............................. 49

7. The Spillane Family............................. 59

8. Foreign Fields.................................. 69

9. Thomond College................................ 89

10. The Glory Years................................ 101

11. Christ, We Were Close to the Five in a Row   109

12. Wounded Knee.................................. 119

13. The Golden Years.............................. 129

14. End of an Era................................. 141

15. Down Under.................................... 149

16. What Made Kerry Great......................... 159

17. Simply the Best............................... 169

18. Templenoe.................................... 179

19. Life after Football........................... 193

20. The GAA in the 21st Century................... 205

21. All Time Teams................................ 219

22. For the Record................................ 231

ACKNOWLEDGEMENTS

The Denims and Diamonds nightclub in the basement of New York's Lexington Hotel was where this book was conceived. A group of us were celebrating Kerry's win over Cavan in the National Football League last October. At the unearthly hour of 2 am the only sober person in the party, Sean McGoldrick asked me whether I ever planned to write my biography. He offered to help. Having seen the finished product I'm glad I accepted his help.

I want to thank Sean for all his hard work and patience in bringing the project to fruition - particularly his achievement in being able to pack all my ramblings into a single volume.

Without the help of many people this book would never have seen the light of day. Thanks to the Bank of Ireland for their generous sponsorship, to Donal Keenan and Storm Books for publishing the book and to everybody who supplied pictures.

Thanks to my club Templenoe for providing me with a mountain of memories and friends. Thanks to all those people who helped in my development as a footballer, particularly the mentors of Templenoe; the GAA trainers at St Brendan's College, Killarney, Dave Weldrick and last, but by no means least, the master himself Mick O'Dwyer.

When my father died in 1964 it left a very big void in our family. Thanks to all my uncles, aunts, relatives and neighbours who rallied to the cause during those difficult years and, in particular, my uncle Gene who nurtured my love of sport.

During my playing career with Kerry I had to get a lot of time off work. For their co-operation and understanding I thank Matt Kingston, the principal and Noreen Deasy, the vice-principal of St Góban's College Bandon, as well as the staff for their patience and help over the years.

Retiring from top level football can be a traumatic experience. Luckily for me the Sunday World and RTE provided me with an opportunity to continue to be indirectly involved in the game I love as a commentator/analyst and journalist. For giving me this golden chance I thank the late Peter O'Neill, Pat Quigley, Michael Brophy and Colm McGinty in the Sunday World while in RTE Tim O'Connor, Maurice Reidy and Bill Lawlor showed great faith in me, although at times I probably gave them a few sleepless nights.

Thanks also to all who helped me recover from my knee injury. In particular the surgeon Mr Dandy who performed the operation in Cambridge, physiotherapist Amy Johnson in Dublin, Mr Brian Hurson in the Blackrock Clinic, Dr Con Murphy in Cork and last but by no means least, the Kerry team physiotherapist Claire Edwards for her endless hours of care.

I hope this books reflects my character. I'm not a complicated person. What you see is what you get and I have never been afraid to speak my mind. Hopefully you will get as much enjoyment from reading *Shooting from the Hip* as I got in compiling it.

Pat Spillane, October 1998

END GAME

THE long shrill on Tommy Howard's whistle signalled the end of the 1991 All-Ireland semi-final. As the Down fans raced onto the pitch I stood still for a few seconds and gazed around at the forty thousand spectators. I drank in the atmosphere one last time. Fleetingly the memories of my great days in Croke Park came flooding back. Although I was sad to be leaving the stage I had no regrets. I had a good innings.

It was both a memorable and sad occasion. It was memorable in the sense I knew I could now bow out of inter-county football on my own terms. It was sad because it was my last ever game at headquarters. A romance which began when I was a teenager was coming to an end.

Nearly two decades of my life had centred around this patch of land in Dublin's north inner-city. I had won eight All-Ireland medals here, been a hero and sometimes a villian. The lad from Templenoe had become a public figure, part of the football team most described as the greatest of all time. Not the team that had lost this game, I might add. This was the dying ember and my spark as a Kerry player was about to be extinguished.

I spent the last twenty minutes of my Kerry career at full-forward. I could have sat down in an armchair because with Kerry persisting with a short passing, running game I saw virtually none of the ball.

I officially announced my retirement from inter-county football in October 1991. Quite honestly had anybody invited me back for the 1992 season I probably would have accepted the invitation.

The Kerry Supporters' Club made me a presentation. But there was no 'thank you' from the County Board and I could count the number of people on one hand who either wrote or telephoned me to wish me well in my retirement. As they say, eaten bread is soon forgotten. My other disappointment was I didn't win an All Star award in 1991.

It was typical of the scheme's inconsistent selection policies. On one or two occasions I was very lucky to get an All Star award. But now, when I believed I deserved one, I was left out. Even though we knocked the holders out of the championship and won the Munster title there was no Kerry player honoured in 1991.

The wisdom of my decision to retire was brought home to me the following July as I watched Clare inflict a shock defeat on Kerry in the Munster final. I was disappointed Kerry lost but I knew I made the right decision to retire the previous October. The loss also ended the managerial career of Mickey O'Sullivan, who had taken over from Mick O'Dwyer in the autumn in 1989.

Regardless of who took over from Mick O'Dwyer, he was on a hiding to nothing. It was worse than succeeding Jack Charlton as Republic of Ireland soccer manager. At the end of the day, Ireland won none of the game's big prizes under Charlton, whereas Micko guided Kerry to eight All-Ireland titles and eleven Munster crowns. The new Kerry boss would be compared with his predecessor and there was simply no way he was going to emulate O'Dwyer's achievements.

The poisoned chalice passed to my neighbour Mickey O'Sullivan, better known as Mickey Ned. Mickey was an absolute gentleman, a teacher, successful businessman and a deep thinker on Gaelic football. He had two significant failings as a manager. He experienced problems translating his excellent theories on Gaelic football into practice and he wasn't authoritative enough. I believe he allowed himself to be dictated to and overruled by his fellow selectors. This quirk in the new management set-up was to have serious consequences for me.

The closest my club Templenoe came to winning a major prize was in 1989, when we reached the Kerry Intermediate championship final which we lost to Dingle. However, I was very happy with my own form at the time. A few days after the final I was on my 11 o'clock tea break in St Góban's College in Bantry when I got a telephone call from the new Kerry manager. Mickey said that the selectors had reluctantly decided I wouldn't be a member of the Kerry squad for the 1989-90 National League campaign.

This news was like a bolt out of the blue. I was so shocked I couldn't talk to him. I just left down the phone and sprinted out of the staff room. I went into my PE room, sat down and cried my eyes out. I was emotional about football but this was the first time I cried about it. Eventually I gathered myself together and went back into the staff room and picked up a newspaper. I will never forget the picture on the front page. It showed a little girl, confined to a wheelchair as the result of an accident.

Just looking at the picture forced me to put my own life in perspective. Up until then it revolved almost exclusively around football. For the first time ever in my life I realised that, in the bigger scheme of things, football was almost trivial. Looking at that girl helped me to get my priorities right. I was a newly married man, in good health, enjoyed my work and was financially secure. Being dropped from the Kerry squad wasn't the end of the world. But I wasn't prepared to just fade away quietly.

I had a physical education class soon afterwards and, given my mood, I was tempted to stay inside and give the students a free period. Instead, I togged out and went outside to the playing field for a training session with the young lads. Out on the field, I decided nobody was going to tell me when I was retiring from inter-county football . I would go on my terms, not when somebody told me my time was up.

I resolved to make even more sacrifices. I would train even harder and force the selectors to bring me back. I believe Mickey O'Sullivan wanted me on the squad, but there were three other selectors who consistently voted against me. So I usually ended up on the wrong side of a 3-2 vote. I trained hard during the winter of 1989 even though I wasn't a member of the county squad. Mickey came to see me in action in the first round of the county league in early 1990. I scored 12 points from play against Derrynane and gave an equally impressive performance in my second match. Word was out in Kerry about how well I was playing.

Evidently Mickey persuaded at least two of his fellow selectors to have a rethink and I was recalled, but I still found some residue of resentment from a number of the selectors. Mickey's training sessions were completely different from what I was used to under O'Dwyer. Predictably, the new manager wanted to bring his own ideas to the job and was anxious to build his own team.

But, in pursuit of this policy, he made the mistake of getting rid of too many of the players from the 1975-1986 era straight away. He brought a lot of youngsters into the squad, but no young team has won an All-Ireland at the first attempt. Wise heads are needed in a young team. For instance, Pa Laide, who won an All Star last year, played championship football for Kerry before he played for Austin Stacks in the Kerry club championships. The experience destroyed his confidence for a long time.

At times Mickey's training sessions lasted up to two and half hours, which was far too long. They were fine in theory, we used cones, bollards and bibs and concentrated on building up skills and working out tactics. But there wasn't enough emphasis on pure physical training. My first comeback game was against Tipperary in a challenge game. Mickey emphasised to me, over and over again, the two reasons why I was dropped from the Kerry squad (a) I was giving out too much to the young players which was shattering their confidence (b) I had become an individualist on the field and wasn't prepared to bring the other forwards into the play.

I was certainly guilty on all counts as regards giving out to players and, indeed, referees. It was one of my big failings on the field: I could never shut-up. I was so passionate about the game that I couldn't tolerate mistakes being made, either by myself or my colleagues. I had no problem if people criticised me but, I suppose, everybody is not as thick skinned as I am. I accept that at times I made life hell for my fellow forwards, particularly at club level. I was forever giving out. However, I didn't accept the idea that I had become an individualist. I was probably guilty of having a 'go on my own style' between 1975 and 1977 but I developed into a team player afterwards. In the twilight of my career in 1990 I was more than willing to bring my colleagues into the game.

We beat Tipperary and I felt my performance justified my recall. I was very conscious of what my new boss told me before the match. So when I got the ball in a scoring position I was looking around for a colleague to pass it to!

Mickey introduced lots of new ideas. Early in 1990 he decided we needed to bond better as a group. He told us one night we were going away for a weekend but didn't reveal the destination. Our only instruction was to assemble in Killorglin for a training session and bring our overnight bags. My wife turned me out in my best finery in anticipation of a relaxing weekend in some hotel. We got a rude awakening when we headed out of Killorglin. We drove to the foothills of Carrantuohill, the highest mountain in Ireland. Half way up the mountain we reached our destination, Cappanalea, an outdoor pursuit centre.

Although our meals were prepared for us, we had to set the tables and wash the dishes afterwards. This was a serious shock to the system of the older guys who were more accustomed to the luxury of five star hotels in far flung places such as Sydney, San Francisco and Hawaii. As Bomber Liston dried the plates he reckoned he had reached the lowest point in his Kerry career. After dinner we did a series of exercises which are now all the rage with stressed out executives and captains of industry. Just picture the scene. Here was I dressed in my good clothes perched on the side of a windswept mountain being asked to get across an eight foot high tarpaulin with the aid of three poles and a rope.

I might have won eight All-Ireland medals but they were of little use to me in this situation. The squad was divided into four groups and thankfully one of our group was a former scout who knew how to tackle these idiotic tasks. Another exercise involved carrying a big telegraph pole through an obstacle course which consisted of ditches, briars and plenty of muck. Hanging from the pole were balloons filled with water. The object of the exercise was to complete the course bursting as few balloons as possible.

Our exploits were videoed and the highlights were shown

to us during the build-up to the Munster final later that year. During the weekend there was an analysis of how we performed in previous matches and we were rated. I was given seven out of ten for my performance against Tipperary.

We slept in dormitories and obviously there was no drink available. However, one player must have had a premonition of what was in store because he smuggled a bottle of whiskey into the dormitory and had a bit of a party. Typical of my luck, I was sleeping in another dormitory and missed it. Before we left, each player received a handout detailing what was expected off them in the coming months. I was given three instructions:

(a) Do not talk to the Press (b) Pass the Ball and (c) Do not give out.

Throughout that spring I tried to follow these instructions. I lined out at full forward in the semi-final of the Munster championship against Clare in Listowel. We won by 13 points (1-23; 0-13) but I failed to score and my shooting left a lot to be desired. In his match report in the *Irish Press* the following day, Gerry McCarthy alluded to this: 'Sadly it must go on record that his accuracy left much to be desired.' Still, I felt I had done enough to hold my place. But the selectors thought otherwise and I was replaced by Eoin Liston for the final. Kerry fielded nine of the team which lost to Cork in 1989 but only four of the 'old guard'- Charlie Nelligan, Ambrose O'Donovan, Liston and my brother, Tommy.

I was really pissed off at being dropped and so made absolutely no contribution to the build-up. I honestly felt I was good enough to be selected. From the moment the team was announced until the day of the match I sulked; I should have been encouraging the younger lads.

In line with his emphasis on new ideas, Mickey changed our traditional pre-match arrangements for Munster finals in Cork. Up until 1990 we always drove to Cork on the morning of the match and met in the Imperial Hotel around noon. After tea and sandwiches we headed down to the ground. This time around we travelled to Cork the evening before. The Saturday night before the 1990 Munster football final was one of the most famous occasions in Irish sport - Ireland played Italy in the quarter-finals of the World Cup.

Everything looked rosy when we arrived at our hotel on the outskirts of Cork city. We checked in, had our meal, watched the match and headed for bed. Then the fun started. Not alone was there a World Cup party in the hotel there was also a wedding reception.

The noise from the two parties was deafening. Two o'clock, three o'clock, four o'clock. The decibel level remained the same. There was complete bedlam and it was simply impossible to sleep. I remember going down to the lobby in my pyjamas at some stage but all the staff seemed to have disappeared into thin air. By now news had spread that the Kerry team were staying the night and the party goers appeared intent on ensuring that we got as little sleep as possible. Chants of Jacko is a W.... rang though the building. A sure sign that I was a forgotten man in Gaelic football was the fact that my name was never mentioned.

Those of us in rooms at the front of the hotel got virtually no sleep. Players staying near the back of the hotel fared better, at least until about five o'clock when the revellers decided to go around to an outdoor pool and wake up everybody. So you can imagine the state this young Kerry team were in for a Munster final against the reigning All-Ireland champions.

Mickey had earmarked our team captain Joe Shannon from Laune Rangers, to do a man marking job on Larry Tompkins. Within fifteen minutes of the start Larry had four points on the board and by half-time we were being routed. I replaced Shannon fifteen minutes before the break. I was on a hiding to nothing because the game was well beyond us at this stage. I was still highly motivated because I wanted to prove to the selectors how wrong they were to drop me.

I played very well for the 40 minutes I was on the field. I scored two points and I was probably Kerry's best player along with Jacko. We lost by 15 points in the end (2-23 to 1-11) but I still wasn't ready to throw in the towel. Having proved the selectors' wrong, I felt I deserved a chance to bow out on my own terms.

There is no escaping the fact we were annihilated by Cork. It was one of the worst defeats ever suffered by a Kerry team in a Munster final. The policies Mickey and his selectors insisted on using had backfired. The young lads we used were not able to cope mentally, physically or in football terms with Cork, who were the best team in the country at the time. My only consolation was I felt I played well enough to earn my place in the squad for the league in the autumn. Lo and behold, I got another phone call from Mickey in October. The message was the same as it was twelve months previously. I was told that myself, Jacko and Charlie Nelligan were been rested for the league.

Given that one of the Kerry selectors, Dave Geaney, was from Castleisland the home club of Charlie, I never thought there was much likelihood of Charlie been kicked off the panel. The shock appointment of Mick O'Dwyer as manager of Kildare rescued Jacko. At the time there were real fears in Kerry that if Jacko was dropped he would jump ship and declare for Kildare. After all, he lived in Leixlip and played his club football in the county for many years.

So when the Kerry panel for the National League campaign of 1990-1991 was announced, the only notable absentee was Pat Spillane. I was back to square one again. It was time to take stock. I was 35 and had eight All-Ireland medals in my back pocket. Was I going to pack it in or give it another go? One factor which influenced my decision was my positive outlook. I absolutely hated losing, be it an All-Ireland final, a club challenge game or the toss of a coin.

I suppose the other factor which swung my decision was that I'm half mad. I'm fanatical about Gaelic football. Whereas I would be hard pressed to remember my wedding anniversary or the dates of my childrens' birthdays, I can reel off all the important dates in my football career without the slightest hesitation. This streak of football madness motivated me to give it one last go.

So I resolved to train even harder still during the winter of

1990-91. From October to the following March I trained at least 12 times a week. My only day of rest was Sunday. Why did I punish myself so much? I suppose deep down, I wanted to turn the clock back. But at the time my aim was to try and finish my career on a high note and watch my 'friends', the Kerry selectors, eat more humble pie.

At times I trained three times a day. This included going for a run when I had a free class during school hours. When I arrived home I went straight for the weights machine in the garage and worked out there for half an hour. Afterwards I sometimes headed down to a muddy field below our house. There was a hill in the field about 50 yards long. I ran up the hill between fifteen and twenty times with ankle weights fitted to my feet. I recently saw a photograph of myself taken during that winter and I looked like one of those ultra distance runners. There wasn't a spare ounce of flesh on me. I was unbelievably fit and, like the previous year, I was playing excellent club football. Once again the selectors relented - one of the three who had consistently voted against me changed his mind - and I was recalled to the squad.

I made my competitive comeback in the quarter-final of the National League in Croke Park. And guess who was plotting Kerry's downfall - our ex-manager, Mick O'Dwyer. In his first season in charge he had guided the Lily Whites into the play-offs. I marked my return by scoring three points but we lost (1-7; 0-9).

The 1991 Munster championship was the inaugural year of a new-look series. After years of campaigning, Clare's Noel Walsh finally persuaded the Munster Council to have an Open Draw. This meant Kerry and Cork were no longer seeded in different halves of the competition. In the very first draw we were drawn in the same half as Cork. Our first championship match was against Clare in Ennis. Traditionally Clare were pushovers - but not in 1991. Now under the management of John Maughan, they were fit, committed, well organised and disciplined. They no longer feared Kerry.

I lined out at left corner-forward but I got little change from Seamus Clancy. Knowing the attitude of some of the

Kerry selectors I'm sure they were thinking about taking me off. Instead I was switched to centre-forward. Even though I wasn't familiar with the position I decided to take the game by the scruff of the neck and roamed all over the field. We eventually saw off the Clare challenge on a 5-16 to 2-12 scoreline.

I held my place at centre-forward for the Munster semi-final in Killarney against Cork. They were seeking their fifth Munster title in a row and a hat-trick of All-Ireland crowns.Having demolished us the year before they were raging hot favourites. By now our training methods had changed somewhat. The sessions were shorter and we were playing a lot more football during them.

The day before the game - remember it wasn't a final - we had a team meeting. For the first time since his appointment Mickey did not dominate it. He allowed the older guys like myself and Jacko to have our say. It was very emotional. Jacko and myself got a chance to explain to the younger lads what it was like to beat Cork and what was required if we were to achieve our goal. Leaving the dressing room that evening I knew we were in the right frame of mind to beat Cork. Overall we were a slightly better team than in 1990 and we were certainly more united and motivated this time around.

Before the match the Cork fans give us a hard time describing us as old men. They were particularly hard on Jacko and his rapidly receding hairline. The tactics we used that day evolved between myself, Jacko and Maurice Fitzgerald on the field. Mickey hadn't imposed any particular game-plan on us so we didn't feel restricted in any way. We caught Cork on the hop and won by two points (1-10 to 0-11).

It was probably my sweetest ever victory over Cork in championship football. I gave an outstanding performance and won the Man of the Match award. I basked in the glory of it all, even when those selectors who had done their utmost to end my career during the previous two years came up and clapped me on the back. I remember when I walked into Molly Darcy's pub on the way home after the match I was given a standing ovation. Even during the peak of Kerry's reign this had never happened before. It was very emotional. The enormous effort I had put into training during the previous two winters had finally paid off.

The 1991 Munster football final between Kerry and Limerick is one of the forgotten games of Gaelic football. Perhaps it was overshadowed by the four-match marathon saga between Dublin and Meath in Leinster. But it deserves more recognition because it was one of the most enjoyable matches I was ever involved in. It was supposed to be a cake walk for Kerry but we got the mother of all frights scraping home by two points in a remarkably high scoring provincial final (0-23 to 3-12). It was also a personal triumph for me as I was one of the Kerry stars and won another Man of the Match award for my contribution.

My former team mate John O'Keeffe was coaching Limerick. He had them very well prepared and naturally he knew the Kerry team like the back of his hand. At half-time it looked dubious for us. Limerick, the 10/1 outsiders, were four points up. I scored a vital point early in the second half which helped to steady the ship and we breathed a huge sigh of relief when the final whistle blew. Limerick lost because they allowed us to play football.

The celebrations were hectic afterwards. The success marked an important milestone for me. I now had 12 senior provincial championship medals - one more than any of the other Kerry players from my era. I was also buzzing in anticipation of what lay ahead. I was just two matches away from a record ninth All-Ireland medal. My dream died in the semi-final against Down.

The match was a disaster, from a Kerry perspective, as Down maintained their proud record of having never lost to us in the championship. Again I lined out at centre-forward. Before the start Down made an astute change moving wing back DJ Kane into the centre in a swap with team captain Paddy O'Rourke. I felt O'Rourke was there for the taking, but Kane was a much more mobile player and he gave me a hard time. I felt I acquitted myself reasonably well by scoring two points.

The contest was tight all through. We led during a ten

minute spell midway through the game. The teams were level with less than ten minutes remaining. When the vital break came it went to Down who scored 1-4 in the closing minutes to clinch a place in the final on a 2-9 to 0-8 scoreline. Maurice Fitzgerald missed a few vital frees during the game which possibly cost us victory. He hit the woodwork three times in the first half. Down missed a penalty but had we got our noses in front before their second goal, I believe we would have held on.

My brother, Tommy, who lined out at full-back, came in for scathing criticism afterwards for his failure to blot out the threat of Peter Withnell, who scored Down's two goals. I believe Tommy was treated unfairly. After picking up an injury in the spring he was dropped from the panel. On his return to club football he was doing very well. But the selectors appeared determined to give him the cold shoulder and he was left out of the squad for the Munster championship.

The difference between Mick O'Dwyer and Mickey O'Sullivan was underlined in the way Tommy's recall was handled. Had O'Dwyer been in charge I'm convinced he would have told Tommy he was the best full-back in Kerry and he planned to build the defence around him. In contrast, Mickey warned Tom that he couldn't guarantee him a place on the team and he would have to work hard in training. It was obvious after the Munster final that Kerry had a problem at full-back and Tommy was brought back to try and sort it out. He was on a hiding to nothing. The whole experience destroyed his confidence and it robbed Kerry of at least three or four more years of service from him. Kerry might have won an All-Ireland in that period had he been around.

2

A BORN FOOTBALLER

THERE was little in the way of organised under-age football when I was growing up in Templenoe in the sixties. Back then the only football field in the area was at the other end of the parish in Dromore, five or six miles away from our house. To me, football meant playing around in the yard or kicking the ball against the garage door.

My first real taste of competitive football came when I enrolled in 'The Sem', or to give it its official name, St. Brendan's College, Killarney. I was twelve at the time. Prior to that I played no more than one or two games a year. Indeed, I saw very few competitive matches and never played outside the Kenmare District Board area. So I had no idea if I was any good.

The only reason I remember my first day at secondary school was because we played a game of Gaelic football. During it I realised I was one of the best players on the field. Fr. Pierce, a teacher in the college, gave me and the rest of my class mates our first ever formal coaching session in the skills of Gaelic football.

Attending St Brendan's as a boarder helped my football education as well as my academic education. If I hadn't gone there, I would never have made it to third level college and qualified as a teacher. Studying was compulsory - three and half hours every evening. It seemed like a terrible chore at the time, but I know had I attended a day school it would have been both impossible and impractical to study for that period of time while living over a bar.

The college was big into sport, particularly Gaelic football. I was very lucky because my first year there coincided with St Brendan's first ever victory in the All-Ireland colleges' final in 1969. John O'Keeffe captained the team and other players included Ger O'Keeffe and his brother Tony, who is now the Kerry County Board GAA secretary. Those guys were our heroes. It made our day when John O'Keeffe nodded to us in the corridor.

The ambition of virtually every youngster in Brendan's was to make the college's senior football team. Observing how the students on the All-Ireland winning team were treated, we quickly realised there were a lot of perks to be had if you were lucky enough to make the senior squad. There were training sessions during study periods, the senior players got better food, they travelled to matches in the best carriages on the train and they were a big hit with the girls from the nearby convent schools.

As first years we were envious of them and this fuelled a desire to be part of this scene. I made the senior team in my last two years there. In 1972 we reached the All-Ireland final. In the semi-final we beat Franciscan College, Gormanstown. Their star midfielder was Ogie Moran - who won an All-Ireland Colleges' medal the following year - while his opposite number on our team was Páidí Ó Sé.

On April 16, 1972 I made my Croke Park debut in the All-Ireland Colleges' final against St Patrick's, Cavan. We felt like professional footballers in the weeks leading up to the final. We travelled to Dublin by train the day before the match and stayed in the Spa Hotel in Lucan. Our coach, Fr. Hegarty, took us to the Phoenix Park for a kick-around before the match.

We worked on a pre-planned move which we put into use straight from the throw-in. It worked and we scored one of the quickest points ever seen in an All-Ireland final at Croke Park. However, it was downhill all the way afterwards. There was no age-limit in colleges football at the time and I think our opponents had a lot of guys who were repeating their Leaving Certificate. They completely dominated us physically, with players like Kieran O'Keeffe and Ollie Brady causing us all kinds of problems. They won by nine points.

It was a particularly forgettable day for me as I was substituted in the second half. Nobody could have envisaged then that Croke Park would eventually become a happy hunting ground for me.Within five months I was back on the Croke Park pitch. But I wasn't supposed to be there. Kerry qualified to play title holders Offaly in the 1972 All-Ireland final. Páidí Ó Sé and myself got permission from the college authorities to attend the game.

After the match, which ended in a draw, Páidí met a few acquaintances from West Kerry and, of course, being a social animal I willingly joined the party. We had a few drinks and missed the train back to Killarney. We didn't panic. We booked into a bed and breakfast on Clonliffe Road. Later that night we attended a dance in the Ierne ballroom on Parnell Square.

Walking back to the B & B after the dance we noticed the gates of Croke Park were still open. So Páidí and I ended up kicking an imaginary ball around the pitch at two o'clock in the morning watched by a bemused female - an old flame of Páidí's if memory serves me right. Little did we realise then that within three years we would be back in the stadium playing with a real football in an All-Ireland final.

Not surprisingly, there was consternation around St Brendan's when we failed to return on Sunday night and the college authorities notified our respective mothers.
Páidí and I hadn't a care in the world. In fact, we didn't even bother making the early train the following day. We eventually got back to Killarney on Monday night. We received what could only be described as a severe verbal warning from the college authorities, but escaped any serious punishment. I'm sure the fact that we were star footballers on the college team helped our case.

In 1973 I was captain of Brendan's and my brother, Mike, was also a member of the team. We retained the Munster title, beating Tralee CBS - who had Mike Sheehy on their their side -in the final. I produced my best ever performance for the Sem in that match and I won the Man of the Match award.

Incidentally on the night of the Munster final a new alcohol-free disco bar was opened in St Mary's Parish Hall in Killarney. The Munster trophy was filled with lemonade and one of the first men to drink from it was the then Bishop of Kerry, Eamonn Casey, who officially opened the new bar. The dormitory I stayed in for three of my five years in St Brendan's was situated in what was known as the new wing. Just a concrete block away from my bed was the Bishop's Palace where Dr. Casey lived and, indeed, it was during my college days that Annie Murphy was entertained there!

We were beaten in the 1973 All-Ireland semi-final by St Jarlath's, Tuam who lost to Gormanstown College in the final. Even though my football career with the Sem ended on a disappointing note, I reckon that the roving tactics I later became famous for evolved during my days in secondary school. Back then, colleges' football was a 13 a-side game. There were two players in the full-back line opposed by two inside forwards. But there were no real set positions. I was one of those inside forwards and during matches I started to drift across the entire full forward line.

I developed a kind of free spirit and I loved to roam, not just along the full forward line, but all over the field. Thankfully nobody ever stopped me. Perhaps, if there was a dictatorial type manager in charge of the Brendan's team, I would have been whipped back into line and told to stay in one position. However, nobody told me to stop and roving became one of my trademarks.

I played on the Kerry minor teams in 1972 and 1973 but we were beaten in successive Munster finals by Cork, who went on to complete a hat-trick of provincial titles. The 1972 Cork team, which included Jimmy Barry Murphy and Tom Creedon, went on to win the All-Ireland. Kerry had quite a good team and many of the players on it had great success later at senior level.

I was unfortunate at under age level because I was born on December 1st, 1956. My brother, Mike, who was born in January 1957 was just 13 months younger than me. But from a football perspective there are two years between us: the GAA use January 1st as the cut off date for under-age competition. This meant I missed out on what should have been my best year as a minor.

Quite honestly, I was nothing more than an average county minor. While I did stand out in my last year at colleges level I don't think the standard was particularly high. There was no indication back then that one day I would became a famous footballer.

I failed to get an honour in Irish in the Leaving Certificate and, while it wasn't my favourite subject, I always blamed football for this. On the day of the oral Irish exam in 1973 we had a trial game as we were busy preparing for the All-Ireland series. Somebody, presumably the team coach, got the time of my exam changed so that I could play in the match. I can only assume the examiner, a female, wasn't impressed at the idea of her schedule being changed because of a football match and she gave me an awful grilling.

I'm often asked how did I manage to reach the top in Gaelic football in such a short space of time. Within two years of failing to impress as a minor I won an All-Ireland at senior level.

I wasn't the kind of footballer who would feature in a coaching manual. I used my left foot for standing on most of the time although, curiously enough, I managed to score a few soft goals with it. I wasn't a tremendous fielder although I played at midfield when I first made my name at club level with Kenmare. In 1973 I was Man of the Match in the county semi-final between Kenmare and Austin Stacks, even though we lost. It was this performance which first brought me to the attention of the Kerry selectors.

Studying physical education at Thomond College in 1973 gave me a head start. But the main reason I became a great footballer was because I worked hard at it. I don't think any player trained as hard as I did. I made unbelievable sacrifices: I constantly practised the various skills, be it picking up the ball, soloing or kicking.

One of the main reasons why the skills levels have dropped in Gaelic football in the last decade is because the majority of players are not prepared to go off on their own and practice the skills.

I regarded myself as a skilful player - although I wasn't perceived as such. I have a theory that the majority of players who are regarded as skilful have a questionable work rate. Southampton soccer player Matt Le Tissier would be a prime example. People seemed to think that because I spent all day running up and down the field it hid weaknesses in my game. It annoyed me that I was regarded as a workaholic type player rather than a skilful one.

I devoured all the manuals written about Gaelic football and, from closely watching other sports, I came to appreciate how important it is for forwards to run off the ball and create space. Even in my current arthritic state, I am still very good at losing my marker and making space for myself. It was one of the strongest characteristics of my game. My chief tutor in this area was Kenny Dalgish. I learned a great deal from watching him play. His work rate off the ball was tremendous and he could lose his marker by a 'shimmy' or running in one direction and then veering off in another.

I simply cannot understand why footballers don't practice kicking the ball more. In golf, if a pro has a bad day on the greens he goes out early the next morning with a hundred balls and practices his putting until he feels he has got his rhythm back. Unfortunately, in Gaelic football, very few players who kick badly go out the next day and practice what is essentially a very simple technique. The reason I was good at kicking was because I tried to practice every day for at least one hour - sometimes two. There are a few simple principles involved. If you are kicking with your right foot then your left foot must be firmly on the ground, you lean towards the target and follow through.

Nowadays many talented under- age players lose interest in Gaelic football once they sample wine, women and song. So why didn't I follow that path? It's not that I wasn't tempted. I'm now 28 years playing for Templenoe. I had my first senior match when I was fourteen. As a result I mixed with adults from a very early age. I had my first drink when I was sixteen. Templenoe won a carnival tournament in Kenmare to capture our first trophy for many years. In true Templenoe fashion, it was an occasion which demanded a major celebration. I drank several pints of cider in recognition of our achievement.

I chose cider because I couldn't be seen drinking Guinness or Smithwicks. Cider looked like cidona so it was all right - or so I thought. Later that night I got as sick as a dog in bed and my mother wasn't too pleased. It was one of the rare times she gave out to me even though it wasn't really a telling off. She just said: "You let me down." I never drank cider again. The other beverage I never touch is wine. My dislike of it was the result of another binge much later in life.

Given the fact that my mother is a devout Catholic the Pope's visit to Ireland in 1979 was a big event in our family . My brother, Mike, presented an oak sampling to the Pope in Galway on behalf of the youth of Ireland, my mother went to see the Holy Father in Limerick and I was sent to Dublin to the open air mass in the Phoenix Park. I travelled up by train and was collected at the station by ex-Republic of Ireland soccer international Ray Treacy and World Superstars champion Brian Budd. They knew each other from playing soccer in Canada and I got friendly with Budd while competing in the World Superstars the previous year.

As far as I can recall all the pubs closed early that night in Dublin and the only drink to be had was wine in the night clubs in Leeson Street. I didn't like the taste of it but somebody suggested I mix orange juice with it. So I ended up drinking pints of wine laced with orange juice. I woke up the following morning in Ray Treacy's house feeling awful. I muttered to Ray that I better head off to the Phoenix Park. He said: "Come in here to the sitting room. There's about ten minutes of it left on television." That was it - I never again drank wine again.

But, even though, I didn't practice a life of temperance it must be remembered that in the early seventies there wasn't nearly as much excessive teenage drinking as there is nowadays. We didn't have as much money in our pockets as youngsters have now and, in general, there wasn't as many distractions as there are now. We might go for a few drinks one night a week. Of course, living at home helped me to keep on the straight and narrow.

Much later, when I should have had sense, the wheels came off the wagon - albeit occasionally. Three weeks before the 1985 All-Ireland final, I wrote off my car returning home from the Rose of Tralee festival in the early hours of the morning. In fact it's not quite accurate to say that I wrote off the car - it was a friend who was driving at the time. After a night at the festival I was so inebriated I couldn't drive so I left the job to a friend. Four of us headed for home in the car and we all fell asleep.

We went off the road at Looscannagh on the Killarney-Kenmare road. The car landed on its four wheels parallel to a lake. When I got out the passenger's door I stepped into water. Had it plunged a few yards further from the road we would probably all have drowned. A local wag reckoned when the black box was recovered the only thing heard on it was snoring!

In general I stayed away from the drink in the run-up to matches. Normally I didn't touch the stuff for three weeks before a big game. Naturally, I had to spend a few days quenching my thirst afterwards.

3

THE EARLY YEARS

EVEN though it's nearly a quarter of a century ago I can still remember the journey from my home in Templenoe to Tralee on March 3, 1974. A neighbour, Harold O'Sullivan drove me in his Ford Capri. Our destination was Austin Stack Park which was hosting Kerry's last home league game of the season against the 1973 beaten All-Ireland finalists, Galway.

I was Kerry's 11th substitute that day but I doubt if there was a prouder 18-year-old in the country. I got a great kick out of producing my free admission ticket to the gate man. I was now officially a member of the Kerry senior squad. Quite honestly I never expected to play even though Kerry were understrength. But after 25 minutes I was handed the famous slip of paper and told I was on. I replaced Frank Russell, father of current Kerry star, Mike Frank Russell.

One of the unusual features of my football career was that I had a habit of doing something to catch the eye as soon as I came on the field. It happened to me at St Brendan's, Thomond College and later with Munster in the Railway Cup. On this occasion I got a chance soon after being introduced and I kicked a point. As a result of that score I settled down quickly; hit another point and played quite well.

The match ended in a draw. We were lucky. Galway's place kicker John Tobin was off target with frees and struck a penalty off the bar. The point was enough to give us a place in the semi-final of the National League. Incidentally my school friend from Dingle, Páidí Ó Sé made his senior debut - as a forward - the same day. It didn't take the selectors too long to realise that Páidí's future as a footballer was further back the field.

The next day the national papers were quite impressed with Kerry's performance and noted the contribution of the two newcomers, Messrs. Ó Sé and Spillane. In my case there was more concentration on my GAA pedigree than my actual performance. In the *Irish Independent* the late John D Hickey pointed out that my late father, Tom and my uncles, the Lynes had played for Kerry and he noted the county's ability to maintain a conveyor belt of football talent. Referring to the debut boys he wrote: 'They will roast many a senior defence in the years ahead.'

For that league campaign the Kerry squad was a combination of the old guard from the double All-Ireland winning team of 1969-70 and a group of new arrivals such as Ger Power, Mike Sheehy and John Egan, who had won All-Ireland U-21 medals with Kerry the previous autumn. Obviously the selectors saw something in my performance against Galway because I was picked for my first full game the following Sunday against Tyrone in the National League semi-final at Croke Park. We stayed in the Skylon Hotel in Drumcondra the night before the game. There were no visits to Leeson Street either before or after the match. We were young and innocent in those days

I was marked by Pat King, the current manager of Fermanagh and father of county players, Shane and Barry. I performed okay and retained my place for the league final against Roscommon. My impact - or to be more precise lack of it - in that contest was perfectly illustrated the following day when a picture of me appeared in one of the national papers bearing the caption JIM Spillane. In truth, my contribution was fairly minimal. I failed to score and was replaced by Eamon O'Donoghue half time. Kerry got away with daylight robbery. After been outplayed for most of the hour John Egan flicked an equalising goal with time almost up.

Predictably I was dropped for the replay. Eamon O' Donoghue kept his place at right half forward. Kerry won comfortably (0-14; 0-8) to claim the county's fourth League title in a row - an achievement which hasn't been equalled since. So less than three months after my call-up to the Kerry squad I had won a national medal. However, the value which the GAA in Kerry place on league success was graphically illustrated by the manner in which I received my medal.

Now in most counties if they won a national GAA senior

title they would hold some kind of function at which the medals would be presented. Not so in Kerry, at least not in 1974. A few months after the game my old school teacher George Rice came into the bar and handed me the first national GAA medal I ever won. He got it from PJ McIntyre, who was the District Board delegate on the County Board.

Even though Kerry won the league neither the selectors or the public thought that the team were good enough to take on Cork, then the reigning All-Ireland champions. There was a trial game staged at Fitzgerald Stadium on Whit Sunday 1974 between a north and a south Kerry selection and many of the 'old guard' like Mick O'Dwyer, Mick O'Connell and Pat Griffin were brought back for this match. Afterwards the squad for the championship was announced with a decided bias towards the longer established players. Against the odds I kept my place.

It wasn't a happy squad, however. There was absolutely no camaraderie or team spirit. Indeed, there was a gulf as wide as Kenmare Bay between the old and young members of the team and there was nobody in between to bridge that gap. The preparations themselves left a lot to be desired.

I remember my first training session for the championship. I was a student at Thomond College and I was picked up from the campus by a Limerick based member of the squad who drove me to Tralee. Everybody wanted to finish early because there was a big soccer match on television later. We adjourned to the Earl of Desmond Hotel after training to watch the match. I can't remember who was playing, which is perhaps understandable given what happened later.

Our next port of call was Castleisland where we stayed until closing time. We had further pitstops in Abbeyfeale and the Highway Restaurant in Limerick where we shared a bottle of wine. For reasons which I won't dwell on I spent the night in a spare bed in the casualty ward of a big Limerick hospital. I crashed out but at some stage during the night there was a big accident and all I remember were nurses and doctors whizzing by. Such was my hangover I was feeling nearly as poorly as the unfortunate people who were involved in the accident. Of course, I had been the author of my own misfortunes.

Things were done differently in football in those days. For example before games one of the selectors used to offer us a swig from his magic bottle into which he had poured brandy and port!

Former All-Ireland winning captain, Johnny Culloty was the team trainer at the time. Basically he was too nice a guy for the job and his authority was fatally undermined because so many of his ex team mates were still playing.

We were often so fresh after a training session that we could go straight back out and play a game. Johnny was an excellent tactician but a poor disciplinarian. He simply wasn't hard enough on us. He allowed himself to be dictated to by the older brigade. Certain fellows escaped training on more than one occasion that summer by complaining about some mysterious pain in the back of the leg. They then proceeded to light up a fag and watch from the sideline. It was a recipe for disaster and it was hardly a major surprise when we flopped.

I wasn't too surprised when I didn't make the team for the 1974 Munster final against Cork. So for my first provincial final as a member of the Kerry squad I sat in the dug out at Fitzgerald Stadium between Mick O'Connell and Pat Griffin, who between them had won six All-Ireland medals. Late in the second half when the game was well beyond our reach - we lost by seven points - the Kerry County GAA secretary, Andy Molyneaux told Mick O'Connell, who was then 37, that he was on. Now most guys of O'Connell's vintage would have been mad to get an opportunity to prove that the selectors' decision to leave him out in the first place was wrong.

Mick was different, however. I will never forget what he said: "Forget about me. There is no point in me going on. Give one of the youngsters a chance." Eventually he was prevailed upon to go on. My other abiding memory of that unhappy afternoon is the sight of O'Connell, who was obviously well past his best, being ridiculed by one of the Cork players.

I vowed that day that if my career ever took off I would make damn sure I bowed out before my sell by date.

Even though we only played together at inter-county level on a handful of occasions Mick O'Connell did have a significant influence on my career. Earlier that summer we were picked together at midfield in a tournament game against Meath to mark the official opening of Seneschalstown GAA pitch. Not surprisingly he opted to anchor our midfield. As a fit 18-year-old I was the right man to do the donkey work and I spent the sixty minutes roaming up and down the field. It was my first time I played such a role at inter-county level.

I can justifiably say that I did it out of necessity on that occasion. I was hardly going to argue with Mick O'Connell. Later in my football career, however, I did have occasion to remonstrate with Mick - in his capacity as a referee. He was in charge of a challenge match between Kerry and Cork and obviously took the job seriously. He visited both dressing rooms beforehand and told the players what to expect. He then proceeded to whistle for every conceivable infringement and the players and spectators quickly got frustrated. I appealed to Mick to let the game flow where upon he turned around and booked my marker, the late Tom Creedon!

I was never slow to try and bend a referee's ear in order to get him to see things from my point of view. Indeed, Kildare GAA official and former referee, Seamus Aldridge once described me as 'King of the Cribbers'. He was right in so far as I always believed in moaning as much as possible to referees. If they were weak characters inevitably they were influenced by my comments. It was a trick I used many times.

Predictably after the 1974 Munster final all the older players such as O'Connell and Mick O'Dwyer retired. The only member of the 'old guard' to stay was Donie O'Sullivan. He hung around and picked up an All-Ireland medal in 1975.

Away from the inter-county scene 1974 was a memorable year, with Kenmare winning the Kerry county championship title for the first time ever. I always regarded the successes I achieved with my club Templenoe and divisional team Kenmare on par with anything I have ever won with Kerry. So you can imagine what this success meant.

It was all the sweeter because we were complete outsiders in the final against Shannon Rangers who had star players such as Paud and Eamon O'Donoghue, Jackie and Barry Walsh and Ogie Moran. For instance, our full forward line consisted of a thirty-something trio of ex-Offaly dual player, PJ McIntyre, Paul O'Sullivan, better known to us all as Paul Paddy, and Paudie Finnegan. Then we had youngsters like myself and my younger brother Mike. Our only established Kerry player was Mickey O'Sullivan.

Leading 2-8 to 0-2 at the break we thought the game was over. But our team manager Denis McCarthy had other ideas. We knew him as 'Top Cross' and he absolutely laced into me at the break for my reluctance to drop back and mark my man when I didn't have possession. Later in my career I came to fear the Thomond College manager, Dave Weldrick and Ireland's Compromise rules tour boss Kevin Heffernan. But this pair never made quite the same dramatic impact on me as Denis McCarthy.

He literally reduced me to tears with his verbal assault and I was very reluctant to come out for the second half because I felt so humiliated. Looking back on it now he was probably spot on in his criticism but I wasn't prepared to accept it. I ended up scoring four points and we won in a canter 2-12 to 1-5. Our fourteen scores all came from play and I can still vividly recall the celebrations in Kenmare that night.

Our short passing style game became Kerry's trademark from 1975 onwards. We were the first club side in the county to adopt this style of football and our success had probably some influence on Mick O'Dwyer's decision to play this type of game once he took charge of Kerry the following year.

Our victory was celebrated in a poem written by John Harrington and printed in the Kerryman. It began:

You're heard of Heffo's Army, Donie O'Donovan's and the rest.

But through GAA circles in Kerry Michael Murphy's are the best.

This year he brought the laurels with his stalwarts brave and true

For the first time to Kenmare this cup long overdue."

I even got a mention:

"And Michael (Ned) and Pat Spillane with craft picked off fine scores.

"Then when the final whistle blew, the Cup was on its way.

For the first time in history to the shores of Kenmare Bay.

All Gaels from Kerry will agree this was the best fifteen.

Well done, young lads, we're proud of you, you brought glory to Neidin."

Kenmare were now the top team in the county and four of us, Mickey O'Sullivan, PJ McIntyre, Michael Murphy and myself, were picked to play for Kerry in their first home national league game of the 1974-75 season against the newly crowned All-Ireland champions, Dublin on November 10.

Over 9,000 turned up in Killarney to see how Kerry - who had lost their first league match by a point to Offaly - would fare against the new kingpins of Gaelic football. It was my first full competitive match for Kerry at home but I remember little about it. I scored a point but a late Jimmy Keaveney free gave the Dubs a share of the spoils.

The only thing I do remember was that PJ McIntyre was replaced in the second half by a gentleman called Dick Spring, who had the rare distinction of playing on the Kerry football and hurling teams, as well as representing Ireland on the rugby field before becoming a TD, Labour Party leader, minister and Tanaiste.

We chalked up wins over Cork and Roscommon in subsequent rounds but the event which was to shape my football life for the next fifteen years happened off the field.

At the Kerry GAA Convention in January 1975 Mick O'Dwyer topped the poll in the contest for new football selectors with 97 votes. He was followed home by Pat O'Shea (84), Donie Sheehan (78), Denis McCarthy (70) and Murty Kelly (68) Initially O'Dwyer had responsibility for training the team - he didn't start coaching us until a few months later. I was picked at midfield for our last league game. We hammered Kildare 3-8 to 1-3 in Killarney. *The Kerryman* suggested afterwards: "This is a great chance for Spillane to stake a claim to a permanent place on the team. He may be young in years, but has football ability and heart in plenty."

Our first big match under O'Dwyer was the league quarter-final against Meath at Croke Park in March 1975. I was selected at centre forward with Ogie Moran coming into midfield to partner Seamus O'Donovan. The night before the match we had a team meeting in the Ashling Hotel. I suspect O'Dwyer and the selectors wanted to take us down a peg or two. The truth was we had started to get cocky.

We had lost just one league match; drawn with the All-Ireland champions Dublin and won our last match by eleven points. As far as the players were concerned we were going places. We needed to be put in our place but the timing - less than 24 hours before one of our biggest games - was all wrong. We were completely demoralised after listening to O'Dwyer spinning the home truths to us.

The match turned into a disaster from a Kerry perspective. Meath, who had won promotion from Division 2, beat us comfortably, 0-11; 0-6. We were woeful and our critics had a field day. That Sunday evening a Munster title, never mind an All-Ireland title, seemed a million miles away.

On a personal level I marked it down as another Croke Park disaster. This, unfortunately, was becoming a habit. I had nightmare matches in the All-Ireland Colleges' final, the National League league final and now the league quarter-final. The common denominator between the three games was they were all played at headquarters. Maybe the ghosts around the stadium were getting their revenge for my late night illegal encroachment on the sacred sod with Páidí Ó Sé during my school days. Certainly there was no hint back then that Croke Park would become my greatest sporting stage in future years.

I was moved into full forward at one stage where I found myself being marked by Jack Quinn. Any ball which came my way arrived via the clouds and I spent most of my time looking up at Quinn's armpits. Whatever chance I had of getting the ball if it came in low, there was absolutely no contest between us for a high ball and I didn't get a sniff of the ball.

Meath went on to beat Dublin in the League final which provided some small consolation for us. We started to think that maybe we were not that bad after all.

4

DREAMS FULFILLED

MUCH has been written about Mick O'Dwyer's legendary training sessions. Quite honestly I don't remember our preparations for the 1975 championship as being particularly savage. Okay the sessions were hard. But we were young and fit and they didn't cause us too many sleepless nights, though by the time it came to getting ready for the All-Ireland final against Dublin we were training five times a week. I have far more painful memories of the sessions O'Dwyer put us through in his latter years as manager.

His regime was totally different from what I had experienced with Johnny Culloty. For a start he didn't accept excuses from players. O'Dwyer was a strict disciplinarian. If training was due to start at 7 o'clock everybody was there at 6.45. He was his own man. For instance, there were several physical education students in the squad including, John O'Keeffe, Jimmy Deenihan, Ogie Moran and myself. We probably knew more about training methods than O'Dwyer. But he never, never asked for advice or guidance from us.

In fact, he probably wished we had all opted to become nuclear physicians. As a result of studying physical education as an academic subject we learned how the various muscle groups in our bodies worked and occasionally malfunctioned. Until then a player would complain about a pain in the back of his leg. Now O'Dwyer was faced with guys telling him they had a tweak in their hamstring - or hammer - as it was popularly known.

John O'Keeffe, for instance, could put a specific name to any injury he had. At times O'Dwyer thought guys were swinging the lead when they piped up with these exotic sounding injuries. Heaven help anybody who mentioned the 'hammer'. Their 'reward' was extra training. On occasions O'Dwyer pushed guys, who were genuinely injured, too hard. As a result they missed key matches. It was a costly lesson, but O'Dwyer eventually learned it.

I made my Munster championship debut in Clonmel against Tipperary on June 14, 1975. We were without our full back John O'Keeffe which was a serious blow. I was selected at left half forward where I went on to play most of my inter- county football. Another player making his championship debut was Kildare based Pat McCarthy, who was to have a significant influence on the campaign. He was an excellent fielder who brought much needed physical strength to the team. In latter years he teamed up again with O'Dwyer as a selector in Kildare.

The tight ground didn't suit our style of play and we got the mother of all frights from a Tipp side which included hurling star Michael 'Babs' Keating. We were a point down at half time. I was switched to the forty at the start of the second half which meant I played at centre-forward in my first and last championship games for Kerry. In 1975, however, I only lasted eight minutes in the position.

The move which swung the match our way was the arrival of John Egan on the forty. He hit a hat-trick of goals which turned what looked like an ignominious defeat into victory.

My football trade mark at the time was my ball carrying ability which I had developed while playing at under age level with Templenoe. I was the team's best player and could carry the ball from one end of the field to the other. Unfortunately it was a trait I took with me into adulthood. During my early seasons with Kerry I was guilty of over carrying the ball. I certainly did it that day against Tipp and I probably continued to do it until 1977. O'Dwyer encouraged and cajoled me into becoming a better team player. But it took time and two bitter disappointments against Dublin in 1976 and 1977 before his message finally struck home.

Anyway, Tipp were out of the way and we were in the Munster final. Three weeks before the showdown against Cork we played All-Ireland champions Dublin in a challenge to raise funds for Sr Consilio's home for Alcoholics. We hammered them by thirteen points. For the first time since O'Dwyer took over we felt we were on the right road.

Even though Cork had lost the 1974 semi-final to Dublin they were raging hot favourites to win a third Munster title in a row. One thing in our favour, however, was that the game was scheduled for Killarney. The 1975 Munster final was due to be played in Cork but as Pairc Ui Chaoimh was being built at the time the game was switched. The wide open spaces of Fitzgerald Stadium were always going to suit us more than the narrow confines of Pairc Ui Chaoimh. The dry sod helped too.

Early in the game we got the kind of break any young team need if they are to cause an upset. I got the ball on the right-hand side of the field and kicked it goalward with my weak left foot. I know there is a theory that a player will never make it to the top unless he can kick equally well with both feet. Well I managed okay, even though I generally only used my left foot to stand on. Anyway my left footed shot dropped into the goal area. Cork corner back Martin O'Doherty - who was a star hurler at the time - got his hand to the ball but only managed to deflect it past Billy Morgan into his own net. We were a goal up and never looked back.

The next day the papers differed on who should be credited with the goal. In the *Irish Times* , for instance, the score went down as an O'Doherty o.g. but elsewhere I was credited with scoring it. I have always suggested that I put a spin on the kick which was the reason Martin was unable to control it. So I can justifiably claim credit for the score. But imagine my disgust at the time. I had scored my first championship goal in my first Munster final and I wasn't getting any credit for it!

Later Mike Sheehy and Jimmy Barry Murphy both missed penalties but it mattered little. We led by seven points at half time and the majority of the 43,295 crowd knew the final outcome long before the final whistle. In the end we won 1-14 to 0-7. And to complete an excellent afternoon my brother, Mike, played on the Kerry minor team which beat Cork by two points. A Kerry and Spillane double.

For the senior team it was a victory based on youth, hunger and determination. I suppose we had learned much from Dublin's victory in 1974 - even though O'Dwyer never admitted that he learned anything from anybody.

Undoubtedly, however, he had taken a leaf out of the Kevin Heffernan manual. The previous year Heffo had brought together a bunch of players - whose football ability was, in most instances, no better than average - and moulded them into a team capable of winning an All-Ireland. They became fit, well organised and highly motivated. O'Dwyer followed the same path.One thing which Micko drummed into us was hunger and appetite and we never lost it.

With an average age of 22.5, the 1975 team was the youngest ever Kerry team to play in the championship. We were also a team of bachelors which was quite unusual in those days. Some of the papers got a bit carried away and said we were 15 non-smokers and non-drinkers as well. But I'm afraid that wasn't quite the case.

Our next opponents were Sligo, who were appearing in their first All-Ireland semi final since 1928. They beat Mayo after a replay in the Connacht final and predictably they celebrated with gusto. Watching the Sligo players during the pre-match parade it suddenly dawned on me that these guys were just happy to be in Croke Park and had no more ambitions left. For instance, while we were totally focussed on the game the Sligo lads were waving to all their friends in he stand. Most of them were there to enjoy themselves.

My abiding memory of the game is receiving what could be described as a verbal warning from Sligo full back John Brennan. I went past him early on and scored a point. Feeling quite chuffed with myself I was running back out to my place at top of the left when John called me back and gave me an ear full. He drew an imaginary circle with his right arm and he advised me not to encroach on this space again. He was one of the strongest men I ever faced on a football field and I heeded his advice.

In the latter stages of the game Sligo moved John out to midfield and we got in for three goals - I scored the second one - and we won 3-13 to 0-5. In terms of fitness we were miles ahead of them but it took us a long time to make our superiority count on the scoreboard. They had a penalty early on but Paudie O'Mahony - who didn't concede a goal during the entire championship - saved Micheal Kearins' kick. Just to complete an excellent day for Kerry the minors hammered Roscommon.

O'Dwyer was also managing the Kerry U-21 team that summer. We had a big win over Waterford in the Munster final and then faced Antrim in the All-Ireland semi-final in Tralee. Up until midway through the second half there was nothing between the teams and Gerry Armstrong, later to emerge as one of the stars for Northern Ireland in the 1982 World Cup, caused us all kinds of problems.

But the game turned on a single incident. The Antrim place kicker Brendan Tully threw a punch at my brother, Mike. I'm not sure whether referee, Tom Cunningham saw what happened. But O'Dwyer did and he certainly made the most of it. He raced on to the field and told Mike to stay down. He even gave him a knee in the back to make sure he didn't get up.Tully was sent off and we won easily. The incident illustrated O'Dwyer's ability to employ gamesmanship when the need arose and this cuteness helped us out of tight corners on many occasions subsequently.

There was a song released in Kerry in the run-up to the 1975 All-Ireland final which began:

'You have heard of Heffo's Army and a great one too but when they meet the Kingdom they will meet their Waterloo.'

It captured the mood in the squad before the game. We were young and eager and not in the least intimidated at the prospect of taking on the Dubs. O'Dwyer made sure we were well prepared.The training schedule was intense with five sessions weekly. But in my view the key to our success was our backs versus forwards games. They were more competitive than many of the matches and nobody slackened off during them. The backs wanted to put one over the forwards and visa versa.

Páidí Ó Sé usually marked me in these sessions. You

might pass Paidi once. But you did so twice at your peril. Nowadays we are loaded down with manuals and videos telling us what coaches should be doing in training. But I believe there is simply no substitute for a backs v forwards game. Another thing which we concentrated on was kicking practice. We spent a half an hour before training started just kicking the ball over the bar.

Fitness, however, was probably the key to our success in 1975. Forwards have always been fit in Gaelic football but O'Dwyer added a new dimension - he had the backs every bit as fit as the forwards. This was a new development. I reckon it was probably the first time ever that a defence was at least as fit as its forward division in an All-Ireland final.

Kerry's team of bachelors were the Boyzone of Gaelic Football at the time. Crowds starting coming to Fitzgerald Stadium just to watch us train. That in itself kept us on our toes. Everybody wanted to impress our new audience.

O'Dwyer changed Kerry's pre-match routine for games in Croke Park in 1975. Traditionally Kerry teams stayed in the Ashling or Skylon hotels. O'Dwyer decided to shield us away from the fans and we stayed in the Grand Hotel in Malahide. Indeed, the format he began in 1975 for big games in Dublin stayed much the same for the next eleven years.

We caught the Saturday afternoon train from Killarney. We ate a steak; had a few games of cards and a bit of craic on the journey to Dublin. Having booked into the hotel we went for a walk on the beach in Malahide. Afterwards we sat on the wall for half an hour and talked about the game and the few tactics we planned to use. But the highlight of the evening was watching 'Match of the Day' on BBC Television.

Back in those days we didn't get the BBC signal down in Kerry so this was a big treat. I remember when Liam O'Murchu was doing his 'Up for the Match' pre All-Ireland programme there was a live link-up with the Grand Hotel on one occasion. Liam assumed we were all watching his programme and he was quite shocked when Jimmy Deenihan told him we were glued to Match of the Day on a foreign channel. These days Jimmy - now a TD - gives more politically correct answers to awkward questions!

Sunday morning was again very well organised. We didn't go out to a crowded church to attend mass. Instead a priest came into the hotel to celebrate mass. Then we had soup and sandwiches at around one o'clock before heading off to Croke Park. We always watched a bit of the minor game before retiring to the dressing rooms.

O'Dwyer's pre-match speeches were always very motivating. He had great passion. We stood around the table and he belted it. After listening to O'Dwyer give a speech before a big game at Croke Park we would be so psyched up we would have gone through the wall if the door wasn't open.I remember before one All-Ireland final his false teeth fell out during his pre-match speech. But the players were concentrating so hard on what he had to say that none of us noticed the flying dentures.

Another example of our new professional approach was that we wore our track suit tops in the kick around before the 1975 final. It was raining quite heavily and there was no way we were going to get wet or cold before the throw-in. Just a small thing. But all these little items add up at the end of the day.

People often wonder how players cope with the noise around Croke Park on the day of an All-Ireland final. I wondered myself how I would react before I experienced it in 1975. The truth was I felt more intimidated by half a dozen spectators at a club match where I could hear nearly every comment they passed than by 60,000 fans at an All-Ireland final.

On All-Ireland final day the minute you hit the pitch after coming out of the dressing room you are confronted by this unmerciful din. It's like turning up a car radio to full volume. I never found it intimidating. What struck me in 1975 was the colour, even it was mostly the Dublin colours. Traditionally Kerry fans were reluctant to wear their colours whereas their Dublin counterparts brought a new life to Gaelic football. I think it motivated us to put on a better performance when we were playing into Hill 16.

The game itself is something of a blur now. But just like

the Munster final we got a lucky break early on and it stood to us. Gay O'Driscoll let the ball slip and John Egan got in to score a beautiful goal with the outside of his right foot. He showed fabulous balance and control to beat Paddy Cullen. The die was cast.

Our captain Mickey O'Sullivan got injured before half time. He was really on song that day and went on a solo run beating several opponents before he was felled by a stiff high arm tackle by Sean Doherty who was very fortunate not to be sent off. Mickey didn't regain consciousness until 45 minutes after the match. Tragically he never again played as well for Kerry. The injury appeared to knock a lot of confidence out of him.

I moved out to wing-forward after Mickey was carried off. It was the best thing that could have happened to me. Left corner-forward was never a position I enjoyed playing in. I felt confined and was often starved of possession. This was another reason why I started to roam all over the field. I had far more space on the wing and it suited my roving game.

I'm inclined to laugh when I hear about the elaborate tactics used by GAA teams nowadays. Back in 1975 Kerry's tactics were very, very simple. They basically consisted of quick movement of ball and man. We never employed specific tactics to deal with particular teams. O'Dwyer, for instance, never suggested that I adopt a roving commission. He never told me to stop it either. It was just something which evolved.

With Mickey O'Sullivan on his way to hospital I was the only player from Kenmare on the team and was now captaining the side. Thankfully I was so wrapped up in the game this never dawned on me. You dream about playing in an All-Ireland final; you dream about winning an All-Ireland medal but I suppose the ultimate dream is to captain a winning team in an All-Ireland final. So here I was at nineteen years of age achieving all these ambitions at the one time and barely recognising the fact.

I learned later that the selectors discussed the possibility of telling me at half time that I would be accepting the trophy if we won. But they thought it wiser not to say anything about it in case it upset my performance. In hindsight it was a good decision. Had I been told I would have spent the next 35 minutes wondering about what I would say in my speech. Instead I was able to concentrate on the game for the full seventy minutes and was very pleased at having kicked three points.

After the final whistle sounded the Kenmare representative on the selection committee, Denis McCarthy told me I was to go up and accept the Cup. I had one problem, however. My Irish was not too good. On the way up to the podium I remember asking a steward what was the Irish for 'on behalf of'. GAA President Dr Donal Keenan presented me with the Sam Maguire Cup and I just about managed the obligatory one sentence in Irish, "Tá an áthas orm an corn seo a ghlachadh ar son foireann Chiarraí." The rest of the speech was a blur.

The captain's role was something I wasn't really prepared for. Thankfully Mickey O'Sullivan was released from St Laurence Hospital the following morning. He was fit to take over as captain again and I was delighted to be relieved of my duties.

For a variety of reasons I got very little sleep on the night of the final. By the time I made it up to the bedroom there was bedlam. I counted 28 people in the double room and it took all my powers of persuasion to secure my bed for a few hours.

The homecoming was unbelievable. Out of the blue we had won an All-Ireland which we didn't expect. We were feted everywhere we went in Kerry. We were the sex symbols of our time and it was a case of wine, woman and song. The highlight of the homecoming was when Sam came to Kenmare on the Wednesday night after the final. Post All-Ireland celebrations always followed a set pattern in Kerry. Monday night we arrived back on the train to Killarney. Tuesday night we visited Tralee and on Wednesday the party moved on to the home town of the captain. What I found strange about the whole experience was when guys who I had grown up with came up to me looking for my autograph.

The Kerry minors beat Tyrone to make a double and it

was also a Spillane family double as Mike was centre back on the team. Exactly a week later both of us were in action for the Kerry U-21's in the All-Ireland decider in Tipperary town. Again Dublin provided the opposition.

What was most unusual about Kerry's U-21 campaign in 1975 was that, as far as I can remember, we had no training sessions! All the players involved were either members of our senior or minor squad. Despite all the celebrations we still managed to account for a Dublin team which included fellow Thomond College students Brian Mullins and Fran Ryder, as well as another future Dublin boss, Gerry McCaul. We won by six points (1-15; 0-12). Kerry had completed the treble for the first time in their history.

We now believed the world was our oyster. We were the team of the future. We were so young we were going to dominate football for the rest of the seventies. The seeds of disaster were already being sown.

5

DOUBLE TROUBLE

ON the surface everything looked in order as Kerry began the defence of their All-Ireland crown in 1976. We bowed out of the National League when we lost to Cork in a play-off at the Mardyke but nobody lost too much sleep over that result. In May we headed for America for the annual All Star tour and enjoyed ourselves thoroughly before then getting down to serious training for the forthcoming championship

John O'Keeffe was team captain in 1976. He was a very polished talker and I can still remember his speech before we played Waterford in the first round of the championship. "Listen lads," he said, " if we don't beat these guys today there isn't much point in playing the Munster final." It seemed to have escaped his attention that if we didn't win we wouldn't be playing in the Munster final! There was no need for alarm, however. We won by 22 points.

Cork's new GAA stadium, Pairc Ui Chaoimh was opened in 1976 and its first big match was the Munster final between ourselves and Cork. There was absolute chaos. Nobody knew for sure how many were in the stadium, but it was dangerously overcrowded with hundreds spilling on to the sidelines. For the first time in my career I was seriously frightened on a football field.

I remember at one point Kerry got a 45 and I was standing on the end line waiting for the ball to come in. I got a belt from an umbrella across the back of my legs from a Cork supporter who said to me: "Don't f... stay in here anymore. If I catch you again you will get the same treatment." Quite honestly I was reluctant to go near where he was standing for the rest of the match.

The atmosphere was very tense. There was a lot of niggling fouls off the ball. Cork felt they hadn't done themselves justice the previous year and they had a point or two to prove. A lot of their tactics that day could best be described as underhand. The majority of the people around the sidelines were Cork fans and the Kerry players were intimidated by them.

I reckon if Kerry had won that day neither us or the referee would have got out safely. A draw was almost the perfect result. Certainly we weren't complaining as we hadn't played well. The result also afforded the Munster Council, the Cork County Board and the Pairc Ui Chaoimh committee an opportunity to do a better organisational job for the replay. As both the 1974 and 1975 Munster finals were in Killarney the replay was fixed for Pairc Ui Chaoimh on August 1.

Predictably from an organisational viewpoint things went smoother the second day. Unfortunately, however, there is a fundamental design fault in the stadium which hasn't been corrected to this day. The GAA seemed to think of everybody but the players when designing the place. The dressing rooms appeared to be built for table tennis rather than GAA teams. It simply was impossible for 15 players, never mind 25, to tog out in comfort in the dressing room. It was hilarious watching guys trying to get changed in this tiny space.

The highlights of the 1976 Munster final replay were shown earlier this year on the 'Action Replay' programme on Network 2 and it has aged well. I would consider it to be one of the greatest Gaelic football games of all times and, dare I say it, it was a better game than the so-called best match of all time, the 1977 semi-final between Kerry and Dublin.

The 1976 replay was a high scoring contest producing 44 scores, including five goals, and a bucket load of controversy. We eventually won it after extra time but it was John Moloney's refereeing which captured most of the headlines afterwards. His decisions didn't find much favour with Cork. In the dying minutes he awarded Kerry a goal when he deemed that Brian Murphy had stepped over his own line after he saved a shot from Sean Walsh. Almost immediately afterwards he disallowed a Declan Barron goal at the other end for a square infringement.

I believe the latter decision was correct as Barron was definitely in the square. We got a lucky break with our goal because I don't think Brian Murphy stepped back over the line with the ball. Aside from the controversy we made a great comeback after conceding a terrible goal early on when Paudie O'Mahony took a short kick out and Jimmy Barry Murphy returned it to the back of the net.

I equalised with a fisted point before Mike Sheehy kicked what looked like been the winning point in normal time. But as the ball was in the air the referee blew the final whistle and extra time had to be played. At that stage I think he was endeavouring to balance the books. But all he was doing was prolonging Cork's agony. Pat McCarthy had a storming 30 minutes in extra time and we won by four points.

It looked like we had the bad performance (in the drawn match) out of our system and we were on the road to All-Ireland glory again. We met Derry in the All-Ireland semi-final and the match turned on an early controversial incident in which I was a central figure.

I was marked by a late replacement in the Derry defence, Gabriel Bradley. But we began our relationship on a sour note. When I put my hand out to shake his before the start he pushed it away. Once the game started he proceeded to hold my jersey and the referee wasn't taking any notice of what was happening. So I did something to make sure he could no longer ignore what was going on. I threw myself down on the ground and stayed down until the referee came over to see what was going on. He warned Bradley. From then on the Derry players, particularly Bradley, were very reluctant to concede any more frees or be caught fouling and we won by sixteen points in the end.

Even though I was criticised for my behaviour - which I might add I repeated on a few other occasions in subsequent years - I have no apologies to make. If an opponent was hanging out of my jersey then it was my job to draw the referee's attention to what was happening - if that meant throwing yourself on the ground well so be it.

Hammering Derry was, in hindsight, the worst possible result from a Kerry perspective. We were now absolutely certain in our own minds that we could handle Dublin in the final. It was just a question of turning up on the day.

The truth was that standards had slipped compared to 1975.

We became celebrities. We were getting invited to festivals and although such invitations didn't extend as far south as Kenmare certainly some of the lads in the north in the county enjoyed themselves, particularly at the Rose of Tralee festival. Discipline slipped and guys were guilty of swinging the lead.

Our complacency was compounded by the fact that Dublin struggled to reach the final. They had stumbled past Meath in the Leinster final and were none too impressive in the All-Ireland semi-final against Galway. In contrast Kerry were the form team.

The reality was that Dublin had strengthened their side since their defeat twelve months previously. The arrival of Kevin Moran was particularly important. Ironically, in an interview before the final, I suggested that Moran's inclusion at centre-back would make Dublin far more difficult to beat. My comment proved alarmingly prophetic. Moran took off virtually from the throw-in and ran straight through our defence. I have often slagged him that while most footballers get noticed when they score goals or points he got famous for kicking the ball wide! In truth, of course, his run set the tone of a game in which nothing went right for Kerry.

We lost our goalkeeper Paudie O'Mahony through injury but we were struggling all over the field. Dublin were first to the ball; they were hungrier and they thoroughly deserved their seven point win. I played as well as I had in 1975 final - as did John Egan - and, indeed, I won my first All Star in 1976 but it was poor consolation.

Dublin were harder, stronger and more physical than us and it wasn't until 1978 that we learned how to deal with this aspect of their game. We caught Dublin on the hop in 1975. A year later they were ready for us, whereas we were not mentally ready for them. I have no hesitation in stating that the Kerry team I was involved in was the greatest team of all time in Gaelic football, but the 1975 -1976 team did not fit into this category. We had weaknesses, particularly at midfield.

Pat McCarthy was not the force he was in 1975. To make matters worse he went off on holidays before the final and put on weight. He went on a crash diet when he returned and while he looked trim in the final his energy levels were depleted. His midfield partner Paudie Lynch was a more natural half-back. We had problems up front as well. Brendan Lynch was a classy footballer who established himself in the team prior to the arrival of the younger brigade. But his style of play didn't really fit into our overall pattern. Mickey O'Sullivan was back but he was only a pale shadow of what he was in 1975.

Former Galway footballer Jack Mahon described our style in the mid-seventies as 'bastardised-football.' His comments were typical of the kind of criticism levelled at us. In a way he was right.

The Kerry team which dominated Gaelic football between 1978 and 1981 used both the long and short ball game. In 1976, however, we over-relied on the hand pass and this played into Dublin's hands. They were as fit as us and had the edge on us in strength so they could counter our short passing game. The warning bells were sounding but unfortunately we chose not to hear them. We had to experience an even more painful lesson the following year before we changed our ways.

Of course it wasn't easy to change because we went through the subsequent league campaign unbeaten. At that time Kerry and Dublin were way ahead of the rest and, although there were major flaws in our team, our fitness levels papered over the cracks. There were over 40,000 fans in Croke Park for the 1977 league final between ourselves and Dublin. But the contest was distorted somewhat by the absence of Brian Mullins. We won by two points in a low scoring game (1-8; 1-6).

I have to confess I have absolutely no memory of the 1977 Munster final. I don't even remember where it was played. For a period in the mid-seventies Cork were probably the second best team in the country. However, because they were being beaten in Munster finals they never got the credit they deserved.

In that era whichever club won the county football

championship in Cork seemed to have an inordinate influence on the selection of the county team. As a result there was no consistency and I don't remember ever being marked by the same Cork player in successive Munster finals in the seventies.

A glance through the record books tells me we beat Cork easily 3-15 to 1-9 in Killarney and I was Man of the Match scoring 1-3. We completed a Munster hat trick but we hadn't solved any of our underlying problems. We were still juggling at midfield, for instance. Jack O'Shea had arrived but we were still looking for a partner for him. Páidí Ó Sé was tried but he lacked height and didn't really fit the bill. But it was an O'Shea-Ó Sé partnership which faced Dublin in the 1977 All-Ireland semi-final.

We were not short on confidence going into the game which was effectively an All-Ireland final. The GAA recognised this by increasing the cost of Hogan Stand tickets. We had beaten Dublin twice since the All-Ireland final and after an impressive Munster final performance we felt we were ready to take them.

The 1977 All-Ireland semi-final has been rated by many people as the greatest Gaelic football match of all time. I have always disagreed with that view. The first half was mediocre. There were missed chances, poor distribution and loads of mistakes from both teams. I agree the second half was outstanding. But 35 minutes of excellence does not entitle the game to be classified as the greatest game of all time. The reason it was labelled with that tag is that it produced the result which the majority of the Dublin based national media wanted - Dublin coming from behind to win.

I have always maintained that the game hinged on one incident ten minutes from the end when we were leading by two points. I made a sliding tackle and the ball went off Brian Mullins and over the sideline. It should have been a Kerry ball and I will invite anybody to watch a video of the game and decide for themselves. The linesman gave the decision to Dublin, however. In those days the linesmen for all big Croke Park matches came from Dublin clubs and they could hardly be regarded as neutral.

Dublin took a quick sideline ball which culminated in a David Hickey goal. Bernard Brogan added a second near the end and our dreams were shattered.

We were roasted at midfield. Sean Walsh missed an open goal whereas Dublin took their chances. There were other reasons too for the Dublin win, not least the fact that they got their tactics spot on. Team captain Tony Hanahoe, who was team manager in 1977, was the on and off the field architect of many of their wins in that era. He was unusual in that he could orchestrate wins on the field despite rarely touching the ball. However, his tactic of pulling the opposing centre-back out of position left a big gap which the Dublin midfield and half-backs raced into and the majority of teams found it hard to counter this ploy. In the 1977 semi-final Dublin used a variation of this tactic. Jimmy Keaveney pulled John O'Keeffe out of position and left loads of space in front of our goal which Dublin exploited to the full.

There was huge fall-out in Kerry afterwards. We were heroes in 1975 and more or less forgiven for what happened in 1976. There was no respite in 1977 and much of the criticism was directed at me personally. I remember one so-called fan coming up to me in a pub afterwards and pouring a pint of beer over me.

Initially I felt the personal criticism I was getting wasn't justified. Admittedly I had failed to score but I had played a lot of ball; won frees which were converted and laid on passes which led to scores. On reflection, however, I hold my hand up and admit that I over indulged in solo runs in the 1977 semi-final. Con Houlihan said I was like a cowboy roaming the prairie without my horse.

As I mentioned in a previous chapter this fault developed during my juvenile football days and I found it hard to rid it from my game. Apart from my ability to kick long range points, solo running was my best skill. My over indulgences didn't matter in under-age or, indeed, in club football. I could solo the length of the field and sell dummies all day. It was different in inter-county football, particularly against the Dubs. It wasn't enough to be fast and skilful against them. I was unable to shake their markers. I wasn't losing the ball but I was being forced into cul de sacs and wasn't creating openings for my colleagues.

I had also off the field worries in the summer of 1977. I had failed my final exams in controversial circumstances in Thomond College. Certain parts of my answer papers had disappeared. So besides preparing for the All-Ireland semi-final I was also studying for my repeats. My future away from football was on the line. All the pressure got to me and I wasn't mentally right for the game.

For the first time in my career and, indeed, the only time until 1990, I was dropped for Kerry's first league game after the 1977 semi-final. I knew I was been made a scapegoat along with a few others for the Dublin debacle. I felt victimised because I believed the decision was wrong and was done for personal rather than football reasons. I came very close to pulling out of the panel. My uncle 'Doad' Spillane advised me: "Don't let them get to you. Quitting is what they want you to do."

I heeded his advice; said nothing and was introduced as a substitute at half time in our next league match against Dublin at Croke Park. I got a fabulous reception from the Dublin fans on Hill 16 when I ran out at the start of the second half. Ever since I have had a soft spot for the Dubs. We lost again but my brief exile was over.

We learned a lot of painful lessons in 1976-77 which proved invaluable later. We quickly realised how fickle our supporters were. Okay some of the criticism we received after the 1977 semi-final was justified. But the reality was that despite weaknesses in the team we were actually unlucky to lose the game.

From then on, however, we adopted a new and different approach. We forgot about playing for the honour of Kerry. We played for ourselves and this united us in a common purpose and it gave us strength in adversity. Mentally it made us stronger. We vowed never again to let ourselves be exposed to such ridicule. We became selfish, maybe even bitter, and we probably developed chips on our shoulders. But the bottom line was: the new approach worked.

6

BACK ON THE SUMMIT

THE knives were out for Mick O'Dwyer after our double defeat by Dublin. But by the time the Kerry Convention was held in January 1978 the criticism had subsided. Kerry's completion of a hat trick of All-Ireland U-21 titles helped assuage some of the anger. O'Dwyer again headed the poll in the election of selectors. Three of the other four selectors, Liam Higgins, Joe Keohane and Bernie O'Callaghan were new. The fifth was Pat O'Shea.

By then O'Dwyer had started to make the changes which were crucial to our subsequent successes. His job was made easier when Jack O'Shea gave up the drink, settled down and got married. Undoubtedly though the single most important factor in turning round the fortunes of the team was the arrival of Eoin 'Bomber' Liston, who made his Kerry debut at full-forward against Offaly in our opening league game in the 1977-'78 season.

Up until then our style of play was based on quick movement of the ball using short passes. We never had a target man. In physically tough matches where the exchanges were tight - such as the clashes against Dublin - we didn't have time to pick out a colleague. As a result we found ourselves in trouble. 'Bomber' brought an extra dimension to our play. Now we had a target man on the edge of the square and his presence resulted in our style of play evolving and the success flowed.

When Liston first arrived on the scene he was overweight. I'm not convinced he ever really got completely fit - but he got close. It was hugely significant that he got a teaching job down in Waterville which meant O'Dwyer could keep a fatherly eye on him. The pair became very close and Micko made sure that 'Bomber' kept his weight under control. Eoin brought size, strength and physique to the forward line. He was an excellent target man and he gave our outfield players the option of kicking the high ball into the danger zone.

He also did a lot of the necessary physical stuff around

the forward line and, in a sector where there were a lot of us who didn't fancy this aspect of the game, his arrival was like manna from heaven. But 'Bomber' was much more than a hard man and an excellent fielder. He was very intelligent and an excellent distributor of the ball. He wasn't, for instance, the kind of player whose first thought when he got the ball was to go for his own score. Instead his first option was to lay it off. If you made a run as he jumped for a high ball nine times out of ten he would flick it to you. He knew all the moves without having to look.

His arrival resulted in Kerry modifying their style. From 1978 on we blended the short game with the more traditional Kerry style of long kicking. For years afterwards our critics labelled us 'Kings of the Hand Pass' and the majority of other teams tried a short passing game themselves. Prior to 1978 the hand pass was Kerry's forte. But by the end of the decade we had travelled a huge distance in terms of the style of football we were playing. My own style of play was a good example of how Kerry's approach changed over the years. I changed from being a ball carrying, short passing and slightly selfish footballer into a much more rounded team player.

Mind you, the results we achieved in the 1977-78 league gave no indication that success lay just around the corner. Having beaten Offaly in our first game we then lost to Dublin, Cork and Galway before drawing with Kildare in our last match. The point we gained in Newbridge was enough to save us from relegation.

Our thoughts that spring were on other issues, however. We had suffered back to back championship defeats to Dublin and we were beginning to wonder why they had the upper hand over us.We started to analyse the differences between ourselves and Dublin to see if we could figure out why they had the edge on us. We believed we were a better football team. Why then were Dublin beating us? We came to the conclusion that we lacked aggression. Kerry were not ready for the physical aspects of the game.We were unwilling to throw our weight around when the going got tough. Perhaps we considered ourselves nice guys. But the reality is that purists may win accolades and awards but they don't win matches.

We noticed too that Dublin's aggression had a different trade mark than that used by any other county. When a Dublin player tackled an opponent he hit him hard be it fairly or illegally. Invariably the stuffing was knocked out of the victim. Okay, he probably got a free, but the chances were he was winded for a long time afterwards - maybe even for the whole match. Quite frankly, Kerry were too nice in the physical stakes. We wanted to play the ball all the time and were reluctant to stop opponents going for the ball. And when we fouled, it was usually no more than a push in the back or a tug on a jersey. We lacked aggression. Provided we could correct this weakness we would have the upper hand.

We got a chance to prove our theory in Gaelic Park in New York on May 15, 1978. Dublin were in the US for the All Star tour and we flew out to play them in another fund raising match for Sister Consilio's home for alcoholics in Cuan Mhuire in Athy. One of the wags in our group suggested it was a very appropriate charity given our fondness for the odd drop. One of our selectors, Joe Keohane was particularly vocal in demanding we shed our Mr. Nice Guy image. This match was going to mark the start of our new approach when we played Dublin. We were going to meet fire with fire. If we got hit we were going to hit them back twice as hard.

The match should never have been played. Gaelic Park was waterlogged. However, the majority of the Kerry team flew out specially for the game - the remainder were on the All Star tour - and a big crowd had gathered. As the event was in aid of such a worthy cause it was decided to go ahead despite the torrential rain.

Surprise, surprise it was an absolutely torrid affair. Dublin were without Brian Mullins and Bobby Doyle but significantly we won by 2-11 to 1-3. Eoin Liston, Páidí Ó Sé and Pat O'Neill were sent off, Paddy Cullen and Ger Power clashed - that incident was to have very serious repercussions for Dublin four months later - while Jimmy Deenihan and myself sustained broken noses. Diplomatic relations between the two camps was at an all time low afterwards. So much so, in fact, that Deenihan and myself had to head for a hospital in the Bronx to have our noses put back into place. Nobody in the Dublin camp offered us their medical expertise that particular day!

The win itself meant nothing but we had gained a huge moral victory. We knew in our hearts and souls it would sink into Dublin over the next few months that we were no longer a soft touch. We were more than a match for them in the physical stakes. If any single match was instrumental in making us the greatest team of all time it was this contest. In essence then there were four factors that elevated us from being an above average team which had won an All-Ireland and league title to be the greatest team of all times. They were:

* The discovery of Eoin Liston.
* Change of attitude towards the use of aggressive tactics.
* Change in our style of play.
* Finally finding an excellent midfield pairing in Jack O'Shea and Sean Walsh.

After the New York trip we knew we were getting our act together and this was confirmed by the nature of our first round Munster championship win over Waterford. We hit 4-28. I contributed 2-5 from play and Mike Sheehy scored 2-8. The movement was superb. We were quite confident before the Munster final against Cork at Pairc Ui Chaoimh. We based this optimism on our belief that the majority of the Cork team were past their sell by date.

Ironically, one of the their veterans Declan Barron was Man of the Match. In a torrid match - Tommy Doyle and Tom Creedon were sent off - Barron's performance wasn't good enough to stop Cork going down by seven points. Sean Walsh had an outstanding game for us and our midfield partnership worked well. He anchored it and did the fetching while Jacko acted as link man.

Having given my marker John Coleman the run around in the first half Cork switched their wing-backs at the break and I found myself marked by Brian McSweeney who was going out with my sister, Margaret at the time. A native of Millstreet, Brian was a quiet guy. We were at college together in Limerick and he played centre back on the Thomond team which I captained to success in the All-Ireland club championship earlier that year.

I remember Brian shook hands with me at the start of the second half and he remarked that whatever happened he would forgive me. I knew in my heart and soul that psychologically he had already thrown in the towel. The one thing you never do to a direct opponent is be nice to him or apologise to him before the game begins.

The pundits were impressed by our performance and so were the bookmakers. They installed us as 5/4 favourites for the All-Ireland with Dublin at 6/4 even though they had beaten us in the previous two championships and were heading for their fourth All-Ireland crown in five seasons.

One of the reasons why Kerry stayed on top for so long was that we didn't have to peak for every match in the championship. From 1978 on, we didn't take the league seriously. We never prepared for it and we stuck to a schedule of not starting our training programme until March. At most, we had to peak for three games in the championship. We never got excited about the Munster semi-final. Basically it was a case of turning up and winning. So our first big match of the year was the provincial final against Cork every July.

Our approach to the All-Ireland semi-final was dictated by whichever team we were playing. For instance, if we were playing the Leinster champions we had to peak for that match particularly if Dublin were the opponents, as was the case in 1977. Unfortunately we probably didn't treat their successors as Leinster champions, Offaly with the same respect. That attitude came back to haunt us in 1982.

However, if we were meeting a Connacht or Ulster team in the All-Ireland semi-final then we didn't peak. In Ulster, Kerry were perceived as being the Manchester United of Gaelic football and there was an aura of invincibility about us. As a result many of the Ulster teams we met in the championship were psyched out even before the game began. They came into the contest with a defeatist attitude. By the time they realised they were as good as us it was too late.

We played Roscommon in the 1978 semi-final. It was a poor match played in pouring rain. With the exception of John 'Jigger ' O'Connor and Michael Finneran, Roscommon were short on quality forwards. And like a lot of teams they made the mistake of believing if they got as fit as us and copied our by then out-dated short passing game they could beat us. Despite the atrocious conditions Roscommon still persisted with the short passing game and really they were going nowhere with such an approach. We were very poor and never got out of second gear yet we still won in a canter, 3-11 to 0-8. The Kerry fans voted with their feet and stayed at home.

There were lot of complaints afterwards about the poor quality of the game, an argument which was underpinned by the fact that 47 frees were awarded. It's an indication of the way Gaelic football has evolved, or to be more accurate degenerated, in the last twenty years that 47 frees would now be below average for a championship match. I scored an impressive looking goal which in reality was a total fluke. I was soloing through when the ball slipped from my hand but I managed to get a boot to it and it flew into the top corner. At the time I maintained I had picked my spot.

The great thing about the match was that it got a bad performance out of our system and we still won by twelve points. Better still, having being labelled as All-Ireland favourites after the Munster final people now suggested that maybe we weren't a great side. As far as the public were concerned there were still question marks hanging over us when we faced into the final against Dublin.

Within the squad itself we possessed a reasonable degree of confidence based on several factors. We felt the Dublin team were past it. Five of them were aged 33. In contrast, our oldest player, John O'Keeffe was 27. In particular we felt their full-back line of Gay O'Driscoll, Sean Doherty and Robbie Kelleher was vulnerable. Their half-back line was rock solid and midfield was okay but we believed they had serious limitations up front.

With the exception of Jimmy Keaveney the rest of the forwards were never likely to score much and were particularly poor at kicking long range points. They had to work the ball in close to their opponents' goals. In 1978 we prevented them from doing this and forced them to shoot from out the field.

Dublin started well in the rain while we looked in trouble. Legend has it that one selector suggested that I be taken off. In fairness, he had reason to doubt me. Sixteen minutes elapsed before I touched the ball. Dublin did all the attacking and raced into a five point lead. I remember Robbie Kelleher popped up in front of our goals at one stage. But they fell into the trap of going too far forward.

As in all big Dublin/Kerry matches the first goal was always going to be decisive. Completely against the run of play we scored it after 24 minutes. Bobby Doyle, whose reason for roving all over the place I could never really figure out, was penalised for over carrying. My brother Mike took a quick free, catching Sean Doherty and Robbie Kelleher out of position. Eoin Liston gathered the ball, passed it to Jack O'Shea who linked up with myself. I passed it to John Egan and he dispatched the ball to the net.

Of course it became the forgotten goal of the 1978 final as our second goal just before half time provoked years of debate and is now part of GAA folklore. Just prior to one of the most famous All-Ireland final goals, Dublin goalkeeper Paddy Cullen tackled Ger Power late and this indiscretion went unpunished. In the goal incident Power was guilty of a late tackle on Cullen. Referee Seamus Aldridge noticed Paddy retaliating and awarded Kerry a free. It certainly wasn't a free. In my view Aldridge was endeavouring to balance the books - it happens all the time. In this case he was punishing Cullen for his earlier indiscretion.

The rest is history. Robbie Kelleher handed the ball to Mike Sheehy while Paddy was still out complaining. There was no whistle and the referee had his back to the kicker. Mike took the kick which went straight into the net and the goal was allowed. Quite honestly Dublin had good reason to feel aggrieved. Con Houlihan's description of the bizarre goal is the one I liked best. Writing in the *Evening Press* the day after the game he described it thus:

"Paddy put on a show of righteous indignation that would get him a card from Equity, throwing up his hands to heaven as the referee kept pointing to the goal. And while all of this was going on, Mike Sheehy came running up to take the kick - and suddenly Paddy dashed back like a woman who smells a cake burning. The ball won the race and it curled inside the near post as Paddy crashed into the outside of the net and lay against it like a fireman who has returned to find his station ablaze. Some time Noel Pearson will make a musical of this final - and as the green flag goes up for that crazy goal he will have a banshee's voice crooning: And that was the end of poor Molly Malone."

We went in at half time totally buoyed up and in the second half we took them to the cleaners. The 'Bomber' scored a hat-trick and we won by an incredible 17 points, 5-11 to 0-9.

Amazingly Liston's three goal salvo wasn't enough to win him the Man of the Match award, which instead went to myself. It was the first of three Man of the Match awards I won for performances in All-Ireland finals, which is a record. Obviously after my slow start I eventually started motoring. There were some interesting statistics published afterwards in the *Cork Evening Echo* about my performance. As I mentioned already I didn't touch the ball during the first 16 minutes. During the remainder of the game I played the ball 32 times - more than any other player. John Egan was next best - he played the ball 28 times.

I had the unique distinction of being the goalkeeper for a few minutes after Charlie Nelligan (and John McCarthy) were sent off in the second half. Jimmy Deenihan took over from me and was later replaced by our official sub-goalkeeper Paudie O'Mahony. It was one hell of a sweet victory and we had one almighty week of celebrations afterwards. The reception afforded us when we came home in 1978 was the greatest ever given to a Kerry team. It copper fastened the idea that one must experience bitter defeat before really appreciating success.

On a personal level 1978 was a magnificent year for me. I captained Thomond College to victory in the All-Ireland club championship; played on the winning Munster Railway Cup team; won Munster and All-Ireland medals with Kerry and named Man of the Match for my performance in the All-Ireland final. I also won All Star and Texaco awards. Last, though certainly not least, I helped Templenoe beat Kenmare in the District Football championship for the first time in 25 years.

There was, however, one sour note to the year. Kerry were bidding for a record fourth consecutive All-Ireland U-21 title. They qualified to play Roscommon in the final. The GAA, in their perceived wisdom, fixed the match for Dr Hyde Park in Roscommon. It was part of a double bill - we played Roscommon in the final of the Ceann Aras tournament in a curtain raiser. I never understood why the Kerry County Board agreed to concede home advantage to their opponents in an All-Ireland final.

Perhaps it had something to do with a row about the date for the U-21 semi-final against Louth. The game was originally to be played before the senior final but Kerry refused to travel. The match was then rescheduled for a week after the senior final.

The arrangements for the entire weekend in Roscommon left much to be desired. The Kerry teams stayed in hotels in Roscommon town and there was an all night party in one of them. In fairness it should be pointed out that Kerry fans - still celebrating our demolition of the Dubs - were as noisy as the locals. In Hyde Park the dressing rooms were well removed from the playing fields with players and officials mingling with the crowds on their way to and from the pitch.

There were bad vibes right from the start. I remember a section of the crowd started chanting "Ogie is a moron." It was the first time I ever heard such a vicious chant being directed at a named GAA player during a match. We lost the Ceann Aras final which we didn't care a toss about. But our U-21 side lost by a point thus depriving Charlie Nelligan, Sean Walsh and my brother, Mike, of four successive All-Ireland medals at this level. I'm convinced had the final been played at a neutral venue Kerry would have prevailed.

From that day on there was always a huge level of animosity between the Roscommon team, their fans, and Kerry. Roscommon became our most bitter rivals. Whereas we became friends with the majority of the Dublin players, we never had a relationship with the Roscommon guys. They appeared intent on never allowing us to play football, too many of their players were negative in their approach while their fans engaged in vicious verbals.

But at least there was a happy ending to an otherwise disastrous weekend. My first cousin, the late Paddy Spillane was Chief Superintendent in Limerick at the time - his son Brian played on Ireland's Triple Crown winning rugby team in 1985. Paddy asked us to call into Henry Street Garda Station in Limerick on the way home from Roscommon. The visit turned into one of the social highlights of 1978.

There were a few barrels of beer set up adjacent to the cells and we had a memorable party. Indeed, before the night was out the prisoners in the cells were pleading with us to keep the noise down because they wanted to get some sleep!

7

THE SPILLANE FAMILY

MY father, Tom Spillane died suddenly on October 1, 1964 from a heart attack. He was forty one. I was eight years old and the eldest in a family of four - the youngest, Tommy, was only two.

I have sketchy memories of my father. He was a big strong man, Mr. Football around Templenoe. During his own playing career he had the unusual distinction of winning a Railway Cup medal with Munster in 1948, without having played a senior championship match for Kerry. Just a few weeks before his death he was a selector on the Kerry team beaten by Galway in the All-Ireland final.

I retain vivid memories of the night he died - he passed away in his sleep. There was fierce commotion in the house. I didn't know what it was all about and I think somebody told me my grandfather was taken ill. Sadly, it was a lot more serious.

None of us were brought to the funeral. We all stayed in a neighbour's house, O'Shea's, on the evening his remains were taken to Templenoe Church. I wasn't in the house when he was coffined but I know the coffin was taken out the upstairs bedroom window as it wasn't possible to bring it down the stairs. I can still hear the church bell ringing as the hearse made the short journey from our house to the church. On the morning of the funeral we were taken by my aunt's husband to a place called the Black Valley. I can still remember the few hours we spent there.

Before his death he gave me my first match in a Templenoe jersey. He ran most of the teams in the club, bringing the players to all the games. I was about six or or seven when I made by debut in an U-14 challenge game against Sneem. I doubt if I merited selection, but nobody was going to argue with my father. The other memory I have of him is when he took me swimming in Kenmare

Bay. He held me on his shoulders as he tried to teach me how to swim.

One of the reasons why both my mother and wife would like to see me packing in football for good is the fact that my father was a very fit man yet he died of a heart attack while still in his forties.

When everything settled down after the funeral my mother, Maura was left with four young kids - myself, Mike, Margaret and Tommy - ranging in ages from eight to two. She also had to run a bar/grocery and petrol pump business, which wasn't exactly thriving at the time. And there was no widows pension in those days.

The sacrifices my mother made over the years were unbelievable. The credit for our achievements lie with her. I know all Irish sons have a soft spot for their mothers. I truly believe my mother was very special. She worked for 35 years in the bar and, even when she was sick, she never took a day off.

She often remarked that when our father died she knew everything rested on her shoulders. There was no point in her wallowing in self-pity. She felt it was important that she looked after herself so she ate well and cooked a dinner every day regardless of how busy the bar was. She was an amazing woman although tragic events in her life hardened her. Apart from my father dying my grand-parents also died soon afterwards..

My mother ran the business for 35 years and reared four children without any help. The kitchen in our house adjoins the bar. While she was cooking she kept an eye on the bar. Sometimes she ate her dinner while standing inside the bar counter talking to customers.

Up until the time she retired she never watched television, she never entertained friends and the only break she got was when the bar was cleared and cleaned at about 1am. She then sat down to do her office work and read the paper. Prayer was a great source of strength to her and I'm sure her religious devotion saw her through many crises. Although she rarely went to bed before two am, she was always first up in the morning. Not alone did she rear us she also developed the business very successfully.One of our best known customers in the late sixties was the late Jefferson Smurfit (Sen), father of Michael Smurfit, who owned a holiday home nearby. He spent a lot of time in the bar.

I remember two things about him. He was always advising my mother to invest any few pound she had to spare in Smurfit shares. Had she followed his advice she would be a very wealthy woman today. He owned a Rolls Royce which he always filled up at our petrol pumps after his drive from Dublin.There were, in fact, two petrol tanks in the car. Our pumps were set for a maximum sale of £10. When we were filling up Mr Smurfit's car and the reading came to £9-19 shillings and 11 pence we had to start again. I think it cost about £13 to fill the Rolls' two tanks.

Everything my mother did was geared towards rearing her children. She knew the chances of us receiving a good education were remote if we didn't go to boarding school because bar life was so irregular and disruptive. Mike, Tommy and I were all sent to St Brendan's Killarney. My sister Margaret, who is in the mould of my mother in terms of the sacrifices she made, stayed at home and went to the secondary school in Kenmare.

Living above a bar is not an ideal set-up. I can never remember us having many family days out. The only days there was any semblance of normal family life were Good Friday and Christmas Day when the bar closed. Even then, while other families were sitting in front of a cosy fire enjoying themselves late on Christmas Eve, we would be washing the floor in the bar. In those days business was much quieter than it is now.There wasn't as much socialising in the sixties as there is now. People might come out for a few drinks once a month.

The big days in the bar were the fair days in Kenmare and August 15th, traditionally the big gathering day in Kenmare. The locals would head into town early and finish up in our pub later that night. There were the inevitable fights and I remember being scared and frightened as I watched men fighting in the yard from my bedroom window upstairs. The bar business is probably the hardest life of all. You are at the beck and call of everybody and it's hard to please all the people all the time. Trying to reason with people who have a lot of drink consumed is not the easiest of tasks.

My mother was a member of one of the most famous GAA families in Kerry, the Lynes from Killarney. All her brothers played with the Legion GAA club in Killarney and two of them, Jackie and Dinny, won All-Ireland medals with Kerry. She never missed a match before she got married. But she stopped going the day my father died. Amazingly she never saw any of her three sons win any of their 19 senior All-Ireland medals. In fact, she never saw us playing in any games.

I often wondered why she didn't go. Initially she didn't have the time. In the eighties she had more time on her hands but at that stage she probably felt it might be bad luck to start going. I have never asked her myself why she didn't go, but when other people pose the question she just shrugs it off.

But she remains a fanatical GAA fan. She never misses a match on television, be it football or hurling and she reads all the match reports and the GAA coverage in the local and national newspapers. But I suppose I'm a little sad that, unlike thousands of other people, she didn't share in our successes by being there on the big occasions.

Football was rarely discussed in our house. But then it was quite rare for all the family to get around the table and have a meal together. Sunday was an exception when the bar closed between two and four o'clock. We dined together then and the only other time we could have a family chat was when the bar was quiet.

My mother always performed two rituals before games. We never left the house for either a training session, a club challenge match or an All-Ireland final before my mother sprinkled holy water on all our gear and it's a tradition I have maintained to this day. And, just before we left for a match, she would always say the same thing to us: "Remember who you are". We would joke with her and say we're the Murphy's from Sneem.

I can only remember one occasion when my mother was overjoyed with a victory we had. In 1987 Kenmare beat Dr Crokes from Killarney in a replay of the county final with a last gasp goal. The Lyne family were stalwarts of the Legion club and their arch rivals were Dr. Crokes. It was the first time ever she asked us to do our best in a game.

Crokes scored a point in injury time in the replay to go two points clear. It looked all over. But within twenty five seconds Kenmare had the ball in the Crokes' net at the other end. It was one of the most memorable victories I achieved in football and one which my mother savoured more than any of our All-Ireland successes. The morning after the game when she came into our bedroom to congratulate us there were tears in her eyes. It was the first time I ever saw her emotional.

After Kerry's All-Ireland success in 1984 when I picked up my sixth medal and won the Man of the Match award I didn't arrive home until the Wednesday after the game. When my mother greeted me there wasn't a word of congratulations as she remarked; 'You should have been here on Monday.'

I cannot put into words the depth of thanks I owe to her for all she has done for me. It is only in in the last few years that she has had time to relax, watch TV or entertain her friends. She no longer lives over the bar but she normally visits every evening. Given the fact that there were strong football genes on both sides of the family, it was almost demanded of the Spillane brothers that we follow in our father and uncle's footsteps and play for Kerry.

Throughout our careers we were constantly compared to the Lyne's and whether we measured up to the standard set by Jackie and Dinny Lyne, both of whom had such distinguished playing careers. After my father died one of my uncles, Gene Spillane, who was a forester in Cork, became a father figure to us. When we were kids he took us to sports days all over the county and we generally arrived home with numerous prizes.

Gene is a football fanatic but he has a blinkered view

whenever Kerry are playing. And when the three Spillane brothers were playing we were the only Kerry players he was really interested in. Whenever I played poorly in the match he would ring me up and insist I had done well. Gene certainly nurtured our interest in sport.

My uncle Jackie Lyne was the Kerry trainer when they won the 1969 and 1970 All-Ireland finals. One of the biggest thrills of my life was when Jackie brought me to one of the All-Ireland semi-finals around that time. I was treated as if I was a Kerry player and that experience fuelled my desire to play for Kerry at Croke Park.

Another of my uncles, Canon Michael Lyne spent most of his adult life as a priest in Glasgow. Indeed, he missed out on what would probably have been a very successful GAA career because of his studies for the priesthood at All Hallows College in Dublin.

While working in Glasgow he got involved with Glasgow Celtic and eventually became the club chaplain. Canon Lyne regularly played golf with the then Celtic manager Jock Stein and the team doctor Mr Fitzsimmons. They arranged with the Celtic kit man to let my uncle have the pick of the squad's old playing gear at the end of each season. So he loaded pairs of football boots, shorts, jerseys and socks into a trunk and brought it back to Ireland with him every summer. We eagerly looked forward to the day of his arrival and for the rest of the summer we wore all the Celtic regalia. I scored a few goals wearing a pair of boots 13.2

better known to the family as Mike. He was an exceptionally good footballer. He won seven senior All-Ireland medals, two U-21's and one minor All-Ireland. But he always went about his business in an unassuming way and never got the credit he deserved.

His club career came to a controversial end. For fifteen years he left his home in Dalkey at around 7 o'clock on a Sunday morning and drove to venues all over Kerry to line out with Templenoe. He rarely got back to Dublin until midnight. He received nominal expenses and turned down numerous offers to join Dublin GAA clubs. He never played for the club again after being left out of the team for a final a few years ago.

The youngest member of the family , Tommy never realised his full potential even though he won four All-Ireland medals and was Man of the Match in the 1985 final against Dublin. He could play at either midfield or centre back - this was probably his best position. He was the most natural athlete of the three brothers, a great fielder and always very fit. However, he didn't work as hard at football as I did or make as many sacrifices. Mind you, he is now a lot wealthier than his two older brothers having established and developed a thriving auctioneering business in Killarney.

I reckon my sister Margaret has been in more arguments than any other Kerry woman defending the honour of her three brothers. She also made the compilation of this book a lot easier as she kept excellent scrapbooks of all my football achievements. The only thing she left out were the big matches we lost and thankfully there weren't too many of those between 1975 and 1986.

I met my wife to be, Rosarii in 1986. She came into the bar one night, played the guitar and sang a song. Tommy and I were both still living at home at the time. As it happened neither of us were behind the counter. We were in the adjoining kitchen which was separated from the bar by a curtain. We always kept an eye on the comings and goings in the bar. As soon as I saw this blonde girl coming in I made a B line for the bar. Who knows how things might have turned out had Tommy spotted her first.

I bought her a vodka - she said afterwards I was so mean she had to buy the tonic herself. Like a typical Kerryman I wasn't going to gamble too much. Rosarii was engaged when we met and I will always remember our first date. She was manageress of the Parknasilla Hotel near Kenmare. I went to the hotel to collect her and while waiting in the foyer I struck up a conversation with another lady. Rosarii passed by and I innocently asked the lady who she was. "Oh that's Rosarii Moloney,' said the lady, 'my daughter will be playing at her wedding'. What a start to our first date!

Rosarii has no interest in football, which turned out to be a blessing in disguise. Up until I met her everything in my life revolved around football and my mother helped me to follow my dream in every way possible. She washed all my gear, cleaned and polished my football boots and bought all my clothes. Indeed, I would be the first to admit that she spoiled me rotten. So much so, in fact, that the only domestic chore I can perform now is to make a cup of tea for myself.

One of the reasons why I was so fit was my mother never got me out of bed before 12 o'clock when I was on holidays. During my playing career I slept an average of eleven hours a day. Everything in my life revolved around football. Before a big match I didn't have to work in the bar. I could sit upstairs and watch TV. I was pampered.

Marriage put things into perspective. For a start it made me realise for the first time ever that there's more to life than football. Football is a selfish game; marriage is about sharing. Rosarii went to one or two matches to see me playing after we started going out. But she soon stopped and I doubt if she ever saw me playing for Kerry. I don't think she could handle seeing me lying on the ground not knowing whether I was seriously injured or just play acting.

Had I met Rosarii in 1976 rather than 1986 I would never have won eight All-Ireland medals. I never imagined myself getting married, settling down and having a family. But now I have a beautiful wife and three lovely children and life couldn't be better. Our first child, Cara, was born on August 8, 1990. There was a lot of publicity about the arrival of a Spillane heir. The local curate congratulated us from the pulpit. But then went on to remark: 'Of course, we are all disappointed that it wasn't a boy. Better luck next time.' Luckily, Rosarii wasn't there because she probably would have flattened him on the spot.

Our second child, Shona arrived two months prematurely on June 18, 1992. It was touch and go for many weeks with her as she weighed less than three pounds when she was born. During the time she wavered between life and death in the intensive unit of Cork's Bon Secours Hospital I finally came to terms with how unimportant football really is in the bigger scheme of things. I prayed more during those few weeks than at any time in my life. Thankfully she survived and is now a very happy six year old.

Then we had a gap of five years before our next child. Traditions die hard in rural Ireland. There is a feeling that when it comes to children it's the boys who matter. I would be a millionaire if I got a pound for every time I listened to people making comments like "Have you the footballer yet?"

I know people don't mean any harm when they make these kind of comments, but they annoyed me and they upset Rosarii even more. But I would be less than honest if I didn't admit that one of the greatest days of my life was when our son, Pat was born in Cork on September 4, 1997. So as far as everything is concerned we now have a footballer in the family. My standard answer to all the speculation on whether he will follow in my footsteps is: "He might want to a ballet dancer."

8

FOREIGN FIELDS

RTE Television ran their first ever Superstars event in 1979. I was invited to compete along with cyclist Pat McQuaid, Dublin GAA midfielder, Brian Mullins, Limerick hurler Pat Hartigan, rugby winger Tom Grace, boxer Mick Dowling, swimmer David Cummins and Republic of Ireland and Arsenal soccer star David O'Leary.

I had no idea what was involved. Either the BBC or ITV had previously run a Superstars competition. But the only television signal we received down in Kerry in the 1970s was from RTE, so I had never seen such a competition until I lined up for a 100m race at Belfield. David O'Leary won that sprint and led the competition after the first day. Luckily for me, he had to return to Highbury to train with Arsenal and missed the second day. This left me in a great position and I was fortunate enough to become the first ever Irish Superstar.

I was then asked by RTE to represent Ireland at the World Superstars in the Bahamas. Unfortunately there was very little time between the Irish event and the competition in the Bahamas. So I had no real opportunity to do any specialist training. I did some cycling on a old style push bike I borrowed from a neighbour of mine, Johnny Bawn. Swimming was out of the question because the water was too cold but I did a bit of road running. I would have liked more time to prepare. I considered it a tremendous honour to be asked to represent my country and, given my competitive streak, I wanted to do as well as possible.

Mind you, I had more pressing matters to attend to on the GAA front before I headed for the Caribbean. The day before flying to the Bahamas, Templenoe had their first county league match of the season.

We were away to Milltown-Castlemaine and they were winning by a comfortable margin with time running out. Then I remembered hearing somewhere that the club was in dispute with the farmer whose land adjoined their playing field. He had a habit of confiscating any football that strayed into his property. It was time to find out whether the story was true. We were awarded a 14 yard free and I told my brother Mike to kick it as high and hard as he possibly could and make sure to look completely disgusted afterwards. He hadn't a clue what I was on about, but he followed my instructions. And, sure enough, the minute the ball flew over the bar and into the next field the farmer appeared, grabbed it and disappeared.

We had our own ball well hidden. Milltown produced a plastic ball which we refused to play with. They then found a soft ball but, on the pretence that we were in a big rush because some of our guys had to catch trains, we rushed off. I think we eventually lost the points in the boardroom. In my case, I was actually heading to Dublin on the train. I slept on the floor of a friend's flat in Harold's Cross the night before making my way to the airport the next morning, March 5, 1979.

The World Superstars was a once in a life time experience. Among those competing were the legendary New Zealand athlete Peter Snell, who won the 800m and 1500m double at the Tokyo Olympics; Mexican-born Rafel Septien, who was the field goal kicker with the Dallas Cowboys; Welsh long jumper Lynn Davies, who won a gold medal at the 1964 Olympics; Brian Budd, a soccer player from Canada who was the defending World Superstars champion; Joe Theismann, the quarterback with the Washington Redskins; former world record high jumper and Olympic medallist Dwight Stones; European welterweight champion, Dave "Boy" Green from England; Greg Pruitt, a running back with the Cleveland Browns; Green Bay Packers fullback Jim Taylor and former F1 world champion Emerson Fittipaldi of Brazil.

It was a long way from Templenoe to the luxurious surroundings of the Princess Hotels in Freeport/Lucaya. We were treated like kings and lived in the lap of luxury for a week. I even had my own minder. It was a fantastic experience to meet and talk with all these world famous sportsmen. Pruitt had just signed a million dollar contract the day before he flew to the Bahamas. Brian Budd was a great character and six months later I bought him several bottles of wine in Leeson Street.

Dwight Stone had eight full-time coaches. At the time, athletics was still supposed to be an amateur sport and any money athletes earned had to go to their club. Stone overcame this little hurdle by forming his own athletic club, Desert Valley AC.

Essentially the World Superstars was a television event organised by the American Network NBC. However, there was serious money available. For instance, Budd took home nearly $40,000 the previous year when he won it. There were ten different competitions spread over three days. The events were tennis - I was probably the first Kerryman to represent Ireland in the sport - gym tests, swimming, weight lifting, 100 yard dash, half mile run, bike race, soccer shooting, rowing and an obstacle course. Each competitor had to choose seven events.

The night before the competition we had to declare the events we were competing in. The first five finishers in each event received prize money ranging from $1,000 for the winner to $300 for fifth place. Being a cute Kerry boy, I let everybody declare before me. I noticed only four people had entered the 200m swimming race. Now, while swimming wasn't exactly my forte - even if I did swim Kenmare Bay later in life - I reckoned I only had to turn up for the race and I would pick up $300. I put my name down and next day I earned the handiest three hundred dollars imaginable.

In this book I refer several times to the use of psychology in sport. It was during the World Superstars that I first saw its value. The Americans were masters of the craft. They had the ability to psyche you out so much, that you were a beaten man before the event even started. I remember warming up before the start of the half mile race when one of the Americans came over to me and said: "Gosh Paddy, if I don't do the first 400 yards in a minute I will not be in the shake up at the finish." I believed him and took it easy during the first lap. By the time I discovered I could have beaten him, and probably the others too, they were gone well past me.

It was also my first experience of drug taking in sport. Mind you, in my innocence, I didn't really realise what was going on. There was a big medical tent set up near the competition area. Guys were going in and out of the tent but I didn't think too much about it. However, I did notice two guys in particular had an extra bounce in their steps after visiting the tent. Remember this was a Mickey Mouse celebrity television competition. Yet there were guys prepared to pump their bodies full of all kind of chemicals in order to improve their performance. I stuck with the local beer.

The Americans had a great interest in my career as a Gaelic footballer, particularly the fact that I was an amateur. NBC organised a kicking competition between myself and Rafel Septien. I matched him for kicks off the ground up to the 50 yard line with an oval ball. On the suggestion of RTE commentator Jimmy Magee I then proceeded to give an exhibition of kicking the ball out of my hands. With my first kick I literally drove the ball out of the ground. Having seen my exploits on American TV, the San Diego Chargers offered me a trial as a 'punt kicker.' I never took up the offer, even though a couple of years later I was in San Diego on an All Star tour.

The one event I expected to do well in was the soccer competition. We had to dribble around two poles and then try and beat the goalkeeper. The rest of the competitors were crap at it. I had psyched myself up and was convinced I was going to win this event. But when I missed the first kick I cracked. I made a mess of the second as well and I think I scored the third. But really I should have got all three. I was so disgusted that I brushed passed current F1 team owner and ex-world champion Jackie Stewart, who was doing commentary work for NBC, and refused to give him an interview. As I had just fluffed the chance of making a grand my mood wasn't great.

I made about 3,000 dollars - I even got a tax return from the US a few months later. The GAA didn't raise any fuss about me keeping the money. As far as I was concerned I was an amateur GAA player, but I was a professional for the purpose of the Superstars competition. Even though I enjoyed the experience, I was disappointed because I missed out on the opportunity to make a lot more money. I really didn't do myself justice because I didn't have sufficient time to prepare. Ideally I would have liked a few months to train specifically for the competition.

I got a trunk load of free gear, most of which I still have: I recently noticed the gear is actually coming back into fashion again. I also made an impression, albeit not a very favourable one, on my future wife Rosarii as a result of my appearance at the World Superstars. Jimmy Magee's daughter, Patricia was a class mate of hers at school in Dublin at the time. After the World Superstars programme was shown on RTE television, Rosarii asked Jimmy's daughter did she know the bloody eejit with the funny suntan who was on the box the night before - yours truly. Due to my fair complexion I burn, rather than tan, and I got what became known as the 'Pat Spillane suntan' while in the Bahamas. I was red from three-quarters way down my arm!

I never defended my title. I was disillusioned with RTE's decision not to send me to the European Superstars competition which was held later that year in Tel Aviv. Even though I was the reigning Irish champion, RTE decided to invite Tony Ward to represent Ireland. I was very, very annoyed. To add insult to injury, Tony wasn't able to compete in all the events in Tel Aviv because he was injured.

The bringing together of top stars from different sports to compete against each other is a great idea. However, the event quickly lost its appeal among the leading stars in American sport who didn't fancy being humiliated in such a competition. The Irish Superstars competition, which was sponsored by the National Dairy Council, continued during most of the eighties. It made good television because it was more light entertainment than a sports programme.

However, people from the main-stream sports quickly lost interest in it, after it was won by guys who were not known nationally and who trained specifically for the event. This, of course, gave them an unfair advantage over the footballer, hurler, rugby or soccer player, who couldn't devote so much time to preparing for the Superstars competition. I believe there would still be a huge television audience for an annual competition between the ten best known sports stars in the country.

The highest honour any sportsman can aim for is to represent their country and I'm proud to have represented Ireland as an individual in the 1979 World Superstars. I later represented Ireland in the Compromise Rules series but the hybrid game was somewhat dubious.

Although I never made it to the Bahamas again for the World Superstars I did make plenty of other trips across the Atlantic during the seventies. During those years the only perks for GAA players were the annual (and illegal) trips to play in the latter stages of the New York championships.

Legend has it that one Kerry player, who wasn't even an established star, earned enough money from his trans-Atlantic trips to build his house. Then there was the Kerry dual player who earned twice the normal fee by playing both football and hurling on his weekend visits to Gaelic Park.

I was just 18 when I made my first trip to the Big Apple in 1974. I let it be known that I was interested and I got fixed up fairly quickly. Looking back on it now, it was a rather harrowing experience, but I didn't worry about it at the time. I was much more interested in this great new American invention - tea bags!

I stayed in an apartment with an IRA man who was on the run from the North. There were regular meetings held in the flat into the small hours of the morning and I imagine those attending weren't discussing the value of the dollar on the stock exchange. Over the years I played in both the junior and senior New York championships with a variety of teams, including Donegal, Clare, Kerry and Tyrone, for whom I probably made the most appearances.

Frank McGuigan was the star player on the team during most of those years. He was one of the best footballers I came across and some of his best ever performances were fashioned at Gaelic Park. I think I ended up with two New York senior championship medals and at least one junior medal. But really, they were fairly accidental in the overall scheme of things.

In my innocence I imagined Gaelic Park to be a fabulous stadium. After all it is situated in one of the most famous cities in the world and one which boasts one of the biggest concentration of Irish emigrants anywhere. Unfortunately the reality couldn't be further removed from the myth. Seeing Gaelic Park for the first time is one of the greatest letdowns any GAA person from Ireland is likely to experience.

In the seventies it was a decrepit, run-down place which hadn't seen a lick of paint in donkey's years. No more than ten players could fit in the dressing rooms where the shower - it rarely worked - and the toilets were situated alongside each other. The majority of the seats around the field were broken and the pitch itself was rough and bereft of grass up through the centre.

Situated close to a subway station in the Bronx, it was basically a large drinking den. There have been marginal improvements to Gaelic Park in recent years. But it's a scandal that in a city like New York this is the public face of the GAA. Thankfully, it's the exception. In other US cities such as Chicago and San Francisco there are excellent GAA facilities which have close ties with the local Irish emigrant community.

My fellow Kerryman, John Kerry O'Donnell, who owned the lease on Gaelic Park for many years, deserves great credit for keeping Gaelic Games alive in New York. Unfortunately there wasn't enough money invested over the years in upgrading the facility.

Football in Gaelic Park was not for the faint-hearted. It was very physical. Understandably, there was much resentment about players from Ireland being flown in for the key matches in the championships.

As a result the opposition thought we were fair game, we got little or no protection from the locally based referees and, at times, our team mates didn't have much sympathy for us. I felt I was a sitting duck and felt more scared playing in New York than anywhere in the world, with the exception of the first Compromise Rules test match between Ireland and Australia in Perth in 1986.

The GAA in New York is the banana republic of the association. Rules mean nothing. I played in one New York final for Donegal during which we made 13 substitutions. Mind you, if there was a touch of lawlessness about the football in Gaelic Park it was a child's picnic compared to what went on in hurling. Having watched a few hurling games over the years I concluded I wouldn't ask my worst enemy to play in the New York hurling championship.

I played no more than a handful of decent games in New York. Once an Irish player arrived in the Big Apple he had a choice: he could either take the whole thing seriously and prepare for the game as he would for an important game at home, or he could hit and the town and enjoy himself. The concluding matches in the New York championship generally coincided with my mid-term break from school. I looked on these trips as a perk and I thoroughly enjoyed myself off the field.

Had I the benefit of four hours sleep before risking life and limb in Gaelic Park I would consider it a bonus. The majority of the matches were played under a blazing sun. Just imagine my condition. I was dehydrated even before I took the field, I was getting belts from all angles and, just for good measure, I was getting sunburned as well. No wonder I never played well.

A doctor was always on duty at Gaelic Park - presumably to fulfil a condition of the venue's insurance policy. On one occasion I stumbled into the medical room with blood pouring from my nose to discover an Italian on duty. He was reading the *New York Times*.

Without glancing up from the paper he asked what was wrong. I replied that I thought I had broken my nose. He told me to go over to the mirror and clean off the blood. "Does it look different than it did this morning," he wondered. "Yes," I replied. "its crooked." "You probably broke your nose then," he replied. End of medical consultation.

Why do players go to New York? The money element is greatly exaggerated. The match fee in 1973 was about $200 plus air fare. By the early nineties the fee had increased to about $500 per game. We were also given free accommodation - usually in somebody's flat or apartment. The main reason why players went out was because it was a short holiday. The reality was you rarely left the Big Apple with too many dollars in your pocket after a few nights on the town.

I did slightly better financially than many of my fellow travellers. A wealthy individual always gave me an envelope with the words: "This is something for the education of the kids."At the time I wasn't married, so I was never too sure whether the dollars were for the kids I taught in Bantry or for my future children. Anyway I didn't jeopardise the arrangement by getting into too much detail. But I ended up getting between $800 to $1,000 for the weekend.

Competition in the New York football championship heated up considerably in the eighties when Cavan and Tyrone clashed in a number of finals. These games featured most of the top players at the time from Ireland. Indeed, there were so many players flown in from Ireland that several sat on the subs' benches. There was one legendary incident involving a Kerry player who agreed to play for Tyrone but changed his mind in the arrivals hall of Kennedy Airport and ended up lining out for Cavan. I can only assume that it hasn't his the love of the blue and white of Cavan which caused him to change sides.

He was reputed to have received $2,000 for playing with Cavan. The truth of the story was never established but it did spawn all the wildly exaggerated stories about the money which we were allegedly getting to play in the New York championship. Once this figure was mentioned, every player felt duty bound to boast that he received a similar sum. Otherwise he was acknowledging the fact that this 'star player' was four times more valuable. Everything got blown out of proportion.

Of course, virtually all the weekend trips were completely illegal. But, apart from the Tony Keady affair in 1989, the GAA have consistently turned a blind eye to what's going on.

The current President of the New York GAA Board, Mike Cassidy once came up with a unique solution to the perennial problem of teams going out 'on the town' the night before a final. He was manager of the Donegal junior team at one time and I travelled over the final. He called a team meeting on the Friday night before the final in his bar, Liquid Assets, just around the corner from the New York Stock Exchange. At the end of the meeting he made a proposition. He promised a free bar for the rest of the night provided we stayed away from the booze the following night. We drank ourselves silly until about 4am the following morning. We were too hung over to touch any drink on Saturday night. We went out the next day and won the final.

All my hair-raising New York experiences did not take place on the field of play. I remember drinking one night in a bar in the Bronx with three or four other Irish guys. An Armenian came in but the barman wouldn't serve him. About two hours later the Armenian returned. He parked his car across the street and proceeded to make tracks for the bar with a gun in his hand. Luckily the barman spotted him. He locked the doors, rang the police and herded us into the basement. But the tension was too much for a father and son from Ireland. They ended up having a digging match after the son criticised the way his father was treating his mother!

One of the reasons why New York football has never developed is its use of 'imported players.' New York based footballers train hard all year. Then, if their team reached a semi-final, they were ditched in order to make way for the big stars from Ireland who couldn't care less who won. Not surprisingly the local players become disillusioned. It's a great shame the money spent on the 'weekend shuttle players' is not invested in the promotion of under- age football in New York. Many American youngsters are natural athletes who could easily be coached in Gaelic football.

In fairness a lot of the dollars spent on bringing players out from Ireland is not what could be described as 'GAA money.' There is a thriving gambling business run in conjunction with the big games in the championship. Wealthy individuals bet heavily on the outcome of matches. Wagers of ten, twenty or thirty thousand dollars were quite common - I even heard of one $100,000 dollar bet . The guys laying these bets were quite willing to throw in a few thousand dollars to bring in a few big named players from Ireland. Once they had the players lined-up, the big monied men could then lay their bets. The guys involved in the betting didn't give a hoot whether the teams were illegal. Bets were paid out on the basis of the score when the referee blew the final whistle. It didn't matter what happened later in the boardroom.

Given all these circumstances, it is admittedly difficult for the Croke Park authorities to police what goes on in New York. Regardless of what regulations are in place, players will always be willing to take a risk once the game remains an amateur sport in Ireland. I always saw my New York adventures as bit of light relief away from the serious business of football.

Holy Pat!
First Holy Communion.

Oh, brother! Pat, Mike
and Tommy (seated).

Little angels, Mike and
myself in pensive mood.

The Spillane Family. That's me
examining my fingers.

My Father Tom and my Grandfather Pat.

**Graduation day in Thomond College with my mother and
my aunt Kathleen (right) in 1977.**

All my dreams fulfilled at 19, I receive the Sam Maguire Cup as the stand-in Kerry captain in 1975

Getting away from the great Tommy Drumm of Dublin,
my most difficult opponent.

Dublin goalkeeper Paddy Cullen denies me a goal in one of the many clashes
against the Dubs.

The Kerry team pictured before the 1975 All-Ireland final. Back row (1-r)
Paudie Lynch, Paudie O'Mahony, Pat Spillane, Tim Kennelly, John O'Keeffe,
John Egan, Brenden Lynch and Ger Power.
Front row (1-r) Ogie Moran, Paidi O'Se, Mike Sheehy, Jimmy Deenihan, Mickey
O'Sullivan, Pat McCarty and Ger O'Keeffe, with Leo Griffin also included.

Mike

Tom

The Good Times... on holiday in the Canaries with Jerry O'Sullivan,
Ger Lynch, John Egan and Tommy

..in the footsteps of Ronnie Delaney. Myself, Diarmuid O'Donovan,
Tommy, Ger Lynch and Bernard O'Sullivan line up at the MCG in
Melbourne during Kerry's Australian tour in 1981

Templenoe under-16s in the mid-sixties. I'm second from left in the back row, Mike is the first on the left in the middle row.

Junior Champions of Kerry. The victorious Templenoe team after our victory in the 1975 final. I'm sixth from the left in the back row.

Kerry 1987-standing: Leo Griffin, Jack O'Shea, Tommy Spillane, Ger Lynch, Charlie Nelligan, Ambrose O'Donovan, Pat Spillane, Ger Power, Sean Walsh, Seated: Eoin Liston, Tommy Doyle, Paidi O'Se, Mike Sheehy, Mike Spillane, Ogie Moran.

Pat (Junior) tries out Sam for size

The Spillane family, October 1998 from right to left: Myself, Rosarii, Pat (junior) Shóna and Cara

9

THOMOND COLLEGE

CAREER guidance wasn't much in vogue in the mid-seventies when I was a student at St Brendan's. I was a fanatic about sport from an early age. Inevitably, therefore, I was hoping for some kind of sports related job when I left school.

The thought of becoming a professional soccer player did cross my mind. During a holiday in London in the early seventies I decided to explore the possibility of going for a soccer trial. I rang Leyton Orient to inquire whether they were having trials: I opted to get in touch with a smaller club because I felt I was wasting my time contacting the likes of Arsenal or Spurs. Anyway Leyton were not having any trials. So their loss became Kerry's gain.

I sought a place in the newly established National College for Physical Education in Limerick - better known later as Thomond College. I also applied for a job as a junior executive officer in the Civil Service. Back then the points race hadn't been heard of and I got a place in Thomond. A few days after I arrived in Limerick I was offered a job in the Civil Service, but I turned it down.

Until the establishment of the National College for Physical Education anybody in Ireland who wanted to become a PE teacher went to places such as Loughborough College or Strawberry Hill in England to study. I was among the first batch of physical education teachers to train in Ireland. There were enormous teething problems at the college and I spent many enjoyable days travelling up to Dublin to take part in marches to the Department of Education.

Amazingly, when I enrolled it still hadn't been decided who would award us our diplomas or degrees when we graduated. Much of the subsequent hassle was about this issue. There were other big problems, not least the fact that, at the time, Limerick city was ill- prepared for an influx of lively third level students.

All the disadvantages, however, were completely

overshadowed by the one big plus about Thomond College in the mid-seventies - Gaelic football. The Thomond College GAA team was the nearest thing to a professional football team I ever played on. We were trained by Dave Weldrick, who was one of the first GAA coaches to introduce scientific tactics.

Sometimes we trained twice a day. We went into great detail about tactics, even going so far as to video our own training sessions. We worked out a system of hand signals so everybody knew where place kicks, from any part of the field, were going to land. No stone was left unturned when it came to team preparation. On one occasion the touring All-Blacks rugby team were training on a adjoining pitch to us in Thomond College. At the end of their session the New Zealanders came over to watch us training and went away suitably impressed.

Dave Weldrick had a major influence on my career, even though, at times, I feared him. The highlight of my third level GAA career was when I captained Thomond College to victory in the 1978 All-Ireland club championship. The entire campaign was nearly aborted before we even played a game in the 1977 Limerick club championship.

In early 1977 we travelled to Cork for a match in the Higher Education Colleges' league. We lost. Our traditional stopping spot in Cork was the Glen Rovers' GAA clubhouse. Dave, who was playing a big soccer match with Pike Rovers the next day, told us to be back on the bus within an hour. But letting students loose in a bar, where the drink was slightly cheaper, was a recipe for chaos. Three hours later we were still in the clubhouse. I was delegated to go out and explain the situation to Dave, who was sitting on the bus for about an hour and half at this stage. I literally crawled into the bus and pleaded for forgiveness. Dave resigned on the spot.

The following Tuesday myself and a few of the other players approached him and pleaded with him to come back. Reluctantly, he agreed. We didn't lose another match during the remainder of my time in college.

We were fortunate that some of the top GAA players in the country were all students there at the time. They included Brian Mullins, Fran Ryder, Brian Talty, John Tobin, Richie Bell, who sadly died suddenly a few years ago, Jimmy Deenihan, Hugo Clerkin, Declan Smyth, Eddie Mahon, Teddy Owens, Tom Donnellan and my brother, Mike.

Thomond College was allowed enter the Limerick senior football championship and, given the quality of our players, it was no surprise that we were more than a match for most teams in the county. Predictably, we were hated by the majority of clubs and nothing much has changed in the intervening years. Last year Thomond College lost the Limerick senior football championship title in the board room. I can't understand why Thomond are not simply banned from competing in the championship. It would mean less hassle all round.

We met with unbelievable resentment everywhere we went. Every possible obstacle was placed in our way in a bid to prevent us from winning the county championship. Club matches were invariably fixed on the same day as big inter-county championship matches which meant we would be missing a key players. In 1976 Thomond College were scheduled to play a club called St. Kieran's, Carrickerry, in the Limerick championship two weeks before the All-Ireland final. Kerry people living in Limerick wrote to the Kerry County Board warning that the Kerry players involved would be in danger. County Board officials tried to persuade us not to play but we lined out.

It would be an understatement to describe the match as a torrid affair. During the game St Kieran's had a player sent off but he came back on near the end. We won, Carrickerry objected - this was typical of what went on - on the grounds that we had failed to transfer from the Limerick city championship to the county championship. We counter objected pointing out that Carrickerry had brought on a player who had been sent off. Our objection was thrown out on the grounds on some spurious technicality. Carrickerry advanced to the next round!

There was so much red tape involved that, when we did reach the Limerick final in 1977, we brought in a legal expert who went through all the GAA rules and Limerick by-laws with a fine comb to make sure that everything was in order. From bitter experience we knew that, while we might win a match on the field, there was no guarantee we would prevail in the subsequent boardroom battle.

There was one Limerick team I purposely avoided during my three years in the college - a city side called Treaty Sarsfields. They consisted mainly of guys who played either soccer or rugby during the winter. I don't know whether they are still in existence - if they have folded I will not be shedding any tears. When ever Thomond were drawn against Treaty Sarsfields I always came up with a convenient excuse to miss the match. Let's say I had a gut feeling that had I lined out against the Treaty men I would not have won 8 All-Ireland medals.

Unfortunately we weren't allowed take part in the Sigerson Cup competition back then . We won every other honour available in Higher Education Football such as the Trench Cup and the Leagues and we finally made our mark in the Limerick championship in 1977, the year I graduated. By then, the likes of Brian Mullins, Fran Ryder and Jimmy Deenihan had already graduated. Ironically, the two Dublin lads played a key role in my election as team captain ahead of Mayo's Richie Bell before they left in the summer of 1976. Making me captain knocked a lot of the individualism out of me and ensured that, by the time I left Thomond, I was a good leader on the field and a much better team player.

Winning the Limerick championship with Thomond was an important boost to me personally because it came at a time when I was being subjected to a lot of criticism in Kerry because of my performance in the 1977 All-Ireland semi-final. I was dropped by Kerry for the opening game in the 1977-78 National League. Instead of lining out against Offaly, I played in the semi-final of the Limerick championship against Claughan.

The abuse we got, on and off the field, was frightening. I remember going into the Claughan dressing room after the game. Now, just like shaking hands with our opponent before a game, the visit of the winning captain to the loser's dressing is a kind of ritual and there is little sincerity involved. As soon as I reached the door of the dressing room I was met with a torrent of verbal abuse the likes of which I have never experienced before or since.

I missed the Limerick county final because it clashed with a National League game - I had been recalled by Kerry at this stage. Our vice-captain Richie Bell led us to victory and accepted the trophy. Our biggest problem was fielding teams in Limerick club competitions during the summer months when the college was closed. The majority of our squad had either gone abroad to work or were very involved with their own county teams.

At times we struggled to get fifteen players together and, on occasions, we had a few hairy looking characters on the bench whose link with the college was very tenuous, indeed. I can't say for certain whether they were ever used; on the law of averages they probably played at some stage.

Back in the late seventies, the provincial and All-Ireland club championship was not nearly as popular as it is now. But the Munster semi-final saga between Thomond College and Austin Stacks, Tralee certainly helped to establish the series. The tie stretched over four games and it produced some of the best matches ever witnessed in the competition and some of the best football I have ever seen.

The saga began on December 11,1987 in the Gaelic Grounds in Limerick . It was 2-6 each at the end of sixty minutes. The first replay took place the following Sunday, December 18 in Pairc Ui Chaoimh. Final score was Thomond College 3-4; Austin Stacks 1-10. We resumed the battle on January 15, again in Pairc Ui Chaoimh, when the final score was Thomond College 2-18; Austin Stacks 3-15. Pairc Ui Chaoimh hosted the fourth and final instalment a week later and, after four and a half hours of dramatic football, we finally got the verdict on a 3-8 to 2-5 scoreline. I scored 2-1 and the *Examiner's* GAA correspondent Jim O'Sullivan was impressed by my performance:

'Classy Thomond College, inspired by their brilliant captain Pat Spillane, did everything right on this occasion and were even more convincing winners than their six-point margin would indicate," he reported the next day.

Austin Stacks had an outstanding team at the time, including Kerry players John and Ger O'Keeffe,Ger Power and Mike Sheehy and Cork's Dinny Long. They were the reigning Kerry, Munster and All-Ireland club champions. I ended up as the leading scorer from play in the four games with a total of 3-8. I was marked in all the matches by a Tralee-based Garda, Noel Power. I always had the edge over him and Stacks probably erred in not trying somebody else on me.

Two weeks later we faced Cork kingpins Nemo Rangers in the Munster final. Like Austin Stacks, they were a star studded outfit backboned by Cork players like Billy Morgan, Dinny Allen, Jimmy Kerrigan, Brian Murphy and Seamus Coughlan. As I said earlier, we were big into tactics. On more than one occasion during training we lined out as we would in a match and just kicked the ball to each other from one end of the field the other.

We got into the habit of doing detailed analysis of all our own performances. We were unable, however, to look back on our winning performance against Austin Stacks because the match video went missing - the word was that Nemo had nobbled it. We were lucky to get past Nemo and were equally fortunate to beat Connacht champions, St Mary's from Sligo in the All-Ireland semi-final.

I was teaching at the time in Ballyvourney, Co Cork and drove up to Limerick a couple of evenings a week to train. It was the same with all the other lads who had graduated. Guys travelled from all over the country and made great sacrifices to prepare together for the All-Ireland series. We did most of our training in the Garryowen rugby grounds because our own pitches were in very bad shape at the time. We did most of it in ankle deep muck but the weather suddenly improved a week before the semi-final and pitches dried up quickly.

We were stuck to the ground for long spells against St. Mary's, who were a top class team at the time with players such as Barnes Murphy, John Kent and former Sligo Rovers' star David Pugh in their ranks. We were damn lucky to beat them.

I smile to myself when I read about the luxury hotels

teams competing nowadays in the All-Ireland club finals use on the eve of St Patrick's Day. Our accommodation arrangements in 1978 were somewhat more mundane. We trained in Limerick on the Saturday and travelled up to Dublin by bus on Sunday morning. Because a lot of us had graduated by then we had no accommodation in Limerick. The night before the final I slept on a floor in somebody's flat, as did several other players.

We fashioned a stunning performance in the final at Croke Park. Even though our opponents, St John's from Belfast, were a decent club side we ran riot, winning by fourteen points (2-14 to 1-3). I scored 1-6. And, despite all our differences with the GAA in Limerick over the years, we ended up wearing the Limerick colours in the final.

Ironically, even though we lived in each other's back pockets for nearly four years we haven't met as a group, on more than one occasion, since. However, I suppose that's typical of college teams. The other curious facet of the team is that aside from myself and my brother, Mike - who was wing forward on the team - and Galway's Brian Talty, none of the other players had successful inter-county careers. They reached their peak in college and found it difficult to reproduce that form once they left.

I have a lot to thank Dave Weldrick for in terms of my development as a Gaelic footballer. During my time in Thomond I matured as a player. I started to think more about the game, analysed my own performances, looked at areas where I might improve and I sought out weaknesses in opposition teams.

Dave went on to coach Clare but didn't achieve the breakthrough with them. If he had a failing - it was that he expected players to accept what he said without question. That was fair enough in our situation, where he was the teacher and we were his students. However, this coaching style was too aggressive and dictatorial for most county teams. However, he was still an outstanding coach and I learned much from him. At their peak Thomond College would have beaten most county teams. As a unit we were very effective; we trained like professional footballers and we were expertly prepared for all our big matches. I also suspect we were the first GAA team to do weight training.

I played soccer while in Limerick and represented Thomond in the Collingwood Cup at centre half and I remember scoring a goal in the competition against UCD. I was picked to play in the final trial for the Irish Technical College side. Among the other players chosen were Kevin Moran and Tommy Drumm. However, Kerry were playing Dublin in a challenge game on the same day as the trial and I opted for the GAA game. I have no doubt I would have made the team had I played in the trial.

While the GAA lads played a lot of soccer in the college we didn't have much contact with the rugby club, whose star performer at the time was Tony Ward. There was a lot of rivalry between the clubs but we liked to think the GAA club was the biggest and best.

Away from the football fields, other aspects of my years in Limerick were less satisfactory. For a start there wasn't enough accommodation in the city to cater for the influx of students, so we had to make do with what was available. The first year I stayed in digs and got a fry every single evening for tea. I got some revenge when I left still owing a week's rent. The next year I moved into a flat, but things weren't much better. Cooking was a skill I never quite mastered. Worst still, when I took the flat I overlooked the small fact that there were no plates or cutlery in the kitchen. One night I ended up eating spaghetti and corn beef from a page of the *Kerryman*.

I thoroughly enjoyed my student days, even if we did encounter a few eccentric lecturers along the way. One gentleman insisted that we present ourselves for his class dressed in spotless white gear. He then marched us out to a playing field and ordered us to roll about in the mud. I could never figure out what the purpose of this exercise was other than an attempt to humiliate us.

The physical education content of the course was long on theory but short on practical advice. For instance, despite having a degree in physical education, I wouldn't consider myself qualified enough to do the physical fitness training for an inter-county team. Much of the course was based on an English model which wasn't particularly suitable in an Irish context. Worst still the course did not prepare us for the harsh realities of teaching. We were never taught what to do when you had a class of forty with one basketball in a gym no bigger than a living room.

Initially there was much fanfare about the fact that the college planned to use continuous assessment, rather than the traditional end of year exams to grade us. So for the first two years we had exams every term but the whole thing was then scrapped.

We were always in dispute, be it with the college authorities or the Department of Education. On one memorable occasion we sent an advance party of three students to Dublin to erect a banner at the top of the Daniel O'Connell monument to publicise yet another protest march to the Department of Education the following day. We certainly got great publicity for the march because after placing the placard one of the lads couldn't get down from the top of the monument and had to be rescued by the fire brigade.

Teaching jobs were not plentiful when I graduated in 1977. And the fact I was a Kerry footballer didn't guarantee anything on the jobs front. I got a job initially as a substitute in Listowel Vocational School. Then two PE jobs came up in the Kerry VEC. I came first in the interview and I chose Rathmore VS because it was relatively close to home. I still have a letter stating when a permanent job arose I would be appointed. Twenty one years later I am still waiting for them to come back to me. Politics reared its ugly head and the job wasn't sanctioned.

In 1978 I got a temporary job in Bonane National School near Kenmare. Then I covered for a year in Colaiste Iosagain in Ballyvourney as a replacement for Mickey O'Sullivan, who took a year out to do a course in career guidance. Colaiste Iosagain is an Irish boarding school. The staff get paid a bonus for teaching through Irish. The farcical thing was my Irish was hopeless. This led to interesting scenes during the year. For instance, all the teachers ate lunch together in a big dining room and conversed through Irish. All I could do was laugh when they laughed, nod my head occasionally and look serious when they looked serious.

Teaching PE through Irish was relatively straigh forward but it was a whole different ball game teaching my other subject, Geography through the mother tongue. Finding Irish names for certain geography terms was a real pain. Every night I had no option but to sit down and write out exactly what lesson I planned to teach the next day. Then I had to get out my battered English-Irish dictionary and look up all the words and rewrite the entire lesson in Irish. The next day I wrote it out again on the blackboard in Irish. It was a tough year.

I took my present position in St Góban's College in Bantry just after I competed in the World Superstars in the spring of 1979. Bantry was a boom town in the mid-seventies because of the oil refinery on nearby Whiddy Island. Wage levels were probably three times the national average. The Betelgeuse oil tanker disaster had just happened when I started teaching in Bantry and there was a lot of salvage work going on.

I have had some marvellous times in Bantry. The college has achieved some success in sport. It was a different story in my early days. During my first week there I looked for volunteers to play in an U-16 match. After about five minutes I realised the only reason they came along was because they wanted to miss class. We decided at half-time to adopt a defensive formation and I pulled all the players back in and around the square. We lost by about 30 points but we didn't concede any goals in the second half.

On another memorable occasion the headmaster, Matt Kingston, refereed a match while sitting in his car overlooking the pitch. One toot on the horn was a free for us; two beeps meant a free for the opposition.

The college's first foreign tour to France was also quite memorable. We all assembled for the scheduled departure time, but when there was no sign of the bus an hour later we knew there was a problem. When somebody telephoned the travel agent they were informed that the bus was booked for the next day!

Even then the trip to Rosslare wasn't without incident as the bus caught fire and burned just outside the port. Thankfully everybody got off safely and the rest of the trip was relatively uneventful.

I am teaching in St Góban's for almost 20 years now. It involves a round trip of 64 miles every day. But I love the job. Once I manage to get out of the bed in the morning I find the rest of the day plain sailing.

10

THE GLORY YEARS

EVEN though we were far more interested in celebrating than playing football in the autumn of 1978 our form never dipped. We fashioned two particularly devastating performances in the National league against Kildare and Laois respectively. A couple of days after winning Kildare's first All Star award, their goalkeeper, Ollie Crinnigan, picked the ball out of the net seven times in Tralee. We won 7-8 to 0-7. Then, in our final league game before Christmas, we scored six goals against Laois who failed to record a single score during the hour.

My hectic social schedule reached its high point in early 1979 when I was presented with the Texaco award. I rubbed shoulders with sportsmen like Northern Ireland goalkeeper Pat Jennings and my ex-Thomond College student colleague Tony Ward.

I learned one important lesson from Tony having watched him practising his kicking. I noticed he always brought at least twenty rugby balls out on the field with him. I followed his example - both in terms of practising my kicks and making sure to bring as many balls as I could find with me whenever I went out for a kicking session. Kicking became the strongest attribute of my game as a result of this practise.

Our old 'friends' Roscommon beat us in the league semi-final in the spring of 1979. But any notion that we were slipping was rudely shattered on July 1 when he travelled to Miltown Malbay and beat Clare in the semi-final of the Munster championship by an incredible 36 points (9-21 to 1-9). The game became known as the 'Miltown Malbay massacre'.

People have often posed the question: Why didn't we ease up against Clare that day? I suppose since becoming involved in coaching underage teams at club and school levels I now realise how demoralising it is to be hammered by a huge margin. For instance, if the team I'm involved with is running away with the game I make a point of asking the referee whether it's okay to sent on a scatter of substitutes in order to try and make it more competitive.

The one reason we didn't take our foot off the pedal against Clare was because nobody, including myself, was guaranteed a place on the team. Nobody was going to let-up. What's often overlooked about the game is we conceded more against Clare than we did against any other team during the remainder of the championship.

I believe Cork people prefer to travel to Killarney for Munster finals than endure the headache of getting near Pairc Ui Chaoimh on a big match day. Indeed, it would be difficult to find a worse location for a major sports stadium. In contrast, there is always a brilliant atmosphere in Killarney which boasts one of the best playing surfaces in the country and its wide open spaces always suited us.

Over 46,000 passed through the turnstiles at Fitzgerald Stadium for the 1979 Munster final which, quite frankly, I could never see us losing. It was a view shared by the rest of the team. Had any of us been gamblers I think we would have made a few quid over the years. It's not that we were arrogant or over confident but at times we felt there was no team around which could beat us. This feeling was particularly prevalent during the 1979 campaign.

I was marked by Johnny Crowley, who was better known as a hurler. Throughout my career I always paid heed to the psychological aspects of the game. I was always interested in how my direct opponent would view the task facing him. He would probably know for some time that he would be marking me. He would get advice from friends, club mates, team mates and coaches on how to handle me. He would be psyched up to the ninety nines about the role. My job was to try and de-psyche him a bit before the game started. I always used the same modus operandi. Start off with a firm handshake, then try and engage him in conversation. The topic didn't matter. It was usually some banal comment about the weather or the size of the crowd. Anything which might distract him slightly.

As it happened Johnny Crowley was on the All Star tour earlier that year and we got on well together off the field. I could see Johnny was all psyched up so I tried my usual tricks. No joy. He was having none of my chit-chat. He just walked away from me. It was time to try Plan B. I broached the subject of an incident which happened to the pair of us in San Francisco. It worked. Johnny engaged me in conversation and, by the time the national anthem was finished, I felt his mask had slipped a bit.

On the day it didn't matter. Overall Cork were poor and we won by ten points with Ger Power giving an awesome performance and finishing up with a personal tally of 2-4. Whereas Cork were virtually as good as us in 1975 and 1976 and would almost certainly have won All-Ireland titles had they beaten us, they were a spent force at this stage.

We met Monaghan in the 1979 All-Ireland semi-final. They were all psyched up. I remember their trainer Paddy Kerr, who was marking me, being asked how he would cope. He replied : "He is a good player. He has everything. But I am looking forward to marking him. Can he fly? He can't fly over me; he can't fly through me. He will have to go around me and that won't be easy." I think Paddy's words came back to haunt him on the day of the match. We won by 22 points, 5-14 to 0-7. Even though we were without Ger Power, who pulled a hamstring in a club game, we were totally confident going into the 1979 final against Dublin.

The Dubs were in transition and had done little since the previous September to suggest they could reverse the 1978 result. Our assessment proved correct. It was as easy as the year before even though John O'Keeffe had to retire injured and Páidí Ó Sé was sent off. We cruised to victory on a 3-13 to 1-8 score line with Mike Sheehy scoring 2-6 which equalled the record which Jimmy Keaveney set in the 1977 final.

I was marked by Tommy Drumm who I consider the best player I ever came up against. I still scored four points. Indeed, I was both fortunate and privileged in my career that I always found my best form on All-Ireland day. I never had a bad final. The big stage seemed to bring out the best in me.

I always believe once a team gets into a winning streak it's easy to keep on winning - just as it's very difficult to get out of a rut once you start losing. So it was with Kerry during the 1979-80 league. Even though we did no training and gave the fringe players a run, we went through the campaign unbeaten before losing by a point to Cork in the league final in Pairc Ui Chaoimh. After their mauling the previous year in the Munster final, Cork had got their act together. The final itself was an ill-tempered affair with a lot of off the ball activity.

I got injured just after half time. Initially, I insisted on staying on but was eventually forced to retire. Perhaps, if I continued, we might have sneaked a win. In retrospect it was just the jolt we needed. The bottom line was we never worried about the league. Even now I'm hard pressed to tell you how many National League medals I have. O'Dwyer realised fairly early on that it would be very difficult to try and win both the league and championship. We looked on league success as a bonus which was achieved more by accident than design.

The 1980 Munster championship was slightly unusual. In the wake of the fall-out from the 'Milltown Malbay massacre' the previous year, the Munster Council made the rather bizarre decision of giving us a bye into the final. Initially it looked like a bad decision from a Kerry perspective as it robbed us of a competitive match before we played Cork. Typically O'Dwyer protested long and hard about the unfairness of it all.

However, the reality was that our backs versus forwards games in training were far more competitive than one-sided championship games against the likes of Waterford, Clare or Tipperary. We did a lot of extra training in the run-up to the final, against a Cork side who were a little cocky after their League final success. Their cause wasn't helped by Declan Barron's absence while Sean Murphy, who had given Páidí Ó Sé a roasting in the league final, had to retire with a knee injury before he touched the ball.

We were always on top in a game which featured a most unusual score. Our centre-back Tim Kennelly kicked the ball over his own bar for a rare 'own point'. The game was over as a contest long before the end with Kerry running out winners on a 3-13 to 0-12 score line.

I rate the 1980 All-Ireland semi-final against Offaly as one of the best matches in terms of sheer entertainment I ever played in. Having become accustomed to Dublin coming out of Leinster we were probably guilty of taking Offaly slightly for granted. The final score line of 4-15 to 4-10 in our favour tells its own story. It was a magnificent spectacle of free flowing football. To their credit Offaly allowed us to pay football and that policy possibly cost them victory. The game will be mostly remembered, however, for the magnificent performance of Matt Connor who scored 2-9 and damn near beat Kerry on his own.

His performance that day ranks as one of the best ever individual displays witnessed at Croke Park. He was an exceptional player. Tragically his career was short lived. Indeed, I often think the disappointment we endured in 1982 when we missed out on the five in a row was trivial compared to the suffering which Matt endures since his car accident.

I had a great tussle with Stephen Darby, scoring 2-2. With about 16 minutes to go we were 3-14 to 2-5 ahead but complacency set in. From a position where we were cruising, suddenly we found ourselves just five points ahead with five minutes left. We were in disarray but, fortunately, John Egan got our fourth goal to steady the ship. Afterwards we maintained it was our own complacency which nearly led to our downfall. Had we given Offaly more credit for what they achieved it might have helped us in the long term. We should have noted that they were a team going places. Within two years they shattered our greatest ever dream.

Having conceded fourteen scores, including four goals, questions were raised about our full back line and there was a lot of speculation about what Kerry would do to rectify the problem.

My brother, Mike, and Ger O'Keeffe - both of whom marked Matt Connor - were dropped. I felt it was a wrong decision as nobody would have held Matt that particular day. Ger O'Keeffe ended up playing in the final at wing back when we were forced into a reshuffle after Eoin Liston cried off. My performance in the 1980 All-Ireland final would not rank as one of my best. Part of the reason was I reacted badly to the dropping of my brother. I was in a sulk during the days leading up to the game because I felt Mike was victimised.

Mick O'Dwyer had other things on his mind, however. On the Thursday before the game Bomber Liston got a sharp pain in his side. He was operated on a few hours later and had his appendix out. We would have problems coping without Liston, who was our most influential forward during the previous three seasons. Our difficulties were compounded when we woke up on the morning of the game to the sound of rain lashing the windows of the Grand Hotel. It dried up during the match and a strong wind blew up. Roscommon had trained unbelievably hard for the game with players taking their holidays before the final in order to devote themselves virtually full time to their preparations.

The animosity between Kerry and Roscommon which started during the 1978 U-21 final reached its peak in this match. We knew from previous experience they would concentrate on stopping us performing rather than playing to their own strengths. Even before the game there were ominous vibes coming from Roscommon with comments like : "We are going to stop them", being bandied around.

Afterwards I spoke to people who were in the Roscommon dressing room before the game and they said the atmosphere was more akin to sending troops into war than preparing amateur sportsmen for a football match. Without doubt it was the toughest of the nine All-Ireland finals I played in. There were elbows and boots flying. There was emphasis on just about everything other than the ball. Of the 64 frees awarded by referee Seamus Murray, 41 went to Kerry. That statistic tells its own story.

Roscommon began in the most positive fashion imaginable - scoring 1-2 without reply in the opening twelve minutes. We weren't at the races. This was the one All-Ireland final we won despite playing poorly. I reckon we only reached about 60% capacity. In truth we sneaked it. There were two main reasons why we succeeded against the odds. Having built up a five point lead it suddenly dawned on Roscommon that they weren't using the tactics they were supposed to. They quickly set about employing them but they backfired.

They also tried to defend their lead which is simply impossible to do in Gaelic football. You can defend a lead in soccer and, with a bit of luck you can close down a rugby match. But such an approach simply does not work in Gaelic football. The only way to consolidate a lead is to try and increase it which puts the opposition under more pressure.

We got a lucky break before half time when Roscommon's centre back Tom Donnellan mis-hit a sideline straight to Tommy Doyle, who had switched from wing back to full forward to replace Liston. Tommy gave me a pass and I combined with Mike Sheehy who hand passed the ball to the net for a crucial goal.

Another turning point came in the second half when Charlie Nelligan made a great reflex save from a John O'Connor snap shot. But in the end the difference between the teams was Mike Sheehy's free taking. He scored six points from placed balls. Roscommon, in contrast, tried three different free takers, Dermot Earley, Micheal Finneran and John O'Connor, who between them only converted two frees.

But there were far too many unsavoury incidents. Gerry Fitzmaurice marked me and, while I wouldn't describe him as being dirty, he certainly wasn't interested in playing positive football that day. Not once during the 70 minutes did he attempt to go for the ball. He spent the whole day holding my jersey or, if I went to make a run, he tried to block me either fairly or unfairly - usually the latter.

Other Kerry players fared worse. Mike Sheehy was punched in the face and knocked to the ground in an off the ball incident which the umpires could hardly have missed. Having felled Sheehy, the Roscommon defender then fell to the ground himself. When the referee looked around he saw two guys on the ground and booked both of them. That was typical of the kind of stuff which was going on and ultimately it cost Roscommon dearly.

It was one of the few occasions I was booked in an All-

Ireland final. Repeating what I had done in the 1975 All-Ireland semi - final against Derry, I lay down on the ground and pretended I was hit. I earned a warning from the referee, who chose to ignore the fact that my jersey was been continually held. The late Micheal O Hehir in his television commentary commented : "Spillane has done this kind of thing before".

Needless to say the Roscommon fans were not amused by my behaviour. I came in for a lot of abuse from them for lying down. But I felt justified in what I did and even now I have no apologies to make. At times in Gaelic football the hard man who makes no attempt to play football is regarded as a hero. In contrast, the guy who wants to play football, but is not allowed, and then tries to do something to highlight his plight is vilified.

I did get a thump later that day. It happened after the match and the assailant was a woman. Coming out of Croke Park I met a Roscommon girl who introduced me to her mother. "You're only an actor," proclaimed the older woman as she hit me a belt with her fist.

Afterwards Roscommon complained about the referee. County Board Chairman Micheal O'Callaghan suggested a Roscommon player couldn't look at a Kerry man or there was a free. The bottom line was the Roscommon tactics were negative. They set out to stop Kerry from playing. It was a more case of Roscommon losing the game than Kerry winning it.

When all the controversy died down the fact remained unaltered. We completed a hat trick of All-Ireland titles and settled into a comfortable pattern of going through the motions in the league and peaking for the key games in the championship.

11

CHRIST, WE WERE CLOSE TO THE FIVE IN A ROW

THE GAA made a ham fisted effort in 1981 to narrow the gap between ourselves and the rest of the Gaelic football world. It was felt in official circles the main reason for the gulf was our exploitation of the hand-pass. Opponents of the hand-pass argued it gave us an unfair advantage and spoiled the game as a spectacle. In an attempt to bridge the gap many counties proposed its abolition. Amazingly one of the motions came from Kerry itself.

Kerry can be a funny county. Our success generated jealousy among an older generation of players and fans. They didn't like the way we dominated football or, more particularly, our style of play. As O'Dwyer often remarked there were thirty one and a half counties against us at times.

At a special Congress the use of the hand-pass was curtailed in a typical 'wishy washy' kind of way. So long as there was a clear 'striking' action we could continue to use it. The wording was vague. It was self evident referees would have difficulty deciding what constituted a legal hand-pass. However, the new ruling reduced the use of the hand-pass during the 1981 championship.

Hand-passed scores were outlawed although, luckily for me, players were still allowed to flick a ball which was in flight either into the net or over the bar. Five years later my flicked goal changed the course of an All-Ireland final.

According to the GAA hierarchy the purpose of the exercise was to improve the standard of Gaelic football. But, as far as I was concerned, it was more a case of trying to bring down Kerry to the level of other teams. It was also a reflection on the poverty of the other teams that we continued to do well in the league. In the 1980-81 season we reached the semi-final before going down by two points (0-10; 0-8) to eventual winners, Galway.

Our first round win over Clare in Listowel marked a

watershed for the Spillane family as my youngest brother Tommy, joined Mike and I on the Kerry team for the first time in the championship.

Before the Munster final against Cork. we were as concerned about the changes to the rule as we were about the ability of our opponents. Then O'Dwyer pulled one of his master strokes. The Munster Council appointed Paddy Collins to referee the game and O'Dwyer invited him down to a Kerry training session in Killarney to demonstrate exactly what a legal hand pass was.

Paddy Collins was unquestionably the game's top referee at the time. Unlike a lot of his colleagues he didn't give the advantage to the losing team in order to 'balance things up'. He refereed games exactly as he saw them and was always very fair. O'Dwyer gathered us all around in a circle, introduced Paddy, and described him as easily the best referee in the country. Collins explained to us how he would interpret the new rule on the hand-pass. He answered a few questions. On O'Dwyer's prompting, each player gave a demonstration of a hand-pass, just to make sure it was correct.

Paddy had hardly reached the gate when O'Dwyer turned to us and said: "We will get away with anything." In a way he was right because having come down to Killarney to show us how the new hand-pass worked Paddy was unlikely to pull us up the following Sunday.

As it transpired there were more frees than usual for illegal hand passes in the match but we won comfortably. I reckon I was very close to my peak as a Gaelic footballer at this time. I certainly needed to be in peak physical condition in the Munster final as my direct opponent Mick Maloney, an Army man, was easily the fittest player who ever marked me.

It was a strange match and Kerry's tactics came in for a lot of criticism afterwards. We won the toss but opted to play against a strong breeze. It was a policy O'Dwyer always insisted upon and I agree with it.

The logic of this approach is that it is easier to contain a team at the beginning of a match rather than be positive right from the throw in. The team which opts to play with the wind must get into their stride straight away in order to take full advantage of the elements. Facing into a very strong breeze in the first half against Cork, we opted to pull nearly everybody behind the ball. As a spectacle it was woeful to watch. Indeed, it was easily the worst 35 minutes of football in any of the Munster finals I was involved in.

We led 0-2 to 0-1 at the break and overwhelmed them in the second half winning by eleven points (1-11 to 0-3) to chalk up a seventh successive provincial crown. Our critics, however, had a field day accusing us of being negative in our approach. My reaction then and now is, we had nothing to apologise for. Our tactics were perfectly legal and effective and that's what counted.

Gaelic football is an amateur game. We were not in the entertainment business - although it was a by-product of many of our performances. We were in the business of eking out a result. Whatever legal means we used to achieve our aim were legitimate as far as I was concerned.

Even though we didn't feel it necessary to peak for our 1981 semi-final clash against Mayo - it was their first appearance in the All-Ireland series since 1969 - we produced one of our better performances. The Connacht champions were marginally better than Sligo (1975) and Monaghan (1979) we still won by sixteen points (2-19 to 1-6). It was a poignant occasion for me, even though I didn't know it at the time. It was my last big match before damaging my knee - an injury which nearly ended my football career. I was 26 and felt on top of my game both physically and mentally.

The following Sunday disaster struck at an intermediate championship game in Kenmare between Templenoe and Waterville. I was playing full-forward. I got the ball, turned and then my left knee went. I was in agony but continued until I was forced to come off. Straight away the knee started to swell up. Up until then I was very lucky with injuries. Indeed, other than a groin strain which forced me to retire during the 1980 league final and a few broken fingers, I never had any problems.

After the match I returned home and worked in the bar for a while before heading to nearby Kilgarvan where the

Fleadh Ceol was in full swing. I had a few pints in Jackie Healy Rae's bar before adjourning to the Gala Ballroom for the Fleadh Ceili. Despite my painful knee I danced the Siege of Ennis and the Walls of Limerick. The next morning the knee looked like an inflated balloon. But I worked in the bar that day and didn't get much sympathy from my mother as I hobbled around.

Nobody knew exactly what the problem was. My leg muscles were quite strong which meant the simple test which specialists normally carry out to determine whether the cruciate ligament has been severed was of little use. The strength of my muscles was masking the problem.

Initially I rested it for a couple of weeks. Then I received intensive physiotherapy before trying electric heat treatment. I was able to take the maximum amount which resulted in an audience gathering to see my leg hopping up and down on the table. I'm sure all this did enormous damage to my knee but I knew no better.

A week before the final against Offaly I tried out the knee in our traditional pre-All-Ireland trial game. Ger Lynch was marking me and I thought I was going okay. Suddenly, just as I was running across the field with no one near me it went again. The next five minutes were the longest and probably the worst moments of my life. I experienced pain the likes of which I never knew even existed. It was unreal. I think my screams could be heard back in Templenoe.

The following Tuesday I went to see a specialist in the Mater Hospital in Dublin. I spent the next two days in the home of physiotherapist Amy Johnston in Blanchardstown receiving intensive treatment. I returned home on Thursday night.

Kerry left a vacancy at left half forward on the team they named for the final. Mick O'Dwyer and our team doctor, Dave Geaney decided I should undergo a fitness test in St Brigid's GAA Ground in Blanchardstown on Saturday afternoon after the squad arrived in Dublin. I wore a heavy bandage on the knee and I passed all the tests. Micko seemed quite satisfied I was fit enough to face Offaly. But in my heart and soul I knew I wasn't right. I sat in on the team talk that night but I heard little of what was said. My mind was elsewhere. I had decided I wouldn't play.

I gave the knee another try on the lawn of the Grand Hotel on the Sunday morning. Had I been selfish I could have played, but I knew I wouldn't be able to give it 100%. I was also conscious of how pointless it would be trying to explain afterwards to the fickle Kerry fans that I had an injury problem. I informed Mick O'Dwyer at 12.30 that I wouldn't be starting. Tommy Doyle took my place at left half-forward.

Viewed from the dug out it looked a poor game. Kerry did not play well but any lingering doubts about the outcome were banished when Jack O'Shea got through for the game's only goal near the end. Even though I didn't start I have two very special memories of the day. Before the match the Kerry lads wouldn't line up for the team photograph unless I stood in as well. I was very reluctant to do so, but I was eventually prevailed upon.

I got very emotional as I hobbled across from the dug out and savoured the applause which came from all sides of the ground. I will never forget the players' gesture or, indeed, the reception I got from the crowd. Equally I will be eternally grateful to Mick O'Dwyer and the rest of the selectors for bringing me on as a substitute with about three minutes remaining. My appearance ensured I got my name into the Guiness Book of Records for having won each of my eight All-Ireland medals on the field of play.

I actually got a few kicks of the ball following my introduction. Looking back on it now I was completely off my head to even think about making an appearance in an All-Ireland final such was the extent of my injury. But I derived as much satisfaction from winning that All-Ireland medal as any of the previous four. As soon as the final whistle blew in the 1981 All-Ireland final attention switched to the '82 campaign and the prospect of Kerry completing the five in a row, which has never been achieved in Gaelic football.

I approached the season with a great deal of trepidation. I knew well my knee wasn't right. But such was the lure of being involved in the historic five in a row campaign that I decided to try the shortest possible recovery route.

Somebody suggested I might get away without having an operation. Their advice was to develop the muscles in my leg which would, in turn, hold my knee in place. So for the next six to eight months I built up the power in my legs. I now know the type of training I was doing was completely wrong. I should have been lifting weights in order to strengthen the knee. Instead all I was doing was improving my stamina levels.

The harsh reality was that I was selfish. I hung in there hoping for either a miracle or another All-Ireland - preferably both. Every couple of weeks the knee would collapse and swell up. After a few days I would get the fluid drained off and begin my training programme again. I was going around in circles.

Kerry won the league. We beat Cork in a replay - I came on as a substitute in the drawn match. I didn't make the team for the second match which was staged a month later because of the All Star tour.

Winning the league was a bad omen. The last time we won it in 1977 we lost the championship. And, sure enough, the problems started straight away.

First of all there was a dispute over the captaincy. I don't agree with the system used in Kerry where the county champions have the right to nominate the team captain. It caused endless problems down through the years.

Ger Lynch, who was a rookie in the squad, was nominated as team captain by the South Kerry divisional team which had won the county championship in 1981. He was put forward because his club Valentia were the divisional champions. Many felt, however, that John Egan - who also played on the South Kerry team - should be the captain. Ger was reluctant to take on the role as he felt it should go to a more senior player. Eventually Egan was given the job. But the affair was the first of many distractions that summer.

Then Jimmy Deenihan broke his leg in a clash with John Egan at a training session in May which ruled him out of the entire championship. Deenihan was a tight, tough, no nonsense defender who did his job without ever being noticed. His loss was a major blow to Kerry and I suppose the fact that I was also missing didn't help.

I played in the first round when we beat Clare in Ennis, but I didn't see any more action until I came on as a substitute in the All-Ireland semi-final. Just over 25,000 turned up for the Munster final at Pairc Ui Chaoimh. We were lucky to escape with a draw. In the replay my brother, Tommy, was man of the match and we won easily. We had a handy enough semi-final win over Armagh. However, as soon as we were in the final, the hype about the five in a row began in earnest in Kerry

The players felt the whole business was a media hyped phenomena and something they were not really concerned about. Initially the media attention was confined to Kerry but eventually the whole country seemed to go bananas. The five in a row T shirts were printed, the infamous song was recorded and the whole thing got completely out of hand. I honestly thought at the time the hype did not get to the players. In retrospect it is inevitable that it had some impact. Worse still, we were portrayed as arrogant, cocky and believing we should be handed the silverware when we turned up on All-Ireland final day.

All of this, of course, was like manna from heaven for Offaly's team manager Eugene McGee. In fact he quoted a verse of the 'five in a row song' recorded by folk group Galleon to the Offaly players before they took the field. "Five in a row, five in a row,

It's hard to believe we've won five in a row."

What greater motivational material could any rival manager hope to get his hands on.

Meanwhile, back in our camp there was controversy over the gear we would wear. We had switched from the traditional O'Neills gear to Adidas manufactured gear. There was a row at County Board level over where the Cup would go to first in the county. It was scheduled to go to Sneem, home town of team captain John Egan on the Wednesday night. All the plans were made to ensure it was going to be the greatest night in the history of Sneem. The bars were stocked up with extra drink to cope with the anticipated crowd. While a few did turn up on the Wednesday night I'm afraid the party was a damp squib.

It was like an incident during the thirties when Kenmare GAA club opened their new pitch. A double header involving Kerry and Laois in football and hurling was arranged to mark the occasion. In anticipation of the huge crowds many of the householders made ham sandwiches to sell at stalls outside their houses. Unfortunately on the day the heavens opened and the crowds stayed at home. For decades afterwards the day was known as 'ham' Sunday in Kenmare.

I came on as a substitute at half time in the final replacing Ogie Moran who lined out at left half-forward. My brother, Tommy, filled Ogie's favourite position - centre-forward. I played okay scoring an early point and getting a few handy balls. But, to be perfectly honest, I had the most wobbly and unstable left leg imaginable which meant physically and mentally I wasn't in any fit state to play in an All-Ireland final.

There were several key moments in the game. Number one was Mike Sheehy's penalty miss which was crucial. Had he scored that penalty I think we would have won. Turning point number two came midway through the second half when we had established a four point lead. Panic set into our play. We were less than twenty minutes away from football immortality. So what did we do? Like Roscommon in the 1980 final we tried to defend our lead.

Jacko abandoned his position at midfield and spent most of the rest of the game back near our goal line which meant as soon as the ball was kicked out it it came straight back. Even Mike Sheehy, who normally never strayed more than 30 yards from the opposing goal line, was back in the defence. In a nutshell we lost our shape.

Then there was referee PJ McGrath. In general Kerry people don't whinge about referees. We have won All-Irelands which we should have lost. I'm thinking in particular about 1980 against Roscommon and again in 1986 against Tyrone. But we should have won in 1982. One of the main reasons we didn't was due to the refereeing performance of PJ McGrath.

McGrath fell into the trap of giving the team who were behind a chance. I remember I was penalised for something trivial, while Sean Lowry manufactured a free out of nothing. Matt Connor duly punished us converting these dubious frees and then, of course, came the tour de force: Seamus Darby's famous last minute goal. The great debate about whether Darby pushed Tommy Doyle raged for years afterwards. I have no doubt it was a push. It should have been a free out but fair dues to Darby he took his goal well. However, had Jimmy Deenihan been fit to play Darby would certainly not have nudged him out of the way and got himself into a goal scoring position.

We had one chance to equalise afterwards when my brother, Tommy, soloed in from the Hogan Stand side. But his immaturity showed. Instead of looking for a better placed colleague he went for a score himself and the ball drifted across the goal.

Initially we were shattered but we got over the disappointment fairly quickly. Our captain, John Egan took the defeat worse than anybody else. Immediately afterwards he was one of the few players who didn't look emotionally distressed. He was cool and calm but I believe it took him a few years to get over the disappointment. After all this was going to be his special year.

For my own part I was over the defeat within a few hours. I remember drinking in Mulligan's of Poolbeg Street the next day by which time we had a new version of the famous song. "Five in a row, five in a row, Christ we were close to the five in a row."

Looking back on it now I'm convinced that had we won in 1982 and completed the five in a row it would have marked the end of the Kerry team. Certainly I don't think I would have played again. Had I collected my sixth All-Ireland medal in eight years I can't imagine I would have put myself through the torture I endured during the next eighteen months in pursuit of another medal.

It was a pity we didn't win the five in a row. It would have officially confirmed us as the greatest team of all time surpassing the achievements of Wexford (1915-1918) and Kerry (1929-1931) - the only other Gaelic football teams to win four All-Irelands in a row. But as I said in an earlier chapter I believe the 1978-81 Kerry team was the greatest side of all time regardless of our misadventure in 1982.

The fact we lost to Offaly spurred me on to have the operation on my knee and it also helped persuade the other lads to stay together and have another go. So while we lost one All-Ireland we actually gained three more in 1984, 1985 and 1986.

Despite the defeat we got a fabulous reception in Killarney when we returned on the Monday night. It was a very emotional occasion. Micko vowed the team would return again as All-Ireland champions. While talk is cheap on these occasions this time his words really did mean something. I believe his emotional speech convinced the players to stick together and give it another go. A lot of players made up their minds that night that they would have another go in 1983. I had made up my mind to go for an operation and try and make a comeback.

12

WOUNDED KNEE

LIGAMENTS are like elastic bands. You can pull and stretch them. But if you over stretch them they will eventually snap. Even though they can be repaired they are never the same again - it's like trying to fix a broken elastic band. The fatal turn I made in the club game in Kenmare in August 1981 was merely the straw which broke the camel's back in terms of severing the cruciate ligament in my left knee. I'm sure it was well frayed around the edges before it finally snapped.

A few years previously I devised a new system for getting past my man. It worked something like this: when going for a ball I allowed my marker to get in as close to me as possible. Just as my opponent reached me I dug my heel into the ground and pivoted on my left knee. So while my foot was stuck in the ground I was turning on my knee. Doing this at full speed you can imagine the amount of damage I did to the joint.

I now believe my 'revolutionary method' of getting past defenders was the main reason the ligament snapped. The funny thing about this injury is you can run for weeks and nothing untold happens. But then your knee is liable to collapse while you're walking down the stairs. I will never forget how I finally found out my cruciate ligament had snapped. Because my leg muscles were so strong the normal tell tale signs associated with the injury did not show up.

I went into the Regional Hospital in Cork to get an arthroscopy done on my knee. The specialist who broke the news to me would not get many marks for sentimentality or, indeed, understanding. Back then, of course, sports medicine in Ireland was still in its infancy. There were very few people in the medical profession specialising in the treatment of sports injuries. Doctors were not used to dealing with sports people and they had no insight into our psyche. They couldn't understand, for instance, why a player who sustained a serious injury would want to go back playing again.

I remember the specialist who performed the arthroscopy coming through the door of my ward. I asked him what was wrong. "You have ruptured your anterior cruciate ligament." "Is that serious," I asked. "It is," he replied, as he walked out and banged the door behind him. I was devastated as I lay in the bed. Prior to the injury I was at the peak of my football career. Now I had just been informed, in the most clinical way imaginable, that I had a very serious injury and from where I lay there didn't seem any way back.

Luckily Dr Con Murphy, the Cork GAA team doctor, came into see me shortly afterwards and he cheered me up a bit. The way the specialist broke the news to me was a shining example of how the mainstream medical profession don't understand how a sports person thinks. I appreciate he was probably a busy man but I think he could have shown a bit more understanding and told me the news more gently. It was like telling me I had six months to live.

The prevailing view about my injury in Ireland at the time was it effectively meant your career was over. I knew nobody in this country who had made a successful return to sport after suffering this injury. Scores of people offered me advice on how I could overcome the injury. They were all well meaning but I'm afraid none of their cures worked.

One old woman from Fermoy sent me a special potion to apply to my knee. She told me to rub the stuff into my knee for three nights in a row but warned me it was very hot. I followed her instructions but woke up in the middle of the second night as my knee appeared to be on fire. I had to get into a cold bath to cool it down. I thought it wiser not to apply the magic potion again. The next time I went to see the surgeon he demanded to know straight away what I had done to my knee - there were third degree burns on it.

A neighbour came up with something called pyramid healing. This involved making a cardboard pyramid and placing it on my knee in a north-south direction with a piece of tin foil between my knee and the actual pyramid. I was to leave this on for three days and three nights. Just imagine the rustling noise which came from my tin foiled wrapped knee. It certainly raised a laugh among my pupils and to avoid too much embarrassment I ended up 'wearing' the pyramid only at night.

Then there was the hi-tech solution contained in an article in the *Readers Digest*. It suggested that carbon fibre could be used as a substitute for tendons. I think nearly everybody in Ireland who read the article sent me a copy of it.

At the time my uncle, Canon Michael Lyne, was chaplain to Glasgow Celtic FC. I asked him to try and find out through his contacts in Celtic whether any soccer player in Scotland or England made a successful comeback after having his cruciate ligament repaired through surgery. My uncle roped in the then Celtic manager, Billy McNeill, who made enquiries throughout Scotland and England. His ex Celtic team mate, David Hay, manager of Chelsea at the time, came up with a name. George Burley, then playing with and now manager of Ipswich Town, had returned to top class football after a cruciate ligament injury.

His knee was repaired by a surgeon called David Dandy. Off my own bat I contacted Mr Dandy and he agreed to do the operation in Cambridge. Financially I put up the money myself. The operation was scheduled for mid-November 1982. But I had one more GAA commitment to fulfil before travelling to England. I flew to the States to line out for Tyrone in the New York GAA final.

At this stage my knee was a mess. I could neither turn or stop suddenly. I travelled out a week before the game but I didn't break the news about the seriousness of the injury to the Tyrone management until the night before the game. I said I would prefer if they didn't select me as a forward, but I was willing to play in defence. I was selected at wing back marking Offaly's John Guinan, who won an All-Ireland medal the previous month.

During the match I got my hand on the ball four or five times. I made the fastest clearances ever seen in Gaelic Park because I couldn't risk anybody coming in to tackle me. We were beaten.

I made it to Cambridge for the operation without any

further mishaps. The anterior cruciate ligament prevents one bone from sliding over another in your knee. During surgery a tendon was removed from another part of my body and stapled into my knee.

The operation itself was a success but a couple of days afterwards a bug was discovered in the wound. It took the doctors several days to identity the particular bug and find the appropriate antibiotic for it. In the meantime I spent four days in intensive care. It transpired the bug was the first of its type ever identified in a British hospital. Funny enough the only other place the bug had previously been identified was Dublin. This story was told to me years later by a doctor who was working in the hospital at the time.

When I was discharged l stayed with a friend of mine, JJ O'Shea in Watford for a few days and he looked after me. I was so weak I nearly fell down the stairs one day which wouldn't have done the knee much good. My gaunt appearance shocked my mother when I came home.

A couple of weeks later I did an interview for *The Kerryman* about the operation in which I said I was lucky I got the bug while in hospital in England. It would have been a lot worse had it happened when I returned to Ireland. One woman, however, took a different meaning from my comments and wrote a long letter to the paper the following week castigating me for criticising the Irish health service. Years later when I started writing for the *Sunday World* I quickly learned how people can take all kinds of different meanings from a seemingly innocent statement.

I was very fortunate that I came across Mr Dandy, who is now the number one orthopaedic surgeon dealing with cruciate ligament injuries in Britain. He did the repair jobs on both Paul Gasoigne and Alan Shearer.

I was lucky in another sense too. I was one of the first patients on whom he tried a new technique, which has now became the norm. He opted not to encase my knee in plaster. This meant I could start light exercises a few weeks after the operation and the muscles did not waste away as much as if the knee was in plaster.

I spent a few months on crutches and I have to confess

they were a great help when I went to the discos. The girls seemed to find me more attractive when I was walking with the aid of crutches! From a footballing perspective, however, it's amazing how quickly you are forgotten. During my time in hospital, and when I was recovering at home, I don't recall any of my Kerry team mates visiting me or telephoning to find out how I was getting on.

The operation in Cambridge cost about £5,000. The VHI covered a quarter of the cost while the GAA Insurance scheme covered another quarter. The Kerry County Board also made a contribution but I was still out of pocket to the tune of about £1,500 which was quite a bit of money in those days.

The late Frank King, Chairman of the Kerry County Board at the time, visited me in hospital in England. Otherwise my contact with anybody involved in the County Board or the team during the eighteen months I was out was minimal. It was certainly a case of out of sight, out of mind. It was up to myself whether I wanted to recovery sufficiently to play football for Kerry again. There was little in the way of encouragement from the powers that be. Just as the criticism heaped on me after the 1977 All-Ireland semi-final had changed me, the whole injury experience made me more selfish, cynical and bitter.

I decided everything I did from then on was strictly for myself. But the episode strengthened my resolve to get back playing The fact that I was able to come back afterwards and play top class football was testimony to (a) my own resolve and determination and (b) my ability to re-educate my body.

There was no guarantee of success with the operation. I knew my knee would never be as strong again so literally I had to learn to do without it. Up until the injury my left peg was my leading foot. After the operation I had to learn to do everything with my right foot. It was a bit like learning to write with your weak hand. But after a while it became routine. Now when ever I'm climbing the stairs I automatically put my right foot on the first step.

The training regime I went through was unbelievable. I pushed my body to the outer limits even though I knew, despite all the torture I was enduring, I might never play football again.

I enrolled in a gym in Killarney and I spent the first few months after the operation lifting weights. Then I bought my own weights machine which I installed in a garage adjoining the pub. It was a cold and drafty building with the dampness rising up through the floor. There were rats and mice around the place. On more than one occasion while lying on my stomach lifting weights I caught sight of a rat scurrying across the floor. I never budged. I just concentrated on the exercise I was doing.

From about January 1983 until I finished my inter-county career in August 1991 I did weight training every second day. It didn't matter whether the day fell on Christmas Day or New Year's Eve I never missed a session during those eight years. Weight training is unbelievably boring and I did it all on my own. Regardless of how bad I was feeling I always finished the session and did every exercise. I was a driven man.

I built up my legs to maximum strength. Eventually I was able to lift the heaviest weight which the machine carried. I reckon I had the strongest legs of any footballer in Ireland for much of the eighties. Mind you, my muscles were a pale shadow of the kind we now see on the world's top sprinters. Given the torture I endured to produce mine, it makes me suspicious of the methods they use. But I cannot stress enough the importance of weight training. It was the key to my success.

Apart from the weight training I also did a lot of running. I did countless circuits of the Templenoe GAA pitch - I could only run on grass - with only the spray from the nearby Atlantic Ocean for company.

Given the nature of the injury I was advised to do as much exercise as possible off my feet which basically meant swimming and cycling. I always needed a challenge in life. Up until I was injured my challenge came on the football field. But now I had to look elsewhere and some of the ideas I came up with were completely hair brained.

The challenge I set myself in the summer of 1983 was to swim Kenmare Bay at its widest point which is close to three miles. I was swimming one evening and the water was quite warm. I decided, there and then, that I would embark on my journey across the bay. A local promised to follow me in a boat.

I was about half way out when I realised he hadn't. Out in the middle of a bay it is very difficult to pick out the nearest point on the coastline and swim towards it. For one awful moment I thought all my months of training were going to come to nothing. I was going to end my days at the bottom of Kenmare Bay. I managed, however, to get across to the opposite side. Afterwards, of course, the story about my swim became something of a legend with reports that I swam Kenmare Bay at least once a week in the summer of 1983. Not true. I only did it once.

Cycling was another recommended exercise. But unfortunately I didn't have a racing bike. The only two wheel vehicle I could lay my hands on was my sister Margaret's old style ladies bike which had two small wheels and a big basket strapped to the front. I commandeered the bike and took it down to Coss Strand near my home. There is a steep 400 yard climb from the strand up to the main road. My aim was to cycle up the hill between twenty and thirty times without getting out of the saddle.

It was difficult enough getting up the hill when you could get out of the saddle. So you can imagine it was damn near impossible to finish the climb and remain in the saddle. But I did it, over and over again, and built up my leg muscles. Margaret's bike ended up a complete wreck.

One person who helped me more than anybody to recover was the Kerry team physiotherapist, Clare Edwards. I became her 'adopted patient' and I probably spent more time in her surgery in Killarney than any of her other patients between 1983 and 1991.

The 1983 Munster final in Pairc Ui Chaoimh was one of the two inter-county matches I attended that Summer. I went through anguish, torture and suffering when Tadgh Murphy scored his famous last minute winning goal for Cork. I think my mood, and that of the Kerry bench, was captured by RTE Television at the time. But I didn't feel involved and I didn't think Kerry wanted me involved.

People suggested I would be ready to come back playing football by the end of 1983. But I was adamant I would play no competitive matches until 1984. My first match back was a challenge game played on the eve of the 1983 All-Ireland final between the 'Old' Kerry and Dublin teams. I scored 2-4. It was fairly tame stuff, with no physical exchanges, but at least it convinced me I could still play football.

In January 1984 I played a few challenge games for Kerry. I was then selected to play against Offaly in a National League game on February 5 1984, a wet and miserable afternoon in Killorglin. I saw Kerry playing in a earlier round and had to fork out £2 like everybody else to get into the game. Okay, I wasn't officially a member of the squad any more, but that incident only fuelled my bitterness and strengthened my resolve to get back playing.

The match against Offaly was like playing in my first All-Ireland again. Over 5,000 turned up and I think my return to the team was responsible for adding a few thousand quid to the gate. Kerry won the match (1-9 to 1-5) to maintain an unbeaten record in the league. The next day the national papers reported I had made a successful return to the Kerry colours. I set up three or four scores and, considering my long lay-off, looked reasonably sharp. However, the reality was I was scared shitless.

The reason I didn't score was simple. As soon as I got possession I treated the ball like a hot potato and got rid of it as fast as possible to ensure I didn't get hit. In truth, I wasn't yet ready for competitive football. Even when I made a successful return there were certain things I had to avoid. I couldn't go into a sliding tackle, I couldn't stop suddenly and I couldn't turn quickly on my left foot.

That evening in Killorglin I didn't think I would be ready for championship football later that year. There was an interesting footnote to that game. The lady who wrote the letter to the Kerryman in 1982 criticising me for my perceived comments about the Irish health service was the first person to come up to me in Killorglin and congratulate me on my return.

The decisive moment in my comeback came in a club league game between Templenoe and Knocknagoshel, which is situated near the county boundary between Kerry and Limerick. I knew if I could survive a trip there - I was really back.

Their pitch is one of the smallest in the county and their teams are invariably tough and physical. As usual when Templenoe and Knocknagoshel clash the match was filthy. There were belts flying everywhere and the tackles were coming in thick and heavy. We won by a point and, just as I was coming off the field it dawned on me, I hadn't thought of my knee during the game.

From then on it was relatively plain sailing, although I went though one unusual routine before every game. I applied a hot water bottle to the knee. Whenever Templenoe played away from home I had to visit a house close to the pitch and ask them to boil the kettle so I could fill my hot water bottle. On the morning after matches the knee rattled so much that I could play the Rose of Tralee on it and, not surprisingly, the knee is now racked with arthritis.

After the match in Knocknogoshel we adjourned to the local bar and got drunk. Guess what the bar was called: 'The Wounded Knee.'

13

THE GOLDEN YEARS

BY the end of the 1983-84 National League campaign I was back as a regular on the team. Despite drawing four of our matches in our group we still got through to the playoffs. In the semi-finals we accounted for Down at Croke Park and then beat Galway by a goal (1-11 to 0-11) in the 1984 league final which was played in Limerick.

I should have been thrilled to be involved in a winning Kerry team again given my experience during the previous 18 months. I believed this league triumph would be the pinnacle of Part Two of my career. Strangely, however, I wasn't in any mood to celebrate afterwards.

I travelled back to Killarney with my brother, Tommy, and Ger Lynch. I had a difference of opinion with my two passengers because they wanted to go to a disco in Killarney whereas I was anxious to go home. We agreed to disagree. I was always a social animal. So why did I refuse point blank to go to the disco after the League final? In many ways it was a reflection of the different attitude I adopted following my knee operation.

For a start, I was more single minded about all football matters post 1984. I became more selfish and cynical, but also more motivated and determined. Micko always maintained we were playing for nobody but ourselves. As a result of what I experienced during my rehabilitation - anything I did now was for myself.

The one regret I had during my 'annus horribilis' period was I felt I never really celebrated our All-Ireland successes. Okay, I had one or two nights out but then life got back to normal very quickly. I vowed if I ever won an All-Ireland medal again I would savour and enjoy it and, of course, celebrate it in style.

Ironically, my best football performances were fashioned after I came back, even though my knee was never 100%. I maintained my form because I did a lot of training on my own, much of it involving weights. I became a fitter and stronger person. Up until the injury I weighed about 13 and a half stone but post 1984 I was tipping the scales at over fourteen stone and I can assure you I wasn't carrying any spare flesh.

Inevitably after two bitterly disappointing campaigns in 1982 and 1983 there were changes to the team when it came to the 1984 championship. Ambrose O'Donovan established himself in the anchor role at midfield with Sean Walsh moving to full-back to replace John O'Keeffe who retired. My brother, Tommy, also settled well into the team at centre-back.

There were other changes too. Páidí Ó Sé moved from right half back to the corner; Tommy Doyle took over from Paidi in the half-back line while Ger Lynch established himself on the opposite flank. Up front John Kennedy and, to a lesser extent, Timmy Dowd were pressing for first team places.

The GAA introduced a new open draw knockout competition in 1984 as part of their centenary celebrations. None of the game's big guns fared too well. Kerry bowed out to Derry in the first round while the then All-Ireland champions, Dublin, suffered a shock exit to Westmeath. Meath beat Monaghan in the final. Incidentally the competition was renamed the Ford Cup the following year and Páidí Ó Sé captained us to victory in the final over Cork. Sadly the competition was never staged again. Rumour has it Páidí still has the cup on display in his home in Ventry.

My comeback championship game in 1984 was against Tipperary in Tralee. We failed to score a goal but hit 23 points and won by 17. So, for only the second time in my career, I faced a Cork team who were the reigning provincial champions in the Munster final. Having finally got over Kerry the previous year at the eighth attempt Cork blew their chance of All-Ireland glory by throwing away a sizable lead against Dublin. Barney Rock hit an equalising goal near the end. Cork managed to persuade the GAA authorities to stage the replay at Pairc Ui Chaoimh but the move backfired spectacularly as a more tactically aware Dublin trounced them.

Even though he was a rookie in the side, Ambrose O'Donovan was team captain in 1984. The county champions, a Killarney Legion-Dr Crokes combination had no player on the team, so the honour fell to Ambrose as he was from the same region, East Kerry. As I said before, it is a crazy system and is still causing problems in Kerry. The whole saga surrounding the Hassett brothers, Mike and Liam, during the last eighteen months has its origins in the captaincy issue and the fact that the county champions have the right to nominate the captain.

Against the odds, however, the fact that Ambrose was captain worked to our advantage in 1984. Even though he was a newcomer he had no difficulty settling into the role. He was a excellent leader, a great motivator and his pre-match speeches - particularly the one before the Munster final - were memorable.

He liked nothing better than getting one over Cork. This owed much to the fact that he is from Gneeveguilla near the county boundary where the Kerry-Cork rivalry is most intense. Rathmore and Gneeveguilla are places which must be either visited or completely avoided on the night of a Munster final. Everything depends on the result because the supporters from the winning team make a point of visiting their neighbours just to slag them off. I doubt if Ambrose hated anything more passionately than the sight of a red jersey and his best performances for Kerry were always fashioned against Cork.

I marked my return to the Munster final stage with two goals - one of them scored with my near redundant left foot which gave me particular pleasure. One of our other rookies, Willie Maher scored another goal, John Kennedy hit four points and we ran out comfortable winners, 3-14 to 2-10.

Galway, who lost to us in the league final a few months earlier, provided the opposition in the All-Ireland semi final. I smiled to myself when I saw Mattie Coleman switching from his normal left half-back position to the opposite flank before the start to mark me. My theory about these pre-match switches is that, far from helping the team which makes them, they give an immediate psychological advantage to their opponent. It's a tell tale sign that the opposition are worried.

Galway had other problems too with Stephen Kinneavy, Peter Lee, Brian Talty and Barry Brennan all ruled out through injury. They led by three points to one early on but, once Mike Sheehy found the net for us sixteen minutes into the second half, it was plain sailing from there to the end and we had 12 points to spare at the finish (2-17 to 0-11)

I always call a spade a spade and, even though it won't win me new friends in the big smoke, I have to be honest and say that I didn't really rate the Dublin teams we played in the 1984 and 1985 All-Ireland finals. By then Brian Mullins was past his peak - indeed he was substituted in the 1985 final and never played for Dublin again. Like all teams managed by Kevin Heffernan they were very fit, committed, well organised and had solid defences but they lacked the flair to win more than one All-Ireland.

Pat Canavan, who was Man of the Match in the 1983 final, marked me in the 1984 decider when, ironically, I was named Man of the Match. This was one of the three All-Ireland finals I derived most personal satisfaction from. The others were 1975 - which was my first - and 1986 which was my last and the game in which I gave my best ever Croke Park display. In terms of performance, however, 1984 was a close second.

During the dark days after my knee operation in 1982 I never thought for one moment I would ever play in an All-Ireland final again. Just to be involved was a special thrill. But then to go on and kick two of the best points I ever scored at Croke Park and win Man of the Match was really special.

The first point came after I picked up a misplaced pass from Brian Mullins about 14 yards out under the Nally Stand. From there I hoisted a high kick which went over the bar. I hit the second point from out near the dugouts on the Old Cusack Stand side. I scored four points in total. Despite failing to score a goal we won comfortably on a 0-14 to 1-6 scoreline.

Only two Dublin forwards managed to get their names on the scoreboard and we were forced to field without the injured Mike Sheehy.

I am amused nowadays when I read about team managers banning their players from giving interviews or reading newspapers before a big game.Throughout my career I made a point of reading as many papers and listening to as many interviews on radio and television about the big games I was involved in.

It helped that I am the most positive thinker imaginable. I wasn't the greatest footballer of all time. But I believed I was much better than my opponent, even if I had no solid ground to back my argument. The day you go out thinking your opponent is better than you - you're in trouble.

I never lacked confidence and I had the capacity to take positive meaning out of anything which was written about me. If a journalist wrote that I was the best footballer in Ireland I would be pleased, but also anxious to prove he was correct. On the other hand, if somebody suggested I was past it - then I would go out and try to prove them wrong.

In their 1984 All-Ireland final preview the Sunday Tribune suggested I would never again reach the football heights I attained in the seventies because of my knee injury. While I wasn't offended by the remark it did spur me on in the game.

The only disappointing aspect of the final was that John Egan was taken off - harshly in my view. He never played for Kerry again. He was a great team mate and a good personal friend but post 1984 he completely cut his links with the squad. It was a sad way to end a magnificent career.

The Sunday night celebration dinner in the Grand Hotel after the final was memorable. I faithfully kept to the promise I made when I was injured and really celebrated in style. But it was team captain Ambrose - affectionately known as 'Rosie' - who was the star of the evening. His rendition of 'Sweet Forget Me Not' brought the house down. Of course, it was an extra little bonus that we came back to win the All-Ireland in the GAA's Centenary Year.

No medical expert needed to tell me I needed to look after my knee if I was to prolong my career beyond 1984. So, for the rest of my days with Kerry I opted out of league football and competitions such as the Railway Cup. It didn't mean I was idle during the winter and spring months. In fact, I probably trained more during these months than any player on the panel. I judged the well being of my knee by its size. It swelled up after a tough training session or a match. I swallowed thousands of Brufen, an anti-flammatory tablet, during the next seven years in order to try and control the swelling.

Mick O'Dwyer knew the team was coming to the end of the road and during the next couple of seasons he fielded experimental teams during the league which give the veterans a chance to recharge their batteries over the winter months.

My memories of the 1985 campaign, particularly in Munster, are very vague. We had a big win over Limerick in the semi-final. We lost Ambrose O'Donovan in the Munster final through injury, following an off the ball incident with Teddy McCarthy, but still prevailed by six points, 2-11 to 0-11.

Current Monaghan manager Eamon McEneaney kicked the equalising point from a '50' near the end of our All-Ireland semi-final against the Ulster champions to send the game into a replay. Coincidentally the other semi-final between Dublin and Mayo also ended level. Whereas I remember little of the detail of the match, I have a very clear recall of an incident before the game when our team picture was been taken.

One of the things which annoyed us intensely over the years was the use commercial companies made of our team picture. In effect they were making money on the back of our success. Mick O'Dwyer argued that we should be like the soccer clubs in England and have a squad picture taken at the start of the season. Then anybody who wanted a copy of the picture or to use it for commercial purposes paid a fee. There are practical problems involved in trying to to this in the GAA, not least the fact that traditionally teams have their pictures taken before every big match.

We felt we would beat Monaghan and O'Dwyer was already plotting for the All-Ireland final and beyond. We decided all 15 players would not stand in the team picture before the semi-final. Ger Power was 'unavoidably' delayed in the dug out while the photographers were busy clicking their cameras. I think in the end only 13 of the 15 players appeared in the team photograph - so it was of no commercial value.

Inevitably there was a big controversy afterwards about our behaviour. The then County Chairman, Frank King tried to pass it off as nothing deliberate. But such was the furore that the day of the replay all fifteen of us lined up for the picture. Mind you, only the fastest lens captured us because barely had our backsides touched the bench than we sprinted away again.

Having been guilty of taking Monaghan for granted in the drawn game, we were more focused in the replay and raced into a 2-3 to no score lead after 25 minutes. Even the dismissal soon afterwards of the Bomber didn't affect us and we won in the end by 2-9 to 0-10. Liston was sent-off for retaliating after a clash with the Monaghan full back Gerry McCarville. The funny thing about the incident is that the referee, umpire or linesman didn't appear to see what happened. Instead, one of the Croke Park stewards brought the incident to the attention of the linesman, who then told the referee. Television pictures clearly show this happening. It served to reinforce our theory that everybody was against us.

We reckoned Dublin were no better in 1985 than they were the previous year. We didn't fear them because their main man, Brian Mullins, was a year older. This complacent attitude nearly cost us the game. I was marked by Dave Synott who kept a tight hold of my jersey for most of the 70 minutes and I didn't have a particularly good game.

An early Jack O'Shea goal from a penalty appeared to set us on our way and we led 1-8 to 0-2 at the break. When Timmy Dowd scored our second goal 15 minutes into the second half we looked safe. However, with John Kearns having a magnificent match for Dublin in the middle of the field they came storming back with two goals from Joe McNally. At one point our lead was cut to one point. Near the end I scored a point from about 50 yards which proved a vital score. It steadied the ship and we were glad to hear the final whistle. We won by four points 2-12 to 2-8.

At this stage we knew the writing was on the wall for Kerry. We were running out of steam. In our old age we became more aware of our own commercial value - the incident over the team picture was an example of our new thinking. We were determined to get as much money together as possible in order to have one last big holiday before the team broke up. The players viewed the infamous sponsorship deal the County Board did with Bendix washing machines before the 1985 final as a kind of down payment on a holiday.

However, we had to threaten strike action the following spring before we got our holiday. The County Board attempted to renege on a deal one of their officers made. We became more militant in our demands. We weren't taking no for an answer.

After it was decided to cancel the team holiday we held a players' meeting. The following Sunday we were due to play Laois, who had just won the National League title, in a game to mark the official reopening of O'Moore Park in Portlaoise. We decided to boycott the match. A number of senior players then had the job of telephoning the GAA correspondents from the national papers and informing them that we were taking strike action. Predictably it was a big story for a few days. The County Board backed down; we got our holidays and I think the week or so we spent in the Canaries played a key role in helping us win one more All-Ireland.

Our 1986 championship campaign began in Clonmel where we overwhelmed Tipperary by 5-19 to 0-12. Ironically, on the same day the newly crowned League champions Laois, who beat us in the tournament game in Portlaoise a few weeks earlier, crashed out of the championship losing to Wicklow in the infamous Battle of Aughrim. Things were altogether less hectic in Clonmel. Indeed, so relaxed was the atmosphere that before the end of the game I signed autographs for young fans while an injured player was attended to at the other end of the field.

We were very, very lucky to scrape through against Cork in the Munster final. I was held scoreless by Niall Cahalane. My brother, Tommy, was man of the match. In a goalless encounter we had just four points to spare (0-12 to 0-8)

By the time the All-Ireland semi-final came around my form was beginning to come back. After many years of trying, Meath finally got the better of Dublin in the Leinster championship and the Royal County was appearing in the All-Ireland series for the first time since 1970. The game turned on an incident midway through the first half. Ogie Moran kicked in a high ball towards Ger Power. Meath full back Mick Lyons came racing out, but instead of hitting Power, he only succeeded in colliding with two of his team mates, goalkeeper Mickey McQuillan and corner back Joe Cassells. The ball broke to Power who calmly kicked it into an empty net. We never looked back winning by seven points, 2-13 to 0-12.

Tyrone provided the opposition in the final. Indeed, they were the first and only Ulster team we ever met in an All-Ireland decider. They brought tremendous hype, expectation and colour to Croke Park. There was great hope in the North that Tyrone were the team who could finally end Ulster's drought in the All-Ireland and bring the title north for the first time since 1968.

A remarkable feature of Kerry's success over the years was that some of our most loyal fans came from County Tyrone. After big matches in Croke Park I regularly met Tyrone people sporting the Kerry colours. Indeed, in the early days it was our fans north of the border and from places like West Limerick, Wicklow and Wexford who brought the Kerry colours into Croke Park on big days. The supporters from our own county were initially reluctant to wear our colours but this, of course, is no longer the case.

The 1986 All-Ireland final was a game Tyrone lost rather than Kerry won. We had eight points to spare (2-15 to 1-10) but they dominated for long periods and we looked in serious trouble early in the second half.

I was marked by Kevin McCabe who was a tremendous athlete and an all-round confident guy. He did things on the field with a swagger. But he was a ball playing wing back rather than a man marker. I met him outside the Cat and Cage Bar in Drumcondra on the evening we beat Meath in the semi-final, in the company of Tyrone businessman Shay McKeown. Tyrone were already through to the final and Kevin was off the drink. In contrast I was knocking back pints to beat the band.

Ulster people are very genuine but in those days many of them were in awe of any statement made by a Kerry footballer. I felt it was an appropriate occasion to launch my first salvo in the psychology battle. I pleaded with Kevin to give me a break in the final and not make a complete eejit of me. I argued I was over the top, drinking heavily and my knee was gone. Everybody was laughing and joking but I suspect Kevin, who was then in the prime of his career, felt he had nothing to fear from me.

This assumption proved incorrect. In the final Kevin played loads of ball all over the field. I was also roaming the field and playing as much ball. McCabe neglected his primary duty which was to mark me. Tyrone erred in not switching somebody like John Lynch on to me. He would have concentrated on stopping me and would probably have succeeded.

Jack O'Shea blazed a penalty off the crossbar after only two minutes but we were on the rack from then on and went in at half time four points behind. Our age was beginning to show. For the first time in ten All-Ireland finals Páidí Ó Sé had problems coping with his direct opponent. Just after half time Ó'Sé's man, Paudge Quinn got in for a goal and Tyrone went six points clear. Worse was to follow five minutes later when Tyrone were awarded a penalty.

There was a lot of debate afterwards about whether Kevin McCabe went for a goal or whether he opted to kick the penalty over the bar. Knowing his make-up, however, I'm sure he went for a goal. But the ball flew over the bar. So instead of finding ourselves nine points behind we were seven in arrears. I know the difference isn't much but it was enough to convince us the game was still within our reach. Had we fallen nine points behind I think we would have given it up as a lost cause.

Within half a minute the fightback began when I scored a point. What happened from then until the final whistle brought me as much pleasure as I ever experienced at Croke Park. My performance in the 1986 final was my greatest ever in an All-Ireland final. But it was more than just a happy coincidence that I played so well that day.

I felt I was going down with the flu on the Friday before the game and I went to see a doctor in Bantry. After checking my pulse rate he informed me that I had a slower rate than Carlos Lopes from Portugal who won the Olympic marathon ahead of our own John Treacy at the Los Angeles Olympics in 1984. That was an indication of just how fit I was.

I rate my 1986 final goal as the greatest I ever scored at Croke Park. Ger Power flicked the ball across the penalty area and I dived full length to push it past Aidan Skelton. It was one of those rare days when everything I tried worked. The guile, craft and experience we gained over the previous 12 years won the game for us because, from a footballing point of view, we were not the better team. Indeed, they held many of the aces. Admittedly there were unfortunate with injuries, key players like Eugene McKenna and John Lynch had to retire. In the final analysis Tyrone's innocence cost them victory.

Now I had eight All-Ireland medals in the bag and even though the warning lights were flashing all round us I think we all believed that evening that we could keep on winning All-Irelands. The reality, of course, was that the 1984-86 Kerry team were not nearly as good as the 1978-81 team. Our standards had slipped. But we still managed to sneak a hat trick of titles primarily because the others counties had still not made up the gap on us.

14

END OF AN ERA

MICK O'DWYER continued his policy of using fringe players during the league campaign of 1986-87. It worked well, with the team winning five of their seven matches to go through to the quarter-final. Mind you, by the time we got to the final against Dublin all the old faces, including my own, were back. The only newcomer was Stephen Stack.

In a marvelously entertaining match an early goal from Ciaran Duff proved the decisive score and we lost (1-11 to 0-11). It proved a particularly unhappy afternoon for Stephen Stack, who got a roasting from Duff in the first 20 minutes. The experience shattered his confidence for years afterwards. It wasn't until last year's All-Ireland final that he exorcised the ghosts of 1987 by giving a superb display against Mayo.

There was wild talk after the league final about the dawn of another era of Kerry/Dublin dominance in Gaelic football. Such optimism was outrageously misplaced. Eight years were to pass before Dublin won an All-Ireland again, while Kerry had to wait until 1997 for their next title.

Straight after the league final Kerry headed to the US for what was to be our last All Star trip. The tours themselves were in serious decline at the time for a variety of reasons, not least the fact that the players treated them as a big social event.

Even allowing for our hectic social life, the scale of the defeats we suffered in the matches in New York and San Francisco set off the alarm bells. After the San Francisco game, O'Dwyer insisted on having a training session the next morning. This never happened before on any tour. The session involved a 30-minute run along the beach. First across the line was County Board Chairman Sean Kelly, who was running in his sandals. Behind him were some of Ireland's finest footballers who, apart from being very hung over, had reached their sell-by date.

All successful teams eventually begin to wonder when they will reach the end of the road. They are the worst judges. Deep down they just want to keep the show on the road just a little longer. So it was with Kerry in 1987. The cracks were papered over as we got down to the business of preparing for a Munster final showdown against Cork at Pairc Ui Chaoimh. There were two notable additions to the Cork side team in 1987, Larry Tompkins and Shea Fahy. They were to prove the difference between the teams during the next four years.

An army officer, Fahy was based in Cork and played club football with Nemo Rangers. The Kildare man was perfectly entitled to play inter-county football with Cork. Tompkins was a completely different case, however.

As far as I was concerned then, and I haven't changed my mind since, he had no right to play with Cork. In my view his transfer from Kildare should never have been sanctioned. Tompkins was working with the Collins brothers from Castlehaven in New York and subsequently got a job in Castlehaven in County Cork. Fair play to him for taking advantage of the situation.

He was arguably the most dedicated footballer in Ireland in the second half of the eighties and if dedication breeds success then Larry deserved it. He was the closest thing Ireland ever had to a professional Gaelic footballer. His whole life revolved around training and games. He was unbelievably fit. He brought a whole new dimension to the Cork team, particularly in the scoring area as he was an accurate free taker and he could also kick long range points from play.

The 1987 Munster final ended in a draw. We were outplayed for most of the game. I was held scoreless by Niall Cahalane and Eoin Liston got little change out of Colman Corrigan. But Mike Sheehy scored what looked like the winning goal deep in injury time. It would have been daylight robbery had we won. We were guilty of a unforgivable lapse of concentration after going a point up. Cork goalkeeper John Kerins took a quick kick-out and the ball was worked down the field. Cork won a free which Tompkins converted. A draw. Had we held out, who knows, the Cork success story featuring Larry, Shea and manager Billy Morgan might never have got off the ground.

So it was back to Killarney for a replay a week later. I had other things on my mind that evening as I inched my way through the inevitable traffic jams to the city centre.

I planned to get engaged in Dublin forty eight hours later. My wife to be, Rosarii, was not a big football fan. She wasn't even at the game and probably didn't appreciate how much it meant to me. In Cork I made my way to a pub called the Office Bar, owned by a Kenmare man, Paudie McSweeney. I asked Paudie whether it would be possible to use his telephone upstairs as I had an important call to make.

I rang Rosarii and explained to her the match ended in a draw and the replay was scheduled for the following Sunday. Eventually I plucked up enough courage to ask her whether it would be possible to postpone the engagement for a week. Her initial response is unprintable. She said the arrangements were in place. Her parents were coming up from Wexford and there was a party planned. The engagement simply had to go ahead.

On the day I got engaged I trained with the Dublin based Kerry lads at Belfield with Micheal O'Muircheartaigh. Then I went and bought the diamonds in Appleby jewellers and I officially proposed in the lounge of the Westbury Hotel. I had one or two drinks but I didn't enjoy them. I felt I was cheating on my team mates. I lived life to the full. But in the two or three weeks leading up to a big game I never took a drink and didn't feel good about enjoying myself. Every waking minute was focused on the game. Momentous as the occasion was, I can't say I particularly enjoyed the engagement party.

Physically I was fit enough but mentally I wasn't prepared to go through the grindstone of another Munster final against a fired-up Cork team. I was again held scoreless by Niall Cahalane and I gave one of my poorest ever Munster final performances. We kicked 18 wides, didn't get our first score until two minutes before the break, had Ger Power sent off and lost by five points (0-13 to 1-5). No Kerry person went near Rathmore or Gneeveguilla that night.

Afterwards O'Dwyer and his selectors came under a lot of pressure to retire. I believe he would have stepped down were it not for the fact that Kenmare won the county championship title in 1987. This meant I would be captain of Kerry in 1988. I always got on extremely well with O'Dwyer and I think he felt he owed it to me to stay on. He then made one of the few mistakes he was guilty of during his long reign. He knew the majority of the players were near the end of the road. Still, he felt he could coax one last hurrah out of us and, to do this, he trained us harder than ever before.

There was much talk over the years about Kerry's legendary training sessions in the early days of O'Dwyer reign. I don't remember them too clearly now, but I am inclined to the view that the stories about the sessions were exaggerated.

The truth is those sessions were not nearly as tough as they were supposed to be. In fact, the most demanding training sessions I ever endured as a Kerry footballer were in 1988. I got married on March 26, 1988 but, even during our honeymoon in Thailand, I was gearing myself up for the season ahead and I trained every day. Now that I was captain I planned to lead by example.

I will never forget the first Kerry training session after I returned from the Far East. It was one of the most crucifying sessions I ever endured and Micko insisted I take a full part in it. Up until then I was cautious and skipped certain drills. O'Dwyer was always very fair about this, even though at times I swung the lead and used my wounded knee to avoid lots of things.

Now I was team captain it was slightly different. I was supposed to be leading by example. Even though I was dying on my feet there was no way I was going to give in. So I stuck it out to the bitter end. I'm sure the fact that O'Dwyer's club Waterville were meeting Templenoe in a county league game a few days later did not influence Micko's decision to be cruel that night! However, he did know the consequences of forcing me to train hard. I could hardly move for a week afterwards as I dragged my swollen knee behind me.

The problem with our overall training strategy was we were leaving our best form on the training field. We simply didn't have the energy or freshness when it came to the matches. Had he done the exact opposite and reduced the training we might have won something.

The Kerry County Board were in debt at the time which added to our problems. Over the years we were always treated extremely well with steak meals after training. Because of the cutbacks we were no longer getting a full meal after training. There were other problems too. The squad were now training in the Kerins O'Rahilly's all-weather sports complex in Tralee three to four times a week. The change of location from Killarney to Tralee meant I spent even more time behind the wheel of a car.

Indeed, looking back on it now, my schedule that spring was horrendous. As well as my football duties, I had also taken over responsibility for running the family bar. In the morning I drove 35 miles to Bantry and spent the day teaching, leaving at around 3.30. When I got home I grabbed a cup of tea and worked in the bar for half an hour to allow my wife time off to have her dinner. Then I drove 45 miles to Tralee and ran what seemed like a thousand times around the pitch. For variety we sometimes ran in the opposite direction!

Afterwards there was a cup of tea and sandwiches available. Then back into the car and another 45 mile drive back to Templenoe. By the time I arrived home at 10.30 I was exhausted. I then worked in the bar until closing time, cleaned and washed up and stumbled into bed some time after midnight. I was usually asleep before I hit the pillow.

We were only a couple months married at the time but it was a case of all work and no play. I was barely able to get up the stairs never mind try and indulge in the normal activities newly married couples get up to when they go to bed. One night Rosarii moved amorously close to me, I pretended to be asleep. She moved away, A couple of minutes later she moved close to me again and I shrugged her off. "For Jaysus sake Rosarii," I blurted out, "what the hell are you up too. I'm exhausted. I haven't the energy to do anything." She turned to me and made a comment which I will never forget: "If Mick O'Dwyer wanted you to do it you wouldn't refuse him."

In a sense she was right: her remark summed up the power Micko had over us when he was manager. Basically we were prepared to do anything he asked us and we never once questioned his methods. Perhaps it was a mistake we didn't do so in 1988 because we were tired men by the time the championship came around.

Mike Sheehy and Sean Walsh retired in the spring of 1988 but we still fielded a very experienced team in the championship. Among the newcomers was Maurice Fitzgerald. It was business as usual in the semi-final as we recorded a 3-19 to 1-7 win over Waterford. Cork, who lost to Meath in the 1987 All-Ireland final, would be a different proposition, particularly in Pairc Ui Chaoimh. Recalled to their team were Dinny Allen and Dave Barry, while Kerry left Páidí Ó Sé, Ger Power, Eoin Liston and Ogie Moran, who between them had 31 All-Ireland medals, on the bench.

Páidí was furious at his demotion and the fact he wasn't introduced during the game. Worse was to follow when it was leaked that the decision to omit Páidí was the result of a 2-3 vote against him at the selectors' meeting. Cork just had the edge over us winning by a single point (1-14 to 0-16). The contest is best remembered for a big flare up near the end, which was sparked by an incident in which the Cork centre back Conor Counihan caught Jack O'Shea in a part of the anatomy that is traditionally off limits in Gaelic Football.

Jacko responded, as any man would, and threw a punch at Counihan and the fracas attracted several participants from both sides before order was restored.

There was further controversy afterwards when one of the Kerry selectors, Liam Higgins, gave an interview on Raidio na Gaeltachta in which he criticised the decision not to introduce Páidí Ó Sé. He also suggested it was time O'Dwyer stepped aside and made way for another coach. The County Board rallied around O'Dwyer and, in a landmark decision, decided that from then on the Board, rather than the County Convention, would elect selectors. O'Dwyer topped the poll in the subsequent election.

The new year began on the best possible note for Kerry. In the first league match of 1989 we beat All-Ireland champions Meath, who had just returned from a holiday in the Canaries, by seven points. We probably overlooked the fact that Meath were still celebrating their All-Ireland win and weren't paying too much heed to the League. We made it to the quarter-finals and, after beating Antrim, ended up with a semi-final date against Cork at Pairc Ui Chaoimh. They taught us a sharp lesson, beat us easily and I retired injured.

We rattled in six goals against Limerick in the Munster semi-final. With home advantage in the final, we were reasonably optimistic we could end Cork's bid for a hat trick of Munster titles. We went three points up early in the match but were three behind when the final whistle blew (1-12; 1-9). In truth we were well beaten and at one stage trailed by eight points. We rallied in the final quarter with Ambrose O'Donovan scoring a goal just before full time. Even then there was never much prospect of an upset.

The one positive feature of the contest, from a Kerry perspective, was the arrival of Maurice Fitzgerald on the national stage. He scored six of our nine points. Little did anybody realise then that the Cahirciveen man would have to wait nearly ten years before he won an All-Ireland medal.

In the wake of our third successive championship defeat by Cork, the criticism mounted. It's amazing how quickly the good days were forgotten. Many Kerry people have short memories. The worst verbal abuse I got from so-called Kerry fans came in the latter years of my career. One suspects Mick O'Dwyer was feeling the pressure too. And, after fourteen years in the job, he stepped down a week after the 1989 Munster final. Like all of us he probably stayed on too long. I think, however, he was annoyed at the way he had to make his exit in the end.

Given his outstanding record, he should have been allowed decide in his own time when he wanted to retire.

Officially he bowed out himself, but I think it's fair to suggest he was slightly pushed. He wasn't even afforded the chance to announce his retirement with any fanfare. The Sunday Independent were all geared up to break the story on Sunday July 31, 1989. O'Dwyer gave Tom O'Riordan an exclusive interview earlier in the week in which he confirmed he was retiring.

But on the Saturday, the Kerry County Board issued a statement to all the media announcing the retirement of the Waterville man. All in all, I doubt if it was the way he wanted to go. I'm convinced that the manner of his departure was one of the reasons why he accepted the offer to manage Kildare two years later. The wheel turned full circle earlier this year when O'Dwyer plotted Kerry's downfall in the All-Ireland semi-final.

15

DOWN UNDER

THE one missing link in Gaelic games is the lack of a meaningful international dimension: the Compromise Rules series was an attempt to fill the vacuum. One of the reasons I made myself available for the 1986 tour to Australia was the chance it afforded me of wearing an Irish jersey. Of course, the trip looked like it would be a fascinating experience and that helped sway my decision.

I didn't play in the inaugural series in 1984, when the Australians came to Ireland, as I felt my dodgy knee would not be up to it. With the wisdom of hindsight, I would have been better to miss the 1986 series as well. There was controversy even before we left Ireland, when the GAA appointed Kevin Heffernan as team manager for the tour. Mick O'Dwyer's failure to land the job caused much resentment among the Kerry squad.

Eoin Liston, who was ideally suited to the Compromise Rules game because of his strength and size, declared himself unavailable for the trip because O'Dwyer was overlooked. Micko was closer to Liston than any other player in the Kerry squad - they travelled together to training when the Bomber was teaching in Waterville. O'Dwyer was the most successful GAA manager of all time and, based on his track record, he should have got the job.

Despite misgivings about the way the GAA handled the Heffernan/O'Dwyer issue, my brother, Tommy, and I declared ourselves available for the tour, as did Jack O'Shea who was appointed team captain. For a variety of reasons Jacko and Micko were never bosom pals. When Jacko accepted the captaincy of the Irish team and later praised Heffernan's managerial ability, I suspect it irked O'Dwyer and, indeed, a lot of people in Kerry.

However, that's not to detract from Jacko's success as team captain in Australia. He was the ideal man for the job. He was universally popular among the players and won our respect right from the start. He was also an excellent ambassador for Ireland off the field. On the pitch, the free flowing nature of the hybrid game suited him. But his relationship with O'Dwyer was never quite the same afterwards.

Due to Kerry's involvement in the All-Ireland final, Tommy and I attended very few of the Irish training sessions prior to the tour. But I cut short my celebrations after the 1986 All-Ireland final - something which I regret now - in order to keep in shape for the final trial.

Kevin Heffernan was an outstanding manager. His track record with Dublin and later with Ireland bears testimony to that. But I had a completely different kind of relationship with O'Dwyer compared to Heffernan. I respected O'Dwyer, but I never feared him. I feared Heffernan. The only other managers I feared were Denis McCarthy, boss of Kenmare when we won the Kerry county final in 1974, and Dave Weldrick, coach of Thomond College. In McCarthy's case, my fear stemmed from the fact that I was young and naive. There was always going to be a chasm between Weldrick and me because he was the lecturer and I was the student. But these experiences did nothing to prepare me for Heffo.

During his years as Dublin coach he was known as a strict disciplinarian and we weren't too long in Australia when Heffo demonstrated who was boss. Prior to the three-match test series there was a warm-up game against the Aussies in a place called Bunbury, south of Perth. I wasn't selected because Heffo didn't want to show all his cards before the real action began. Instead, along with the other guys who weren't togged out, I had the job of keeping notes on what certain Australian players were doing during the match.

Ireland lost this game but it didn't stop us from celebrating afterwards. There was an almighty session which went on into the early hours and culminated in a lot of boisterous behaviour along the corridors of the hotel.

Heffo obviously heard the racket. First thing the following morning he called a team meeting. It was like an entire class being hauled up in front of the worst headmaster imaginable. By the time he finished castigating us for our behaviour we were as quiet as mice. The tone for the entire tour was established at that meeting. Any notion that the trip was going to be like an All Star tour was banished for ever. We now knew who the boss was and it suddenly dawned on us this was serious business. From then on we trained twice a day.

Heffo had done much of his homework on the Aussies before we even arrived in Australia. He analysed their performances during their trip to Ireland in 1984. He noticed, in particular, how they behaved when a row started. There were numerous fights in the first match on the 1984 tour in Cork. When the rows erupted all the Aussies joined in. 'Bomber' Liston got involved in a scrap in Cork. Suddenly he found himself surrounded by Aussies and isolated from his own team mates. This was not going to happen in Australia.

Heffo decided in the event of any trouble starting the Irish would adopt an 'all-in policy'. Predictably this contributed to the tempestuous nature of the games. The worst violence occurred in the first test in Perth, but there were also unsavoury incidents in the other two tests in Melbourne and Adelaide.

The Irish media blamed the Aussies for the violence. But, to be perfectly honest, it was the Irish who started the majority of the fights and, of course, the Aussies were more than happy to join in. Looking back at videos of the three games it is particularly noticeable how our lads were always first on the scene when there was trouble.

The tour was punctuated by an inordinate number of team meetings, many of which lasted for more than three hours. Quite frankly I felt they were far too long. We analysed their strengths and failings and looked at our own play. Everything was done in a thorough way with nothing taken for granted.

Prior to the first test in Perth we were psyched up to expect trouble. In the early stages of the game there was a minor incident. Had it happened in a GAA match it would have passed off unnoticed. However, we felt it was time to utilise our 'all-in policy' and, inevitably, a big row developed. Five players were sent off including my brother, Tommy, and Pat O'Byrne. The three Aussies dismissed were Robert Di Pierdominico - better known as the Dipper - Gary Pert and Gary McIntosh. It was the first of many fracas during that game.

Another one of Heffo's tactical ploys caused uproar with the Aussies. In Australian Rules, players are allowed pick the ball off the ground with their hands. There is an unwritten code in the sport that when a player is bending down to gain possession his opponent doesn't use his boot to kick the ball away. Heffo drummed it into us that we were not to allow the Australians get easy pick-ups. If there was a 50/50 ball we were to pull on it which, of course, is perfectly legal in Gaelic football and was not outlawed in the Compromise Rules.

This tactic drove the Aussies mad. While they found it perfectly acceptable to punch an opponent, they thought it was the worst kind of thuggery for us to draw on a loose ball when they were trying to pick it up.This meant the Aussies didn't contest many of the 50/50 balls because they were afraid of an Irish boot arriving just as they were bending down to get it.

For all their macho man image, the Aussies were quite timid. Sure they set out to intimidate us. They wore tight, sleeveless jerseys which created the impression they were hard men and they stared menacingly at us during the National Anthems. Once the game began they weren't slow to push us out of their way and assert their physical presence. If they were allowed get away with it, they would have walked all over us.

But Heffo decided to face fire with fire. When it was put up to them by our strong men such as Pat O'Byrne and Brian McGilligan, it was the Aussies who turned out to be the wimps. Heffo came up with a rallying call which we roared at them during their national anthem. We used an Irish phrase 'Fior Gael' which means 'True Irish'. I remember one amusing incident before a match when we were attempting to outstare the Aussies and shouting Fior Gael at the top of our voices. I was standing beside Dermot McNicholl from Derry whose pronunciation of our rallying call sounded like Fine Gael. So, even though we were 12,000 miles away from Ireland, we didn't leave the politics behind us!

The WACA in Perth - venue for the first test match - is a cricket ground so it wasn't the most suitable place for a football game under floodlights. I didn't start the match. After the first row there were bad undercurrents for the rest of the evening. It was the kind of game which was liable to erupt into violence at any time.

In theory, my mobility, stamina and speed, allied to my ability to kick long range points, should have resulted in me making a positive contribution to the game. But, when I eventually made my appearance, I had two problems straight away. I was wearing contact lenses and the glare off the floodlights meant I had difficulty judging the flight of the ball. The second, and more critical difficulty, was I simply didn't feel at home in a match so dominated by naked aggression. It was an aspect of football I was never comfortable with. I didn't really get into the game and Ireland were beaten 64-57.

We flew to Adelaide the morning after the game and a few days later moved on to Melbourne. A few nights later Heffo called me up to his suite in the Old Melbourne Hotel. He offered me a drink, but bearing in mind the rollicking we received in Bunbury I opted for a orange juice.

"Tell me this," he said, as he handed me a glass of orange, "what do you think of this game." I said I enjoyed it. But that was a lie.

We quickly got down to the core issue. "What about the physical end of it. Do you like it ?," he asked. I was more truthful this time around. "To be quite honest," I replied, "I'm not into the physical stuff."

It felt like a pupil being spoken to by a headmaster. It wasn't that Heffernan was being dictatorial. But the reality was I was in fear of this man. The discussion rambled on. He emphasised the fact that he admired my football skills. But I quickly realised I didn't fit into the role model he wanted. He had his mind set on the kind of players he needed. He wanted guys who were prepared to throw their weight around and hit opponents. I wasn't going to compromise my principles in Australia. So I knew before

I left the room that, from a playing perspective, my tour had run its course.

Ironically, another big name player who didn't figure in Heffo's plan after the first test was Meath's Colm O'Rourke. In fairness to Heffernan, he picked horses for courses.

Ireland won the second test in Melbourne which set up the series for a final showdown in Adelaide. We knew there was much hype and controversy about the tour back in Ireland. Australian coach John Todd accused the Irish of being "a bunch of wimps". His remark did little to foster good relations between the two squads.

And what did I do for the rest of the tour? I thoroughly enjoyed myself. The night before the second test I went on a massive booze-up and missed the team meeting. I remember coming in the back gate of the Old Melbourne Hotel in the early hours of the morning and sneaking up to my bedroom trying not to create too much of a fuss. Heffo sought me out before the game and asked me to be the team's official 'runner'. Under the rules of the series each team was allowed a 'runner' who could go on the field and give drinks to his team mates and make any switches the manager wanted.

Until he offered me this job, I was sulking because of my omission from the playing squad. He felt, because of my record, the players would respect me when I came on the field and gave them instructions. There and then I decided to compromise. Perhaps I could make a positive contribution to the tour after all. So, even though I didn't play in the last two tests, I was on the field for longer than some of the players and, more importantly, I felt part of the Irish set-up. Mind you, had I been breathalysed at any stage during the second test I would probably have blown the gauge off the chart.

I ended up enjoying my role and I was disappointed when an attempt to introduce a 'runner' in Gaelic football, a few years later, failed at the final hurdle. Given the noise levels at big games nowadays I think a 'runner' could play a very useful role.

Ireland, of course, ultimately won the series 2-1 and the

trip made heroes out of several players. Jacko's star rating went into orbit, but it was the relatively unknown players who emerged as the real heroes. I'm thinking in particular of Wicklow's Pat O'Byrne and Derry's Brian McGilligan- a relatively unknown footballer then. They were two of the strongest footballers I ever came across - particularly O'Byrne. A sheep farmer, O'Byrne was the strongest man I ever saw togged off on a GAA field. He could push the Irish front row from one end of the field to the other without breaking into a sweat.

There was a hilarious incident during one match when Heffernan instructed me to tell Brian McGilligan to hit some Aussie. "Tell McGilligan to 'lamp' Mr X," said Heffo. Obviously the phrase didn't mean anything to Brian. He hadn't a clue what I was talking about even though I shouted the instruction to him several times. So I put him straight: "Fucking hit him Brian," I shouted, which he did.

Cork's John O'Driscoll was another young player who starred on the tour. He was just starting out his career as a Gaelic footballer and he came home from Australia a star, but he never reached the same heights again. People sometimes forget that the Compromise Rules and Gaelic football are different games.

Then we had guys like Noel Roche and Spike Fagan who ran and ran all day. The combination of physical force and constant running created the space for the skilful players such as Jacko and John O'Driscoll to do the business.

Apart from my brief appearance in the first test, the only other matches I played were two ordinary GAA games. The Australasia GAA championships were played while we were on tour and an Irish team played a side drawn from the competing teams. It was harmless stuff - we won 4-9 to 2-3 - but our opponents' centre forward Bernie McCahill later played for the All Blacks. Near the end of the tour, in a suburb of Sydney we also played a GAA match against a New South Wales selection. The only notable feature about it was I recorded one of the highest individual scores I ever managed in a GAA match. The Irish papers reported my tally was 2-5 but I believe it was much higher. I was marked by Seamus Clancy from Clare who got his revenge on myself and Kerry a few years later.

Despite obvious difficulties, the series has potential and I'm delighted it has been revived. However, it will always be very difficult to develop a hybrid game with a country at the other end of the world. Australian Rules are in the same predicament as the GAA - they have no meaningful international outlet for their semi-professional game. The two markets they are really interested in cracking are Japan and the US. They haven't managed to do this and perhaps this is one of the reasons why they have renewed their relationship with the GAA.

A weakness of the Compromise Rules series, so far, is the Aussies have had to concede too much to the Irish. For instance, had the GAA agreed to use the oval ball, particularly for the two tours in Australia, it would have made the series more attractive to the Aussie public who showed little interest in the hybrid game. The Aussies found it very difficult to control the round ball. I'm sure we would have found it just as hard to master the oval ball.

The idea of having two referees was fine in theory but there was one big problem. At one end of the field the Irish referee Paddy Collins attempted to be impartial at all times. But the Aussie official, Rowan Sawers was so blinkered it was embarrassing. He let the Aussies get away with murder. I can accept being the victim of an act of thuggery on a GAA field because, in general, the perpetrator will be punished by the referee. In the Compromise Rules, however, this was never going to happen. An Aussie certainly wouldn't be punished if he committed the offence at the end of the field where his fellow countryman was officiating and I think both referees were reluctant to dismiss players.

The GAA did learn a lot, and could learn even more from the Aussie Rules games. When Aussie Rules hit our TV screens in the early eighties it was very neatly packaged. What we saw were the spectacular high catches and the physical exchanges. However, the average 80 minute Aussie Rules game is no better than a poor junior GAA match in Ireland. There are missed catches, too much broken play and too many melees.

While they deliberately try and hype up this aspect of the game, the truth is it's nothing more than handbagging stuff. Despite all the brawls, players rarely get injured or leave the field as a result of injuries received in these rows; there is rarely any real blood spilled. But promotion is all about presenting the right package and the GAA could use a lesson or two in this area.

I believe the GAA will eventually follow the path taken by the Australian Football League where the leading players are on semi-professional contracts. In return they do promotional and coaching work for the clubs.

The facilities for players in the stadia and training grounds we used were top class. The dressing rooms were huge. There were well equipped with weight training rooms in all the stadia and big warm up areas. Thankfully there is now an excellent warm-up area for teams under the new stand in Croke Park. Hopefully this facility will be incorporated into other major stadia throughout the country.

Despite my personal disappointment, the tour was a great success. Everything was done in a very professional manner. It was a new and rewarding experience to meet and tour with players from other counties and be looked after so well.

In 1987 the Aussies toured Ireland. Eugene McGee was the Irish manager and I was selected again. There was a consensus that, if the series was to be viable, there would have to be less violence and more emphasis on football. McGee, in particular, was anxious to prove we could match the Aussies in terms of skills without having to resort to the physical stuff. Even though we lost the series 2-1, I was the leading Irish scorer although I didn't play exceptionally well. I derived much satisfaction from proving my style of play could be adopted to the Compromise Rules.

The other representative series I played in was, of course, the Railway Cup. How many medals did I win? The honest answer is I didn't know until I saw the records section at the end of this book. I won four: 1976, 1977, 1978 and 1981.

Even in the mid-seventies the competition was dying,

although I remember one final I was involved in against Leinster attracted a crowd of over 30,000. I think on that occasion the GAA offered free admission to all youngsters. It was a good example of what a simple marketing initiative can achieve. Unfortunately, there is a lack of such marketing ploys when it comes to the Railway Cup, or the Inter-provincial series as it is now called.

Nowadays the competition has become a bit of a joke. I remember one year while I was still playing with Kerry there was a few Cork players selected on the Munster team who hadn't even played for their county. I still think the competition has a future - but it must be made more attractive to spectators and players alike.

While players insist they want to participate in the competition the reality is they don't train for it. Nowadays it is usually staged at a time when county teams are in the middle of their stamina training programmes for the season ahead. The players treat it as a welcome diversion from the really serious football business.

In my day I never attended a Munster training session - in fact I don't remember one ever been held. Basically, it was a matter of picking the bulk of the Kerry team and adding a few players from the other counties. The Railway Cup did give me the opportunity to play in what was possibly the greatest forward line I ever saw. We took on Leinster in the 1976 final and won by seven points. The Munster attack consisted of four Kerry players, Mike Sheehy, Mickey O'Sullivan, John Egan and myself alongside Cork's Jimmy Barry Murphy and Dinny Allen. The success of the Kerry forward division was based on team-work and understanding. The two Cork lads fitted into our system with the minimum of fuss which underlined their ability.

I also recall scoring a great goal in a Railway Cup match with a soccer like volley from out the field. Otherwise, I'm afraid, I have few memories of my days in a Munster jersey. It was a case of being there, done that and got the jersey.

16

WHAT MADE KERRY GREAT

THE 1978-81 Kerry team was the greatest GAA side of all time. Our unbeaten run in the championship, which stretched from June 1978 until September 1982, was probably one of the longest runs at the top by any team, in any sport, in modern times. It's easier for a professional soccer team to stay at the top for a long stretch. They can go out and buy players when the need arises. And, of course, the longer professionals stay on top the more money they make. Contrast their situation to what faced us.

We were an amateur team which appeared in ten All-Ireland finals in twelve years. We won eight of them, as well as eleven Munster titles and three National Leagues. What motivated us to stay together was not a financial windfall, rather it was the pursuit of another All-Ireland medal. In that context what we achieved was remarkable.

What was the key to our success? The first significant element in the jigsaw was fitness. O'Dwyer recognised that the arrival of the Dubs in 1974 was the catalyst for a sea change in Gaelic football. I have consistently argued over the years that, individually, the 1974 Dublin team were not brilliant footballers. But they were superbly fit and were well organised as a unit.

The Dublin team, managed by Kevin Heffernan, established a benchmark in the area of fitness and organisation which other teams had to reach if they were to challenge them.

The first thing O'Dwyer did when he took over in 1975 was to get us fit. But he wasn't content to leave it at that. He wanted us to be fitter than Dublin; ultimately we achieved his target. But it wasn't just fitness that O'Dwyer looked for in players. He wanted players who thought as quickly as they moved. Traditionally managers looked for speedy forwards, midfielders with a fair bit of mobility and a back line filled with 'hard men'. The stereotype defence of the early seventies consisted of two small but speedy wing backs, a big solid centre back with the 'hard men' on the full-back line. O'Dwyer got rid of this type of defence. It was this move which eventually played a key role in our domination of the Dubs.

The Kerry defence which O'Dwyer assembled was the fastest ever in the history of Gaelic football. It was very rare in those days to have backs who were faster than forwards. In our squad, John O'Keeffe and Ger Power consistently out sprinted the forwards. There were no weak links in our defence and we built our team from the back up. In contrast, there were weaknesses in the Dublin rearguard. For instance, neither Sean Doherty or Gay O'Driscoll were particularly fast. This lack of pace in the Dublin full-back line eventually came to haunt them in the 1978 All-Ireland final.

One of the unique features of both the Kerry and Dublin teams was that most of the players had college degrees. Indeed, it's more than a coincidence that many of the Dublin and Kerry players from this era are very successful in their chosen professions. Intelligent players think a lot about football and are good readers of games. Kerry and Dublin had enough self belief to change tactics to suit the occasion without any prompting from the sideline. It might sound easy, but it's amazing the number of teams in recent years who are unable to adopt a new approach when the need arises.

The majority of us involved in football at third level colleges were training like professional footballers and this sector is a proven breeding ground for inter-county players. In recent years successful football teams revolved around one individual, like Maurice Fitzgerald in Kerry or Peter Canavan in Tyrone, our strength lay in our overall unity. We were never dependent on one or two players to be match winners in every big game. One day it might be Liston and Sheehy who would be the stars; the next day it could be Jacko and myself and the third day Ogie Moran and Sean Walsh. As a unit we were very evenly balanced.

Having come together at a very young age, we developed an excellent understanding on the field. The main emphasis in training was on games between the backs and forwards. These sessions helped forge an understanding that flourished to such an extent that there was a kind of telepathy between us out on the field. For instance, if the 'Bomber' got the ball he didn't have to look around to see where the other forwards were. He knew precisely what positions we would be running into.

All our play was based on movement and possession. O'Dwyer wanted quick movement of the ball and constant movement of players. We were never tied down to set positions. We switched around all the time. The half- backs were encouraged to come upfield; the left corner-forward switched with his colleague on the right and I roamed all over the field. All this movement meant we were a difficult team to defend against.

Since Kerry won the All-Ireland in 1997 a favourite GAA pub debating topic is: Who would Maurice Fitzgerald replace on our team? I believe he would not replace any of us. Maurice is a more skilful footballer than anybody on the 1978-81 team. Circumstances, however, have forced him to be an individualist, who holds the ball and takes his own scores. This was never part of the O'Dwyer strategy and, unless he changed his ways, he would not have fitted into our style of play.

Even though we were the most successful team in the history of the game, it's a complete myth to describe us as one big happy family off the field. The guys I got close to were my club mates in Templenoe who I went to school with and later socialised with.

Apart from team holidays and the occasional drink together after a match, the players from the great Kerry teams did not socialise much together. The Tralee boys formed their own group, the north Kerry players formed another group, Páidí Ó Sé and Paudie Lynch hung around together and Jacko was in Dublin. As a result I never really got close to any of my team mates on a social basis. Now it's only in the event of a bereavement or some anniversary that we get together.

One of O'Dwyer's great achievements was his ability to get fifteen guys from different backgrounds, with different temperaments and differing opinions to stay together for so long. The excellent treatment we received from the Kerry County Board helped us to stay at the top also. We were one of the few teams which had steak dinners after every training session - there were some cutbacks in the later years. Although our travelling expenses weren't great - they averaged 12p to 15p per mile - they were paid promptly. Our medical expenses were generally looked after as well.

Of course the fact we were so successful meant we, or more precisely O'Dwyer, was in a strong negotiating position with the County Board. We called the shots most of the time and that doesn't happen in too many counties. Indeed, reflecting on it now, the longer we stayed on top the more we demanded. We knew the chances of the County Board pushing us around were slim. For instance, when we threatened strike action in 1986 they backed down rapidly.

We had all kind of characters in the team. Here is a brief pen picture of the main men in the four-in-a row team:

Paudie O'Mahony: Nicknamed 'The Boot' because he wore size 13 football boots. Conceded no goals in the 1975 championship. His kickouts were long, apart from one he sent straight to Jimmy Barry Murphy in the 1976 Munster final replay which JBM returned to the Kerry net. He may not have looked a spectacular keeper but one glare from him was enough to scare off most forwards.

Charlie Nelligan: An extrovert, always shouting and, invariably, he managed to antagonise opposing forwards. He was the kind of guy liable to shout an unflattering comment to an opposing player in the pre-match parade and if there was trouble around our goals it was a banker Charlie would be in the thick of it.

Ger O'Keeffe: Ger was never slow to give his opinion on any subject. He was a very confident player and he talked a terrific game. His Kerry career ended prematurely after he suffered a series of bad injuries.

Mike Spillane: Mike is probably the forgotten man of Kerry football even though he won seven All-Ireland medals. A famous ex-Kerry footballer once asked Mike who he was. A much quieter guy than his older brother! He wasn't a flamboyant performer, he just marked his man in an efficient manner. He was very unlucky to be dropped for the 1980 All-Ireland final.

John O'Keeffe: Johnno was the team's thinker and one of the serious men in the side. He trained exceptionally hard and did a lot of work with weights. He had the finest physique of any player on the team. He was prone to injuries.

Jimmy Deenihan: In terms of football ability Deenihan had probably less skill than any other player in our defence. But what he lacked in skill he made up for in grit and determination. He was one of the tightest markers I ever came across - he marked me in a number of local championship games. He was a made footballer prepared to hand out punishment which Cork's Jimmy Barry Murphy, among others, will vouch for. I'm convinced if Deenihan played in the 1982 All-Ireland final there is no way Seamus Darby would have got inside him for that famous goal. Deenihan was a man about town in his younger days. He dressed casually and enjoyed the social life. This all changed when he entered politics. Shortly after he was selected as a Fine Gael candidate he turned up for a match in a suit and tie.

Páidí Ó Sé: He was the extrovert extraordinary on the team. He always wintered well but got himself into peak condition for the championship. He epitomised the Kerry spirit more than anybody else. He was our chief motivator and would go through a wall for the cause. So many of his direct opponents ended up scoreless in All-Ireland finals is testimony to his ability, temperament and value to Kerry.

On the nights before All-Ireland finals Páidí would be so hyped up that he couldn't sleep and he would patrol up and down the corridor in the Grand Hotel using his pillow as a football. He was also one of the hard men in our defence. Páidí was a bit of a loose cannon and for years the Kerry County Board were reluctant to trust him with the job of senior team manager. Eventually his patience and persistence paid off and his motivational powers played a key role in Kerry's All-Ireland success in 1997.

Tim Kennelly: He was the strongest man in the team. He was not the greatest footballer ever to wear the number six shirt but he was very inspirational. He was always very solid and gave a man of the match performance in the 1980 All-Ireland final. Now his son Noel, who has already won an All-Ireland U-21 medal, is a member of the Kerry senior squad.

Ger Power: The fastest man on the team, Ger could carry the ball at great speed. He had to be careful, however, because his hamstrings were very suspect. A versatile footballer, he began his career at wing back before moving to the forward division. I'm not sure which position suited him best.

Paudie Lynch: One of the team's quiet men, he never got full credit for his contribution. He was the coolest man around and never appeared rattled. His greatest asset was his accurate distribution. He was the the unsung hero of the forward division as he consistently put the ball on a plate for us.

Jack O'Shea: He dominated the headlines, particularly during our second coming between 1984 and 1986 when there was much debate over whether he was the greatest footballer of all time. Strictly speaking he wasn't a midfielder in the traditional sense because he didn't catch many high balls. His greatest attributes were his work rate and mobility.

It's fair to say there was a certain animosity - perhaps jealousy might be a more accurate description of it - among the team towards him. He was based in Leixlip and the darling of the national media. There were allegations he was picking up a few bob as a result of his numerous personal appearances around the country. This caused some resentment, although the truth was, if any of us were in the same position as Jacko, we would have done exactly the same thing.

Sean Walsh: He was the great under-achiever. Apart from John O'Keeffe, he was the most complete athlete on the team. Over six foot tall, he had strength, stamina and speed. But we rarely saw him at his best. There was a long running in-house team joke that if there wasn't at least 50,000 spectators at the match Sean would not play well. As a result his best performances were fashioned in Munster and All-Ireland finals. He was rarely at his best in semi-finals and definitely not in mid-winter league matches. He had an unbelievable spring off his foot, well illustrated in a newspaper picture of him jumping way above Brian Mullins to catch a ball in an All-Ireland final.

Tommy Doyle: Better known as the 'Private' to his team mates, he was the fittest player in the squad. He trained harder than any Olympic athlete. Unbelievably strong, he didn't score much, but did a lot of the hitting in the forward division. Tommy was a bit like John O'Keeffe, always complaining about having pulled hamstrings and a tweak in his calf muscle. Given his extraordinary fitness levels, he should have made a bigger impact.

Ogie Moran: The gentleman of the team, he was our lucky mascot. The eight times he lined out at centre forward in All-Ireland finals we won. Ogie was one of the greatest ever under-age footballers to come out of Kerry. At senior level he lacked height and his scoring rate wasn't exemplary. However, when his club mate, ''Bomber' Liston arrived on the scene a great telepathy developed between the pair of them.

I resented this because I felt when Ogie gave the ball into the 'Bomber' he invariably got a return pass, whereas if I linked up with the Bomber he didn't necessarily give the ball back to me! In later years Ogie managed the Kerry team. Like his predecessor Mickey O'Sullivan, he was on a hiding to nothing as he lacked managerial experience. In fact he was too nice and wasn't nearly ruthless enough. One of the mistakes he made was to bring the 'Bomber' out of retirement in 1993. There was enormous pressure on him to deliver but he never got fit enough again to make an impact in championship football.

I criticised Ogie and the selectors after the 1995 Munster final for failing to make changes. Although it wasn't meant to be personal, he took it badly and there is a coolness between us since, which I regret very much.

Mike Sheehy: He was the most skilful player on the team and a real gentleman. Some of his scores, such as a chipped point in an All-Ireland final and, of course, his famous goal in the 1978 decider when he caught Paddy Cullen off his line and chipped him from a free, bear testimony to this. He was a very accurate free taker but his record from penalty kicks was not as good. His miss in the 1982 final proved very costly. His skills levels were such he could have made it in cross channel soccer.

Eoin Liston: He was the key player in the set-up and his arrival on the scene in the autumn of 1977 meant that we had found the last and most important part of the jigsaw. His physique made him an ideal target man. He was never selfish when he got the ball and he excelled at bringing the other forwards into the game. I never got on well with him because I looked for the ball all the time and the 'Bomber' didn't always give it to me. We had countless effing matches during both training and games.

John Egan: The quiet man in the forward line. He was overweight when he arrived into training each Spring. But he was immensely strong and he endured any amount of punishment on the training field. In fact, the harder the session, the more he relished it.

He had great balance and was a very intelligent reader of the game. He is another player who never got the full credit for his contribution. He was the one guy on the team who didn't seek to exploit his fame off the field. Most of us benefited in our businesses from our involvement in football. In contrast, John Egan is a member of the Gardai all his life.

When we became the youngest Kerry team ever to win an All-Ireland in 1975 we hadn't a clue how to handle success. Then we suffered two successive setbacks against Dublin in 1976 and 1977. We were subjected to savage criticism in Kerry, particularly after the second defeat.

This brought home to us how fickle the Kerry public are and how thin the line between success and failure. The whole experience made us much stronger characters. When we won in 1978 we knew how to handle success and that played an important role in keeping us at the top for the next four years.

One of the less redeeming features of Irish life is that people rarely get the recognition they deserve for their achievements when they are still alive So I'm resigned to the fact that we will all probably be dead and buried before our achievements as a football team are truly recognised.

17

SIMPLY THE BEST

TINA Turner's hit record, 'Simply the Best', immediately springs to mind when I think about Mick O'Dwyer - or 'Dwyer' as we called him. It was his man-management skills which set him apart as the greatest team boss in the history of Gaelic football. If he was not gifted in this way there is no way he would have kept the same bunch of players together and motivated over a 12-year period.

Remember all that was on offer at the end of each season was a medal, a few night's drinking and a tour to the United States. Then it was back to the grindstone for another season. He was fortunate that a particularly talented bunch of players came together around the same time in Kerry. Regardless of who was team manager the chances are we would have won two or three All-Ireland titles. But without O'Dwyer there is no way Kerry would have appeared in ten All-Ireland finals in twelve years and won eight of them.

Of course, he had his failings. If he was judged only on his ability as a team trainer he would probably fall into the 'above average' category. In the early years and, more particularly, in his latter years he probably fell into the trap of over training us. But in between he always had us fresh for the big matches. It helped, of course, that we had only two or three games to peak for every year.

As a tactician, his game plan was simple. It could be written on the back of a postage stamp. We didn't analyse our opponent's play or watched their games on video. Having experienced the other side of the coin during Mickey O'Sullivan's reign, there was a lot of merit in O'Dwyer's approach. For instance, prior to the 1991 All-Ireland semi-final we watched all of Down's matches in the Ulster championship. But the more we watched, the more we believed they were very good. We would have been far better off just concentrating on our own game.

Watching videos of your opponents' games is now regarded as a normal part of the build-up to big matches. It is completely overused and is responsible for much of the negative tactics we now see in Gaelic football. Having studied your opposition, there is a growing tendency to go out and try to stop them playing football. O'Dwyer preached the gospel of forgetting about the opposition and playing to our own strengths. He rarely sought out weaknesses in teams we met or instructed us to play to a set pattern. We were the last 'free spirit' team in Gaelic football.

He insisted on two things, quick movement of both ball and player. He emphasised, again and again, that he didn't want guys looking at the O'Neills logo on the ball. In other words, the minute you got the ball you looked for a better placed colleague and passed it to him. He wanted players to be moving all the time, regardless of whether they had the ball or not. The strategies he used were somewhat similar to those pioneered by the great Dutch team beaten in the 1974 World Cup final. It was a kind of 'total' football. Everybody went forward when we had the ball, but as soon as we lost possession all fifteen players became defenders.

By the end of the seventies, O'Dwyer probably realised that he needed something more to keep us motivated than just the prospect of chasing another All-Ireland medal. The carrot he dangled in front of us was team holidays. His plan worked. In addition to the annual All Star tour to the United States we could also look forward to a holiday in the sun provided, of course, we won the All-Ireland. Initially we went to places like the Canaries but we soon set our sights on faraway horizons.

We put in a huge effort in 1980 to win a hat-trick of All-Ireland titles and O'Dwyer sensed that he needed to dangle a really big carrot in front of us in order to get us in the right frame of mind for yet another campaign. He mooted the idea of a tour to the United States, Hawaii and Australia and recruited a top businessman called Tom McCarthy to help us with the fund raising.

Tom met us after a league match in the spring of 1981 The first question he asked us was how much money did we think we needed to raise for such a tour. Somebody said £60,000. McCarthy said "Peanuts, let's aim for £100,000," which was massive money at that time. He told us to forget about the traditional fund-raising methods like raffles and dances. He suggested, instead, that we organise just three or four events.

He staged three. There was a King of the County competition, featuring eight candidates, and which proved very successful. Then we commissioned a handpainted portrait of the three in a row team and offered copies of it for sale at £100 each. It wasn't a standard team picture. Perhaps the artist decided to take some poetic licence because when the picture was unveiled, John O'Keeffe looked like the smallest man on the team, while Ogie Moran was a giant. My mother didn't recognise her son, Mike, in the picture.

Kerry people had more artistic appreciation than we gave them credit for. We made somewhere in the region of £34,000 from selling it; the picture is now a collectors' item. It was unheard of at the time to charge £100 for what was essentially a team photograph. We targeted the business community in our sales drive. The hangers-on who followed the team during the previous three years melted away like snow in May. We quickly found out who our real supporters were; an education in itself.

The other fund-raising venture we undertook were two weekend trips to the North. One weekend we played under floodlights in Burren, Co Down before heading to Glenravel, Co Antrim for a match on Saturday and we finished up the weekend with a game in Donegal. We took the gate receipts and we also sold autographed pictures of the team. The average attendance at each game was around 5,000 and a favourable exchange rate with sterling at the time boosted our coffers further.

During the second weekend trip we played under lights in Castleblaney. On Saturday we travelled to Carrickmore in County Tyrone where 6,000 people paid £2 sterling each to see us play. The RUC didn't visit Carrickmore too often in those days; the bars stayed open all night and the Kerry team were the best customers. Despite having got virtually no sleep, we travelled down to Dundalk and played Louth on the Sunday. We were lucky to win by a couple of points and this led the Louth fans to think their team would be challenging for major honours that year.

The three fund-raising projects raised £109,000 in total which was absolutely huge money back in 1981. Inevitably there was a lot of controversy about how the money should be shared out. But typical of O'Dwyer, he made sure that after the tour costs were paid, the remainder of the money was divided among the players. We ended up getting £1,400 pocket money each. O'Dwyer proved as able a financial manager as he was a team boss. He was the banker on the trip and he doled out the money in instalments so we didn't spend it all in the first week.

Looking back on it now it was a trip of a lifetime but I suppose it is the funny incidents which stand out. We booked into a hotel in Adelaide in Australia after a long overnight flight. Soon afterwards a member of the party rang reception to complain about the lack of air conditioning in his room. He threatened to pull the entire Kerry party out of the hotel if the problem was not fixed immediately. The service man came up to the room and took a quick look around before looking at our friend straight in the eye and remarking: "Why not try and plug it in buddy," There were no further complaints from that gentleman.

I had my first real taste of journalism during the tour doing a series of articles for *The Irish Press* . The practice of GAA players writing columns for newspapers was relatively new at the time. It is only recently I was told my scribblings did not please the National Union of Journalists who threatened industrial action. Evidently the problem was sorted out because the column continued to appear.

We were involved in what would probably be described nowadays as a 'Royal security alert' during the trip. One night while we were in Melbourne a group of us dressed in our Kerry blazers headed off to a disco. We were refused admission and a few burly looking bouncers insisted that we be on our way. We heard later that Captain Mark

Phillips, who was then married to Princess Anne, was a guest at the disco that night and obviously the doormen felt that blue blood might not mix with Kerry blood.

The tour kept us motivated for another season because we won our fourth All-Ireland title in a row the following September. Incidentally had we won the five in a row in 1982 we planned to holiday in Bali in the Far East. I remember the day after the 1982 final, fellows were saying that the only Bali we would be going to would be Bally f......bunion!!!!.

One of O'Dwyer's other significant achievements was to ensure the star players did not grab all the off the field endorsements. To the best of his ability, he made sure everybody got a share of the spoils. Considering what has happened in other counties since, his achievement should not be underestimated. In the late seventies several players - including myself - had boot contracts. My contract was with Puma, but Adidas were after me for years to sign up with them.

Eventually I agreed. A few days before the 1980 All-Ireland final I broke all the GAA rules on amateur status when I accepted a cheque for £400 outside Fitzgerald Stadium from an Adidas representative in return for wearing Adidas manufactured boot in the final.

There was no cash element in a deal I had with another company. Instead I could get as much of their gear for free as I wanted. About a week after the final, I received a bill for £2,000 from my former brand for all the gear I received from them over the years. I felt the figure was wildly exaggerated. I immediately handed the bill to my new friend from Adidas. He assured me that as an amateur player any contract I had was not binding. So I was off the hook and I never heard anything more about it.

There were at least two other Kerry players who received money from Adidas at that time in return for wearing their boots. O'Dwyer realised what was going on straight away and he knew that, unless he acted, the whole thing could get out of hand. It was through O'Dwyer's prompting that the County Board did a deal with Adidas, who now supply all the gear to the Kerry teams. Although the link-up remains a source of controversy right up to the present day, it has stood the test of time.

As far as I remember Adidas initially paid somewhere between £10,000 and £15,000 to secure the gear contract and this money went into a players' holiday fund. The GAA insist that any gear worn by county teams must be manufactured in Ireland. Kerry managed to circumvent the rule by pointing out that the jersey and togs we wore were manufactured in County Donegal under licence from Adidas. So, in effect, they were an Irish product.

Perhaps the most famous (or should that be infamous) sponsorship deal we were involved in was with Bendix washing machines before the 1985 All-Ireland final. We were ridiculed when the advert, featuring the half naked Kerry squad, appeared in the newspapers. We didn't give a toss, however, because we were getting good money - somewhere between £10,000 and £15,000 - for our holiday fund from the company. There was also some talk that all the players would get a free washing machine but I'm afraid I'm still waiting for the delivery.

I would argue that it was far more honourable to squeeze a few pound out of the corporate sector than charge bars or other GAA clubs, for the privilege of visiting them with the Sam Maguire Cup. This is a lucrative circuit nowadays but in our day all these visits were free of charge.

O'Dwyer never criticised his players in public and rarely did it in private either. He used a different kind of psychology. He would take a player aside and tell him that he was the best footballer in his position in the country, he would compliment him on his magnificent performance the previous Sunday and indicate that he planned to build the team around him. Even though he was always positive in his comments, when he wasn't happy with you it was very easy to pick up the negative vibes from him.

I suppose he was the ultimate 'cute hoor'. I remember when I was dropped after the 1977 All-Ireland semi-final O'Dwyer conveniently missed the selection meeting which, I suspect, wasn't entirely a coincidence. He was unbelievably competitive. He had to be first at everything.

For instance, when we went on trips abroad O'Dwyer would be the first man off the bus at the airport, first to check in at the airport, the first on and off the plane and the first to check into the hotel. So much so, that even on long trips he generally brought only one bag with him which he brought on to the plane.

He was equally competitive in training. His speciality was press-ups. He was very fit himself and he loved to have press-up competitions with the players. He knew in his heart and soul he was way better than most of us in this particular discipline.When we were running laps in Fitzgerald Stadium O'Dwyer would invariably join us for the last circuit and beat most of us. This was good for his ego as anybody watching would spread the news that O'Dwyer was still fitter than any of his players. "Didn't I see him with my own eyes beating them all in a race".

Micko would never be caught making outlandish statements during interviews. He was always the perfect diplomat and he never missed an opportunity to play down Kerry's chances regardless of who we were playing. He still does it and it amazes me how some commentators still swallow the spin he puts on things.

I remember before one big championship match we got word during a training session that spies from the opposing camp were watching us. What was O'Dwyer response? He instructed us to play what he called 'ground football' - soccer - for the remainder of the session. So the poor devils who came to see us training went home somewhat bemused.

I suppose he could be described as a Football Fanatic. How else can you explain a man in his sixties making a 400 mile round trip from Waterville to Newbridge several times a week to train Kildare. I assume he is paid generous expenses but it's his love of football which really drives him on. The most feared drill during an O'Dwyer training session was known as 'wire to wire' which, as the name suggests, was a sprint across the pitch. We often did up to twenty of them in rapid succession.

Then we had what we called the 'Heavy Gang' who were overweight when they turned up for training every year.

Among its members were Tim Kennelly, Jimmy Deenihan, John Egan, Bomber Liston and Paidi O Se. O'Dwyer would bring this group in for two extra training sessions per week for a month in late Spring until they shed the extra pounds. He also recruited Ogie Moran, Ger Power and myself for these sessions. We were known as the 'Rabbits.' Our job was to push the 'Heavy Gang' in training until they had a spring in their step.

Kerry and Dublin were the fittest team in any sport in Ireland in the mid to late seventies. Indeed, Kevin Moran remarked to me recently that the training he did with Dublin was much harder than anything he ever endured with either Manchester United or Blackburn Rovers. Back then there was no such thing as bleep tests, measuring body fat, nutron diets or anything like that. O'Dwyer (and Kevin Heffernan) got us fit using simple effective methods.

But, unlike the majority of current day managers, Micko never fell into the trap of forgetting that the ball is the most important item in Gaelic football. He was a great believer in using the ball as much as possible. For instance, he didn't neglect the humble kick around before training. Our backs versus forwards games in training were often more intensive than anything we experienced in a competitive match situation.

Nearly all successful teams have a manager who has complete control. O'Dwyer worked with four selectors in Kerry but nobody had any doubt who was in charge. The selectors, particularly the late Joe Keohane did, however, play an important role during matches. O'Dwyer tended to get very caught up in the games whereas Keohane was the essence of coolness. I suspect when changes were made during matches the selectors had at least as much input into the decision as O'Dwyer. They noticed things he missed because he was so wound up.

There was a certain amount of tension between O'Dwyer and Keohane as the latter came from the traditional school of Kerry football. I'm sure he didn't agree with some of the tactics O'Dwyer used but they still worked well together. It's vital for any team manager to leave his County Board under no illusions about who is boss. Generally speaking where there is a dominant County Board Chairman and a weak team manager the county team suffers because the County Board can't keep its nose out of team business.

In Kerry, Ger McKenna and the late Frank King let O'Dwyer get on with the business of managing the team and dictate his conditions. He had total responsibility as regards how many training sessions we had, when and where we organised challenge games and where we went on holidays. But O'Dwyer used his power well and enjoyed an excellent working relationship with the County Board.

All the Kerry players pushed their bodies to the limit, and beyond, during their careers. Inevitably some of us are now suffering the consequences of what we did. At times our training was so intense that players broke down during sessions. In the event of this happening we were allowed take pain-killing injections. In the early years we went to one particular specialist in Dublin to be injected.

These trips were viewed as part and parcel of the lead-up to big games. We were so committed and dedicated we wanted to play in every big match. We feared if we missed a game we might not get back on the team because the competition for places was so intense. Predictably, the combination of pushing ourselves to the limit and beyond, and taking pain killing injections, is now causing problems.

I have severe arthritis in both legs and according to a specialist I visited last year my left knee resembles that of a 70 year old farmer. Others are suffering too. Sean Walsh needs a hip replacement and such is the condition of Mike Sheehy's knees that he can do very little now in the way of any sporting activity. Don't get me wrong, however. Not one of us blame O'Dwyer for the condition we now find ourselves in. We were willing to push our bodies beyond the limit and agreed to have pain killing injections administered. Between the time I had my knee operation and the end of my inter-county career I survived on a diet of Brufen - an anti-inflammatory tablet

O'Dwyer had his favourite players. Bomber was his

number one, but I was also well up his list of favourites. He was always good to me, he gave me breaks and rarely criticised me. But there were certain players he was very hard on - particularly fellows who arrived into the squad during the latter years of his reign. I always felt that John Kennedy got rough justice at times from him.

He pushed the new guys very hard in training and if they made a mistake he came down on them like a ton of bricks. He made the mistake of not blooding enough young players when we were on top. While he was always willing to experiment during the league, he rarely gave the newcomers a real chance in crunch championship matches. They were the first in the firing line when things were going poorly. Paradoxically his loyalty to the older players, which we admired him so much for, ultimately led to his downfall.

These were minor faults. His record speaks for itself and I think it's safe to predict that no other manager will ever equal his feats. As I said at the start, he was Simply the Best and his success this year with Kildare suggests that he hasn't lost his magic touch.

18

TEMPLENOE

THERE is a sign erected on the western approach road to our bar which reads: Drive slowly through village. Somebody has scrawled underneath it 'or you'll miss it'. In fact, Templenoe is not a village in the strictest meaning of the word. The pub and church are separated by a couple of hundred yards and there is no main street. Indeed, sadly and scandalously, there is no national school in the parish either.

At one time there were two, but then there was this daft drive in the sixties to centralise national schools. Both were closed, even though there were enough students around to keep them open. We now have the ludicrous situation where more than 100 young children are being bussed into Kenmare. For some it means a daily journey of 30 miles.

Geographically, Templenoe covers a wide area but, like many rural parts of Ireland, was ravaged by emigration. Down through the decades people from the parish went to three foreign cities in particular -London, Boston and New York to earn a living. I remember entire families left. Templenoe depends on agriculture and tourism for economic survival. There are no industries here.

The area has been completely neglected by successive governments down through the years. Our biggest handicap was we never had a TD to press our case in Dublin. Maybe that will now change after the election in 1997 of Independent candidate Jackie Healy-Rae from nearby Kilgarvan. Already we are beginning to see the results of his lobbying.

Just like everywhere else, Templenoe has benefited from the Celtic Tiger in recent years. The population is steadily increasing and there are a lot of youngsters growing up in the parish now. We see evidence of this in the GAA club where we can now field two adult teams and have decent sides at under-age level. The absence of a national school is a huge drawback to the GAA club. Traditionally national schools are the breeding ground of future footballers, while teachers often play a pivotal role in the affairs of the local club. But we are deprived of all this because of a very short-sighted policy.

Templenoe is a completely laid back place and I have no intention of ever leaving it. I could write a book about the many characters who come into the bar. Indeed, it's easy to see where another Kerry publican, John B Keane, gets such rich material for his books and plays. The people are fantastic but they don't tolerate prima donnas. I had first hand experience of this myself. They were less fazed with my successful football career than virtually any other parish in Ireland. I have seen Albert Reynolds, Bertie Ahern and other famous people drop into the bar for a drink and none of the locals pass much heed on them.

During my teenage years I had little, or no success, at under-age level with Templenoe. We reached an U-14 county final but were beaten. Indeed, we were having so little success that we succumbed to the temptation of using over-age players. In those days the enforcement of the regulations wasn't as strict as it is nowadays.

There were still a myriad of complications when illegal players were used. Say for instance, the under- age player we wanted to use was called Paddy Murphy. We would search around for a player who was eligible and shared the same surname. So Paddy Murphy was rechristened Michael Murphy for an hour.

But, even though the paper work might look correct, there were practical problems once the game began, particularly when we had up to half a dozen over-age players in action. We had to remember to call all the illegals by their assumed names. Otherwise the opposition would smell a rat straight away. Of course, what happened was guys started getting excited as the match wore on and forgot what they were supposed to call each other. It was a recipe for chaos and, predictably, it didn't make the slightest difference. We still couldn't win anyway.

One of my fondest memories of those times is when Templenoe joined with Kenmare at U-16 level and the team reached the county final. I can still see two of our players actually driving into the ground. This was in an era when cars were not as plentiful as they are now. Certainly there were no sixteen year olds driving cars around Kerry. But we still lost.

At senior level, Templenoe float between Division 2 and 6 of the county league in Kerry - our natural home is somewhere between Division 3 and 4. The club became famous, not because of its achievements but because Mike, Tommy and I played with them. But, for all our problems, we did have a few days in the sun. We won a county novice title in 1974, a junior title in 1975 but lost to Dingle in an Intermediate final in 1989. We also won a Division 5 league title.

In truth having the three Spillane brothers on the team was a double-edged sword. The team suffered a lot because of our involvement with Kerry. Every year the season would follow a set pattern. We would start well in the county league but then Mike, Tommy and I would have to devote more time to Kerry. We missed matches, the team started losing and interest fizzled out until the following year.

Yet I cherish the memory of my modest achievements with Templenoe more than any other aspect of my football career. What I won with the club means more to me than most of my successes at inter-county level. With Templenoe I played alongside my friends - the lads I grew up with. While I had marvellous times with Kerry, I didn't make lasting friendships with more than a couple of my inter-county colleagues.

I have devoted 28 years of my life to Templenoe GAA club. I trained their senior team, acted as club secretary, served as a district board delegate, a county board delegate and organised an annual trip to London. Currently I train all the juvenile teams and for years I was the club's star player. But in Ireland one is rarely appreciated in their own parish. I received dozens of presentations from GAA clubs all over the country in recognition of my achievements on the football field. The only gift I ever received from my own club was a wedding present.

Don't get me wrong, it's not that I wanted anything. But we're all human and, I would be less than honest if I didn't say I'm disappointed my achievements were not recognised by Templenoe in some formal way. But in Templenoe one is never allowed to become too big for your boots - which, in many respects, is a good thing. There are so many people in Kerry with All-Ireland medals that winning one or two is no big deal. I was always treated as one of the lads and was never allowed to feel any different from the rest.

Of course, I managed to antagonise virtually all my club mates over the years because of my attitude on the field. I am the first to admit that I was one of the most annoying footballers ever to play alongside. I was constantly bickering and giving out to my team mates. It was an aspect of my game which I'm not proud - but I couldn't help it. I hated losing. I gave every game, regardless of how important it was, my total commitment. The minute the game was over I forgot what all the petty rows were about. However, other people who were on the receiving end of my comments were not as forgiving and carried chips on their shoulders.

One year Templenoe won a district championship beating Kenmare in the final. I had one of my best ever games for the club scoring something like twelve points. I imagined everybody would be happy. But afterwards in the bar fellows were carping - though not to my face - that I wouldn't pass them the ball. I was guilty as charged. But I was one of the best forwards in the country and I felt I could get most of the scores myself. Football was a matter of life and death. My club mates resented the fact that I was always giving out. I remember one day berating a colleague for kicking high balls towards me. His comment was "I won it, now you go and earn it."

Club football in Kerry is quite clean. Many people outside the county imagined I would be a target for 'special treatment' in club football. In fact, nothing could be further from the truth. Indeed, I can only recall two matches in my playing career when I felt I was being targeted.

The first was a league game against Ballylongford in North Kerry. Apart from my own marker, all the other

Ballylongford players seemed to be lining up to take hits off me. It was the only time I drew a belt on a guy right under the gaze of the referee. For the first time ever I knew there was a possibility I would be sent off, but the referee didn't take any action. I remember afterwards there was an item in the Ballylongford club notes in the paper apologising for the tactics used against me.

The second time I was scared on a football field in Kerry was near the end of my inter-county career during another county league game against Scartaglen. Not alone was I afraid of the guys I was facing on the field but there was an angry mob on the sideline baying for my blood as well. Kerry were going poorly at the time and, as I said before, Kerry GAA fans can be very fickle or perhaps they have short memories. Anyway, this particular evening I was getting dog's abuse from so-called supporters on the sideline and in club football you can hear every comment made.

Sean Kelly, who is now Munster Council GAA Chairman, took charge of the game when the appointed official didn't turn up. Sean just let the play flow and the guy who was marking me was giving me a right thumping. Ironically, we have since become close friends. With about seven minutes left I walked off . I felt if I stayed around any longer there was a danger I would get badly injured.

The other bad experience I had in club football was in a county championship match between Kenmare and John Mitchels. The previous Sunday I played well in a Munster final but that didn't stop the John Mitchels 'fans' from shouting obscenities at me. In fairness the manager of the John Mitchels team, Buddy Grady, came into our dressing room afterwards and apologised on behalf of the club.

Like the majority of rural GAA clubs, the only meeting which attracts a decent attendance is the annual general meeting. It takes all day to get people to fill the various officer positions. But in between there is no shortage of talk. Indeed, if talking could produce results on the field we would have won several All-Ireland club titles. I often describe Templenoe as a social more than a sporting club. Certainly, whenever Templenoe play a game away from home, it's a major disappointment if anybody is back at base before closing time.

Training mainly consists of playing among ourselves. We are resigned to the fact that the majority of our players like to play instead of running 25 laps of the pitch. At one time in the seventies, when we were going quite well, we had a problem with our kick outs - we never knew where they might land. We devised a tactic where the kicker would shout a signal and the outfield players then knew where the ball was heading for - much like you see in a rugby line out.

Initially we started off using place names. But the problem with using place names is that they are long winded. Imagine trying to get you tongue around somewhere like Derrygerrane or Slieve a Dubh. We decided we needed a quicker signal so we opted for car registration numbers. So we had PZI 901 if the ball was going to the right flank, or NZO 120 if the kick was dropping short. The problem with car registrations numbers is that most people cannot remember their own, never mind remembering three or four more.

The last thing we tried was using a name associated with a player's work. For instance, the call word for my brother, Tommy was cidona - a reference to the fact that we had the bar. If the shout was 'cidona' it meant the kick out was heading for Tommy who played at midfield. I remember telling this story to 'Bomber' Liston and, fair play to him, he used it to good effect in a Railway Cup semi-final against Ulster at Croke Park. He was fouled around the middle of the field and shouted 'cidona'. I immediately turned around, he hit a short free to me and I kicked the ball over the bar.

There was one club member who considered himself an expert on the rules of the game. We were playing in a junior final on a miserable wet day and our friend made a hole in the top of a sponge and attempted to place the ball in this hole when he was taking a kick out. When challenged by the referee he pointed out the rule stated the kick out had to be taken from either the 14 or 21 yard line. It didn't say, 'on the line' so he was quite entitled to use the sponge. Unfortunately the referee had a different interpretation and the sponge had to be removed.

In the seventies we had a very good team and came very close to making the breakthrough. One season we were lying second in Division 2 of the county league and needed another win to clinch promotion to Division 1 for the first time in our history. Our last game was against Laune Rangers, who were third or fourth in the table, but had no chance of winning promotion. They offered us a deal. They were preparing for the Mid-Kerry championship and they badly wanted a competitive game. Would we travel to Killorglin for the match on a Saturday evening on the understanding that they would allow us win it? At least, that was my understanding of the agreement.

So we headed off to Killorglin with an understrength team. Mike, for instance, didn't bother travelling down from Dublin for the match. With 15 minutes to go a Laune Rangers selector called out to our secretary who was playing : "Timmy the deal is off." We lost by a point and missed out on promotion. Ironically, Laune Rangers went from strength to strength afterwards and won the All-Ireland club title in 1996.

Some of our more memorable escapades happened off the field. For years we organised an annual trip to London. Usually we went across on the ferry from Rosslare to Swansea. On our first ever trip, two of our fellows managed to get arrested in Swansea. They were so drunk when they stumbled into the customs hall, not only did they walk into the barrier, but they managed to knock it over.

We still played some of our best football on those tours. One year we participated in a tournament involving London club Round Towers and Skerries from Dublin. Round Towers beat Skerries and we then beat Towers in what we understood to be the final. Afterwards however there was no sign of the trophy. The organisers explained that the cup was for the winners of the game between between Skerries and Round Towers. We were bitterly disappointed having to come home empty-handed.

Round Towers brought in players from all over London to

bolster their side. Their full-back was giving me plenty of belts, but I was getting even more grief from a woman on the sideline, who was calling me every name under the sun. I turned to the full back and remarked "She's a terrible bitch." He replied "Yes she is." Afterwards in the pub I met my marker again. He made a point of introducing me to his wife. I nearly dropped dead when I saw her - the woman who had been roaring at me from the sideline!

Another year we played on a pitch outside Wormwood Scrubs prison. The chant from behind the bars remained constant throughout the match: "Go home Paddy, somebody is screwing your wife" We chanted back: "At least we know it is isn't you, you Limey bollix". Our verbal exchanges with Her Majesty prisoners was by no means the only highlight of that tour, which took place on the coldest weekend in February for about fifty years.

Our problems began almost as soon as we left Templenoe. The heater on the bus packed up. I remember one of the girls on the trip fell asleep with her head resting on the window. When she woke up her hair was frozen solid to the glass. It was the first in a catalogue of disasters. After stopping at a cafe somewhere in Wales we took the wrong turn when we got back on the motorway. After about two hours he discovered we were no nearer the Severn Bridge than when we left Ireland.

We finally reached London only for the bus to break down as we headed up Kensington High Street. I can still picture us pushing the coach which had a big poster stuck on the window: Templenoe GAA Club on Tour. On our last London tour two of our players were so drunk they were taken off the field for their own safety.

Prior to all the tours we did some fund-raising to help finance the trip. Normally we organised a dance but one year we decided to auction the jersey I wore in the Centenary All-Ireland final in 1984.

The room was full and the drink was flowing when Tommy, my brother, started the bidding. People get carried away in these situations and the jersey was sold for a couple of hundred quid. We were thrilled until the purchaser came to see me the next day. He complained that the jersey he bought wasn't in fact the one I wore in the Centenary final. He had checked the video of the final and noticed the numbering used on the 1984 jersey was different from what was usually on the Kerry jerseys. He was 100% correct but, fair play to him, he still gave us the money.

Last year I decided I would give football one last crack before throwing my boots into Kenmare Bay. I faithfully promised my wife it would definitely be my last season. I trained really hard - even if I cheated a little. I bought a running machine at Christmas and installed it in our bedroom. I did most of my training in the evening keeping one eye on Coronation Street and Sky Sport. But I over did it. After playing the first match against Castlegregory my knee blew up like a balloon and I had to go for surgery.

Afterwards the surgeon presented me with a jar full of bones and little bits of gristle which were floating around in my knee. It wasn't a pretty sight. The surgeon had some good news, however. The knee was in such poor condition I couldn't do it any more damage! Once I recovered from surgery I decided to go back training with the lads. I was enjoying the backs versus forwards games so much I made myself available for the Cahill Cup - a competition for players who didn't play in the club championship.

I played a couple of matches and we qualified for the semi-final. Then I started to have back trouble and I couldn't train or play. The day before the game I went to a doctor and he gave me a pain killing injection. Just to be doubly sure, I decided to have two pain killing injections on the morning of the game. Twenty minutes into the first half my back went again. The pain was ferocious. But, being a complete eejit when it comes to football, I decided to continue.

Afterwards I couldn't move which was a mite inconvenient given that my wife had just arrived home from hospital with a baby boy. Eventually in November last year I had another operation - this time on my back. So my efforts to play in Division 4 of the County League and the B football championship last year resulted in me having two operations, not to mention all the grief and pain

I endured. Mad, of course I am.

So what did I do this year? I resumed training in June and one evening I caught Rosarii in a soft mood and got permission to play again. I started my comeback coming on as a substitute in a B match. Since then I have graduated to the senior team and in September I scored six points in a county league game against Listowel Emmets.

People ask me what am I doing playing football at the age of 42 when I should be on the golf course. I should be playing golf. But, of all the sports I tried, I enjoy Gaelic football best of all. I don't like golf because I don't give it enough time and I can't understand why I can't get birdies when I occasionally play. I still get enjoyment from going down to the football field with two balls and kicking them in and out of the goals. It may seem boring but I like it.

It's amazing how my attitude has changed over the years. When I was in my twenties I remember looking at older guys and wondering what the hell they were doing playing football at their age. But as I got older I came around to their way of thinking.

I met countless guys over the years who retired from football in the their late twenties or early thirties. They all regretted their decision - they quit too early. I want to be remembered as somebody who is still able to play well and be one of the better players on the team, even if it's B football. There will come a time when I won't be able to play any longer. That moment is fast approaching. Meanwhile, as long as I can get enjoyment out of it, I will continue.

Kerry footballers are very attached to their clubs and it is virtually unheard of for any county player to change clubs. Unlike many counties where a player has to be playing with a big club to get a chance of playing for the county, in Kerry, you will get your chance regardless of what club you play with.

Templenoe never made it to senior grade, so I played with a divisional side Kenmare in the Kerry senior club championship. They drew players from four clubs, Kenmare, Kilgarvan, Twosist and Templenoe. I won two county championship medals with Kenmare in 1974 and

1987 but, like the majority of divisional teams, there was a lot of jealously among the four clubs, particularly ourselves and Kenmare, who at one time were bitter rivals. Before my time, clashes between the two clubs in the district board championship generally featured rows on the field and later in the pub.

When the Kenmare divisional team was selected we judged its merits on how many Templenoe players were selected. If we had more players than the Kenmare club then it was a good side - it didn't matter really whether the team was any use.

It actually suited my inter-county career that Templenoe was such a small club. Had I been playing with one of the top clubs in the county I would have had to devote more time to them. As it was, I wasn't involved in too many make or break games with Templenoe so I could concentrate all my energies on Kerry. In a way playing with the club was a welcome relief from the pressures of inter - county football. There was a relaxed atmosphere with everybody enjoying themselves.

I get more feedback from an article I do every year in the *Sunday World* about the life and times of Templenoe GAA club than from any other piece. The reaction is not always favourable as I discovered some years ago when I recalled an infamous incident involving ourselves and the Castlegregory GAA club. The Templenoe U-16 team that I was managing at the time reached the county final. Unfortunately the date of the match clashed with our annual trip to London. The County Board were prepared to refix the final but our opponents Castlegregory wouldn't budge. We didn't turn up because all our officials were in London on the date of the game.

Castlegregory claimed the game. It was an unbelievably selfish decision on their part and we lost a lot of good players who were very disillusioned by what happened. It was hard to blame them. Two years ago we played Castlegregory at senior level. Spurred on by revenge for what happened years before we beat them for the first time ever. Later I wrote about the incident and the game in my Templenoe diary. They had their revenge on Templenoe and myself a year later. They tore into us and I got lots of verbals about what they thought of my article.

On an altogether more pleasant note a former Limerick hurler Dermot Kelly wrote a song in my honour called the Templenoe Hare. It went like this:

Near the town of Kenmare
There's a footballer there
Well known to the whole countryside
He had a bad knee which between you and me
Was the cause of much of sorrow and pain
When he played against Dublin
He heard a great rumbling
His legs were reduced to a trot
The thought to himself I'll wind up on the shelf
If I cannot unravel this knot.

Chorus:
The Templenoe hare he did not despair
He ran through the field like the wind
There was never a hound that could turn him around
He left all opponents behind.

Verse 2
A girl from the Barrow
was so full of sorrow
for Pat that she send him a cure
Hot poultice and ginger rubbed on with a finger
Would get his knee going for sure
Pat took no notice 'till one night the poultice
Set fire to the blankets and bed
Only Mick and big Tom stopped the fire going on
I'm afraid that poor Pat would be dead.

Verse 3
On the Late Late Show
He was asked by Gaybo
To drop in one night for a chat
No trouble at all he would give him a call
A decent young Kerryman Pat

He told him of stories of all sort of theories
Of cabbage, of tin-foil and paint
When he finally asked are you cured at last
Pat said, Gay I am and I ain't.

Verse 4
So come one and all who kick the football
Have courage and do not give in
If your ribs or your thighs
Or the balls of your eyes
Are battered by elbows and shins
Just think of how Pat conquered ailments like that
and with one knee came home with the cup
So hats in the air to the Templenoe Hare
Spillane who never gave up.

19

LIFE AFTER FOOTBALL

THE ultimate goal for any person is to be paid to pursue their hobby. I played Gaelic football for nearly twenty years at the highest level but never earned any real money from my involvement in the game - in fact, it probably cost me. I have no regrets - it was worth every lost penny.

I find it mildly ironic that now, having hung up my boots, I'm actually being paid to talk about the game on television and write about it in the *Sunday World* . I suppose it's the next best thing to getting paid for playing. Talking about football comes naturally to me. I guess I owe my gift of the gab to the fact I was born and reared in a bar where there was non-stop talk about football.

All during the O'Dwyer era the Kerry team were very media friendly. We never had media bans - they are counter productive in my view. Far from relieving the pressure on individual players, they create more because players get paranoid about simple things like answering the telephone.

O'Dwyer's strategy was to use the media as a tool in our psychological battle against our opponents. While I was well known for my forthright views on all kinds of issues, I never ran down our opponents in any interview. Like all Kerry players, I never said we would win any game. We always beat around the bush. What we were doing was building up the opposition and the strategy worked for us over the years.

When I retired from inter-county football in 1991 a couple of national newspapers approached me about the possibility of contributing articles about Gaelic football. I suppose they recognised me as somebody who was not afraid to air his views. I opted for the *Sunday World*

Since then I have applied the same qualities I displayed on the football field - complete commitment, dedication, determination and single mindedness What you see with Pat Spillane is what you get. I'm straightforward and honest.

During the summer of 1992 I also started doing some television work for RTE and one of my first jobs was co-commentator with Clare man Marty Morrissey, when his county beat Kerry to win the Munster football title for the first time in 75 years. Marty was so excited I thought at times he would tumble out of the broadcasting box at Limerick's Gaelic Grounds.

The power of the media is amazing. The day after winning my eighth All-Ireland medal in 1986 I could have walked down Grafton Street in Dublin and perhaps half a dozen people might have recognised me. Now as a result of my media work, I am recognised more often than when I was a player. Going on holidays in Ireland, or even going out for a drink anywhere outside Kerry, is a chore. I have become something of a celebrity since I retired, which I find rather strange.

Up until the time I started doing a weekly column in the *Sunday World* I felt the majority of GAA journalists had to adopt a cautious approach to what they wrote in order to maintain a working relationship with County Boards, managers and players. Unless they had such a relationship they would find it virtually impossible to do their job. I believed there was a niche in the market to be filled. I was a retired footballer. I was never going to become a full-time GAA journalist, so I didn't have to stay on side with the powers that be in the GAA.

I never set out to be critical just for the sake of it, even though most people accuse me of being either over critical or cynical. I call everything as I see it. If I see a guy hitting somebody off the ball then I will name the culprit. If I see a player making mistakes then I will refer to it. I believe that's my job as an analyst. I accept I have changed my views on whether amateur GAA players should be criticised about their performances in the newspapers or on television. During my playing career I argued that as amateurs playing football as a hobby we did not deserve to be criticised. Indeed, I made this point quite forcibly in an interview on the *Late Late Show* in 1985.

Since retiring I have come around to the view that once anybody, be they professional or amateur, goes on to the centre stage performing a song, acting in a play or playing football or hurling then they are open to criticism - be it good, bad or indifferent. GAA players have one of the biggest stages in Ireland and are now watched by a huge audience. If they play badly or are guilty of some misdemeanour then I believe it should be highlighted.

Nowadays, when I go to major matches, I get the same message from many fans. 'Stop being negative', 'Stop being so critical' or 'Don't be cynical'. At times I am probably too smart for my own good. But if I am cynical I'm merely reflecting much of what is going on in Gaelic football at present. We have witnessed teams adopting negative tactics and being more interested in stopping the opposition than playing to their own strengths.

I have offended many people and counties over the years. To my cost I learned there is a world of difference between how people take criticism in the Republic of Ireland compared to the six Northern counties. Criticising any aspect of GAA activity north of the border is interpreted as an attack on the ethos of the whole community. It's not just an attack on a GAA player, it's a criticism of his club, his county, nationalism and Catholicism. What a lot of people don't realise in the south is that Gaelic football (and hurling) are more than just games to the nationalist community in the six counties.

My harshest critics come from the North. For instance, I have met people from Ulster who can quote me chapter and verse of something I wrote in the Sunday World or said on television years ago. Down here the majority of people would not remember what I wrote or said a week ago. My stock answer to people who ask me why did I slag off player x or y is that they are not customers in my bar. And it's true. I never criticise the customers that frequent the bar here in Templenoe. I suppose it's relatively safe to criticise people from a distance. Or is it?

One of the few times I criticised Kerry was during Ogie Moran's reign as team manager after they lost to Cork in the 1995 Munster final. The longer the game went on the more obvious it became that Kerry had a problem at midfield. Wearing my Kerry supporters' hat I was getting more and more frustrated that nothing was being done about it. In the end the moves were made too late and on the *Sunday Game* programme that night I commented about this issue.

The following Sunday a Fr Tomas O'Chaoimh, who is a brother of Kerry County GAA secretary Tony O'Keeffe, gave a sermon in Irish at mass in Carraig Church in the West Kerry Gaeltacht during which he alluded to my comments on television. According to a front page story in the *Cork Examiner* the next day, Fr O'Chaoimh said: "What he had to say on RTE television disappointed many people. I don't know why he did it and I don't think it was good enough."

In the letter, which was later published in the paper, Fr O'Chaoimh pointed out that he referred to me for twenty seconds in a six minute sermon. According to the *Examiner* report the congregation applauded at the end of the sermon. Their reaction was in keeping with the prevailing mood in Kerry at the time because I received ferocious criticism in the county over my comments. I still maintain that while many people in the county agreed with my remarks they didn't want to hear a native Kerry person making them.

I can understand their view but I always try to be neutral when I make my comments. I honestly felt the Kerry selectors made a mistake that day which possibly cost us the match. I would have been dishonest if I hadn't made that point. Despite the furore it caused I have no regrets.

I have lost count of the number of abusive letters and phone calls I have received over the years. I had to get rid of my answering machine because it gave every Tom, Dick and Harry an ideal opportunity to leave long, rambling and sometimes abusive messages.

One thing I find fascinating about the abusive letters I receive is that so many of them are unsigned. I cannot understand the logic of sitting down and writing three or four pages containing all forms of venom and then not bothering to sign it. Sometimes I read them, but more often than not I chuck them into the bin - particularly the unsigned ones. Even before I open the envelope I have a fair idea whether it's a tirade of abuse.

It seems when people are mad at me they cannot bring themselves to write my address on an envelope in a civilised manner. I have received letters addressed to 'Pat Bollix, County Kerry', or 'Pat Spillane, So Called Former Great'. These are real giveaways so I don't even bother opening them.

The first county I had a serious run-in with was Clare. And to this day I am not welcome in the county for two reasons. Firstly, I highlighted an off the ball incident in the 1992 All-Ireland semi-final between Dublin and Clare in which Tom Morrissey and Dave Foran exchanged punches. It was partially because I drew attention to the incident that Morrissey and Foran were suspended by the Games Administration Committee.

On the day of the match itself RTE were short of material near the end of the transmission and the presenter Michael Lyster told me to keep talking. During the course of my monologue I suggested it would be many a long day before Clare would be back in Croke Park in an All-Ireland semi-final.The you know what hit the fan. I got numerous letters and phone calls from Clare people berating me for my comments.

The funny thing about the phone calls was they all came through to the phone in the bar. I was living over the bar at the time. Nine times out of ten it was a customer who picked it up because the phone is outside the counter and close to the door.The callers on the other end of the line were in such an animated state they rarely bothered to ask who they were speaking to, so it was my customers who took most of the abuse. My prediction turned out to be accurate because until Martin Daly's late, late goal against Cork last year, Clare hadn't won a championship match since 1992.

The Mayo fans were another group who fell out with me as a result of an article in the *Sunday World* . In the 1996 Connacht championship Mayo struggled to beat Roscommon in the semi-final. When previewing the final I suggested in the opening line that if Mayo played as badly as they did against Roscommon they needn't bother getting out of bed. Mayo people went mad. The Mayo papers had a field day. My comments were used by John Maughan to extract a few ounces of extra effort from his players. Of course, what all my Mayo critics conveniently ignored was my very next sentence: 'Any team trained by John Maughan will be fit, determined and committed and cannot be ruled out of the equation.'

The Mayo fans had sweet revenge when, not alone did they beat Galway in the Connacht final they went on to knock Kerry out of the championship in the All-Ireland semi-final. This led to me experiencing one of the most scary moments in my life. On the day of the Mayo-Kerry match I was working for RTE in what's called the Crow's Nest which is situated high up in the Nally Stand, with Michael Lyster and Martin Carney. After the game between 500 and 600 Mayo fans gathered underneath the Crow's Nest. They all apparently wanted a friendly word with me!

The Gardai were called to clear the crowd and fair play to Martin Carney, he escorted me out of Croke Park. The verbal abuse I got was quite frightening. The RTE match commentator Ger Canning then gave me a lift in his car and I literally had to lie low in the back seat any time we stopped near Mayo supporters. We headed straight for Dublin Airport and I got the first plane heading south. There was a humorous side to it as well. I know of at least one pub in Mayo where my picture was superimposed on their dart board and the thrower got an extra prize if he managed to hit my nose which wasn't too difficult a task because it's fairly big!

I got the red card in Donegal when I suggested they hadn't an asses hope of beating Dublin in the 1992 final following their laboured win over Mayo in the All-Ireland semi-final. I still believe my comments were justified as the two teams were woeful with Donegal, as usual, over indulging in the short-passing game. What happened when it came to the final? They played a completely different brand of football and thoroughly deserved to beat the Dubs.

During the last few minutes some of the Donegal fans appeared more interested in roaring abuse at me and giving me the two- fingered salute up in the Crow's Nest than watching history unfold down on the pitch. Then some entrepreneur produced a new line in T-shirts which sold like hot cakes in the county during the post All-Ireland celebrations. My name was written on the front while printed on the back was : 'Knows Fuck All About Football'.

Nowadays it's almost obligatory for all the pre All-Ireland football songs to include one snide remark about me. I reckon I should patent my name and make a few bob out of it. But I suppose the bottom line is that at least people are reading my column or watching me on television. It's the day the postman has no deliveries for me that I should be concerned about.

Sligo was the latest county I got into trouble with. After their 1997 Connacht final between Sligo and Mayo I said on television it was such an awful match that any pupils I wanted to punish I would have them watch a video of the entire match. A lot of people, including high ranking officials in the GAA, were very vexed about that remark. As luck would have it Sligo played Kerry in the League in Tralee at the tail end of 1997 and, in a big upset, beat the All-Ireland champions. I was at the game and during the last ten minutes the big contingent of visiting fans invented a new chant : 'Are you watching Pat Spillane' Are you watching Pat Spillane.'

But probably the worst scrape I got into was as a result of comments I made on television after an Ulster championship match between Derry and Armagh in 1996. It was a violent game in which Armagh, in particular, seemed hell bent on stopping their opponents from playing. There were several off the ball incidents and I used the word 'thuggery' to describe some of what happened.

I refused to give a Man of the Match award. The real reason I didn't pick a player was because nobody told me it was my job until the *Sunday Game* programme was about to go on air. Not surprisingly, my comments got a big reaction. But worse still there was a suggestion that my remarks bordered on slander.

I was approached by the powers that be in RTE and they suggested I withdraw the word 'thuggery' but not to apologise. It was a tricky assignment at the best of times and I made the fatal mistake of not scripting exactly what I wanted to say. I did it off the cuff and, while I took one step forward, I went about two miles back. I compounded the whole problem by suggesting that if some of what went on during the game took place outside the ground those involved would be branded criminals.

The next morning the manure really hit the fan. It was one of the worst days of my life. RTE were sued by members of the Irish Rugby Football Union over remarks made by Mick Doyle. The people involved received about £30,000 each in settlement of their claim. RTE senior management feared that I had slandered all the Armagh and Derry players and they were expecting an avalanche of claims. Based on the pay out made to the IRFU people they could be facing a £1m bill on this one. While they accepted I was good for the programme they reckoned I was a loose cannon.

At that point my TV career looked over. I suggested that I apologise on the *Monday Game* programme. This time I wrote out exactly what I wanted to say, stuck with it and thankfully no legal proceedings were initiated. Ever since I am more careful in what I say - particularly on television. Up until then I believed that if somebody punched another person while the ball was fifty yards away, or kicked an opponent while they are lying on the ground you could describe the perpetrator as a 'thug'. I approached a barrister friend afterwards for advice on this specific issue. His view was that it was slanderous to suggest that a person guilty of these offences was a 'thug' but they could be described as 'blackguards'.

Writing a weekly column for the *Sunday World* is an enjoyable experience and I think it works well for both myself and the paper, whose sales have been increasing steadily in recent years. The big difference between writing for a newspaper and making comments on television is that you have a lot more time to think about what you write. What you submit is checked by the editorial staff and maybe looked at by a solicitor before it is put into the paper. Television is a completely different medium.

In recent years I have tended not to go to big games. Instead I stay in the studio and watch the match on television. I don't really miss going to the game because I generally get dog's abuse from both sets of fans. The *Sunday Game* programme is done live and there is very little time for rehearsal. You end up with maybe two minutes to summarise a major talking point. Even for somebody like myself, who talks very fast, it is a very difficult thing to do.

One of the few times I was criticised for not calling a spade a spade was after the 1996 All-Ireland semi-final between Meath and Tyrone which featured a number of controversial incidents. While the programme was on air such was the volume of calls to the RTE switch board complaining about Meath's so-called 'rough house tactics' that the programme executives decided that we should highlight a number of specific incidents.

Normally if we were doing this we would have studied the incidents in slow motion. There were three, in particular, tackles on Peter Canavan, Ciaran McBride and Brian Dooher. The panelists viewed the tackles on a small television about twenty feet away from us. It was virtually impossible to say what happened and accordingly I had to be very careful about what I said. Mind you, even if I had the benefit of studying the incidents closely - as I have done since - I still find it impossible to say whether any of the tackles were deliberate.

The Man of the Match award is one of the big features on the *Sunday Game* programme. During my playing career I was the recipient of more Man of the Match awards in All-Ireland finals than any other player.

At the time I always felt individual awards took away from the gloss of the team's achievement. I felt that was wrong because Gaelic football is a team game and without the help of your team mates you would win nothing. I don't think individuals should be honoured. Despite my personal reservations the award is now a permanent feature of Gaelic games. Indeed, as soon as a match is over one of the first questions the fans will ask is: 'Who do you think will get Man of the Match?'

I am now regarded as an enemy of the GAA by many in the higher echelons of the Association which, in reality, couldn't be further from the truth. In 1997 during contract discussions between RTE and the GAA, the GAA suggested I that I should be dropped from the *Sunday Game* programme. RTE stuck to their guns and kept me on. Once again this year more overtures were made by the GAA to get rid of me but I survived the chop again.

Even though the GAA want me off the television it didn't stop them asking me to supply material to their new museum at Croke Park. I was more than willing to help - on one condition. I specifically asked that a named member of the GAA staff at Croke Park contact me. Six months later I'm still waiting for the call.

Over the years I have been courted by the political parties to stand as a candidate in South Kerry in a General Election. I am not a member of any political party and I never intend to be. Over the years I have voted for a variety of candidates, but my family are regarded as Fine Gael people.

At some point in the 1980s the Fine Gael General Secretary Finbar Fitzpatrick approached me about the possibility of standing as a second Fine Gael candidate in the South Kerry constituency. I would have shared the party ticket with the sitting Fine Gael TD Michael Begley.

His support base was slipping away at the time and the party needed me to sweep up extra votes to bolster his candidature and ensure his election. Even though I didn't fancy the idea of being used to get somebody else elected, I was willing to play ball. I told the party if they could do something for me then I would owe them one. I asked about the possibility of being made a director of Aer Rianta - I reckoned there was plenty of perks in that job. But there was no vacancy.

In the heel of the hunt I settled for a place on the Sports

Council. At the time Fine Gael were in Coalition with Labour and their leader was my old friend Dick Spring. He smelt a rat straight away. Labour also had ambitions of taking a seat in South Kerry but they reckoned my entry into the field would scupper their plans. Sources in Fine Gael suggested to me later that Spring vetoed my appointment.

A few years later after Fine Gael lost their seat in South Kerry they approached me again. I eventually agreed to meet a delegation from the constituency in Kenmare. There was a frank exchange of views. The Saturday after the meeting Templenoe were playing a league game in Scartaglen. An individual approached me after the game and introduced himself as a member of the delegation who met me the previous week.

He asked me whether we were going for a drink afterwards. I asked the lads where they were heading for and they shouted back 'Fleming's Bar.' My friend turned to me and said: "Murphy's is the Fine Gael bar in this town and if you want to get elected you should go there."

There and then I decided a career in politics wasn't for me. If somebody was going to tell me what pub I should go to, I knew politics wasn't for me. I have absolutely no regrets about that decision. Going into political life would mean an end to whatever privacy and family life I have. I simply wouldn't tolerate that. Anyway, Jackie Healy-Rae is doing a fabulous job for us at the moment.

20

The GAA in the 21st Century.

IT is to the immense credit of the GAA that as we reach the end of the 20th century, it remains the most successful, innovative, organised, supported and powerful sports organisation in Ireland. It has achieved this high standing despite having very conservative people in key positions throughout the country.

Even though I am critical of the GAA, it still stands as a model for all other sporting organisations. Much of the criticism levelled by outsiders at the GAA stems from nothing but jealously. For instance, those who suggest that the GAA is the 'grab all association' are completely wide of the mark.

Unlike the FAI which has invested money in white elephant projects such as floodlighting at places like Abbeycarton and Gortakeegan and the IRFU, which spend an increasing percentage of their budget to meet the inflated salaries of fairly average players, the GAA has, by and large, invested its money wisely. They have developed an excellent infrastructure both at local and national level. The situation in Kerry is mirrored throughout the country. There are probably more registered soccer teams in Kerry than GAA clubs, yet no more than half a dozen of them own a pitch or have changing rooms.

In contrast, virtually every GAA club in the county has its own playing field and dressing rooms: many have state of the art facilities. All these projects are granted aided by either the Provincial or Central Council of the GAA - or in some cases both. The GAA had to cope with high levels of emigration during much of the eighties, while the nineties brought a huge upsurge in the popularity of soccer in this country due to the success of the Republic of Ireland soccer team under Jack Charlton and more recently, the blanket TV coverage British soccer receives on Sky Television.

The GAA appear to have coped well with these

challenges, but there are many more just around the corner. At grass roots level the conveyor belt which provided the association with an abundance of talented young players over the decades is beginning to dry up. There is increased competition from a variety of other sports, not to mention the fact that many youngsters nowadays prefer to sit down and use a Play Station or watch a video than play football or hurling.

There is a decreasing number of people willing to give up their free time in order to coach GAA teams. This problem has been exacerbated in recent years by the number of child abuse scandals which have been uncovered in Ireland. For decades national teachers and, in particular, Christian Brothers, gave up much of their free time to coach youngsters in the skills of football and hurling. The Brothers have virtually disappeared from our schools, while lay teachers are no longer willing to give up so much of their free time.

The GAA must realise that they will have to compete in a crowded market place to get youngsters to play their games. More coaches need to be employed and the games have to be made more attractive for young people.

At the other end of the spectrum I applaud the GAA's growing links with the corporate world. Much of the finance to build the new Cusack Stand at Croke Park was raised from the corporate sector. This project will stand as a lasting monument to the Presidency of Peter Quinn. Provided a fair percentage of the seats within Croke Park continue to be made available to the ordinary punter, I have no problem with the association accepting finance from the Captain's of Industry.

The decision made a few years ago to finally accept sponsorship from alcohol companies was long overdue and another step in the right direction. The bottom line is that the money accruing from these sponsorship deals is ploughed back into the association.

Whereas the GAA has excelled in this area, it is still very poor at marketing the products. It has yet to catch on to what's happening at international level in this area. On a practical level, I would wager a considerable bet that the majority of Irish teenagers do not identify with the top GAA players, either within their own county or nationally. Ask any youngster between the age of eight and eighteen to name their top five sportsmen and the chances are they will pick overseas soccer players.

The structure of the GAA season makes it difficult to market GAA stars. Dublin, one of the glamour GAA football teams in Ireland, had three major games in the last two years; every Premiership club in England is guaranteed forty matches per season. I agree 100% with people like former Wexford hurling manager Liam Griffin and St Patrick's Athletic chairman Pat Dolan who have questioned the reason anybody from Ireland wears, say, a Leicester City replica jersey.

It's all down to marketing. Anybody who receives Sky Sport knows how the station hypes up the Premiership. The hype factor will get worse if Wimbledon are allowed relocate in Ireland under a new name like Dublin City FC.

The GAA, in association with its major sponsors - Guinness and the Bank of Ireland - must market themselves and their products more aggressively. The television advertising campaigns devised by the Bank of Ireland and Guinness are a step in the right direction but much more could be done. At the very least, there should be a shop in every county selling GAA merchandise like jerseys, hats, posters and all the other items which a visitor to the Manchester United mega store at Old Trafford can purchase.

Ultimately the GAA will have to reform the structure of the All-Ireland championships to maximise its return from any marketing drive. No system is sacred and the decision to allow the beaten finalists in the Munster and Leinster hurling finals back into the All-Ireland series was a welcome move for three reasons. Firstly, it generated extra revenue. Secondly, it provided extra matches which heightened the profile of Gaelic Games and, thirdly, the quality of some of the matches was excellent. The 1997 quarter-final clash between Kilkenny v Galway last year and the second replay between Offaly and Clare this summer were two of the best hurling games seen in the last two seasons.

Apart from the argument about marketing, there is another more practical reason why the championship structure needs to be reviewed. At present teams are training eight months of the year for one guaranteed match. It's completely illogical. Other than the tradition which dictates that the All-Ireland champions must win every game in the competition there is no reason why it should not be changed.

At least the Rubicon has been crossed in hurling - a team beaten in the series can be crowned All-Ireland champions. Major world sporting events such as the World Cups in both rugby and soccer are decided on a combined round robin-knock out format and there is no reason why the GAA can't follow that path.

Given the power which the four Provincial Councils wield within the GAA, it is unrealistic to expect that the provincial championships will ever be abolished. I believe they should be retained, with the All-Ireland series run as a different competition with the provincial winners and runners-up being seeded. With 32 counties participating in the All-Ireland championship they could be divided, on an Open Draw basis, into eight groups each consisting of four teams. The provincial winners and, perhaps, the beaten finalists could be kept apart.

There could be a series of round robin matches. Each team would be guaranteed three games with the group winners advancing to the quarter-finals. From then on it could be a knock out competition down to the final. Everybody would benefit. The weaker teams would have an opportunity of making progress with a guarantee of four matches - three in the All-Ireland series and one in the provincial championship. The extra matches would guarantee more revenue and television coverage and the most consistent team in the country would emerge as the All-Ireland champions.

Perhaps the GAA's experience with live television will convince them to take the plunge and go for a new look championship. For years the Association was vehemently opposed to the whole concept of live TV coverage for matches other than the All-Ireland semi-finals and finals. The argument was that it would reduce attendances and affect the scheduling of club games throughout the country. Now, three years into fully fledged live TV every Sunday during the championship season, the opposite is the case.

The GAA has captured a whole new audience as a result of having its games shown live week in week out. Better still, people want to go to see matches live which has meant a significant increase in attendance at virtually all championship games.

But the GAA cannot have its bread buttered on both sides. Once they allow live television coverage of their games they cannot expect the station or the panelists, like myself, to gloss over controversial incidents. The fact that I'm not prepared to 'toe the so called GAA line' is perhaps the reason the GAA made overtures to RTE in the last two years to drop me from their panel.

The other issue which the GAA have yet to address is the refusal of the Ulster and Munster Councils to schedule major games for any time other than Sunday afternoon. As a result we continually have some of the biggest games in the provincial championships being played in direct opposition to each other. Last summer four major games, the Ulster and Connacht footballs finals, the Munster hurling final replay and the Leinster football semi-final were all played on the same Sunday afternoon in July. The only concession to common sense was the starting times of the Ulster and Connacht final were staggered in order to allow both to be shown live on television.

Had Sky Sports the TV rights for Gaelic Games this wouldn't happen. Neither does it happen in the World Cup. The Provincial Councils will have to wise up on this issue and stop behaving like independent republics. There is a wider picture and the sooner the GAA starts scheduling matches for Saturday afternoon/evening the better. In the longer term, the GAA ought to look at the possibility of installing floodlighting in at least one venue in each province and open the way for night matches, which I believe would attract a new audience for Gaelic Games

The GAA hierarchy is at its hypocritical worst when it comes to dealing with the thorny issue of not allowing soccer to be played in Croke Park. While banning soccer, the GAA have allowed American football, professional boxing and rock concerts to be staged in the stadium. There is no logical argument against allowing the Republic of Ireland soccer team to play matches at Croke Park. With Dublin no longer playing National League matches there, Croke Park is virtually idle between September and May apart from the All-Ireland Clubs finals and the Primary Schools finals. The latter finals could be readily accommodated elsewhere. Why should Dublin be allowed stage their schools finals at Croke Park when no other county is allowed this privilege?

Allowing soccer to be played at Croke Park won't result in hundreds of GAA players suddenly deserting Gaelic Games and taking up soccer and it won't do undue damage to the surface - certainly not as much as the concerts do each year. The GAA should follow the example of the IRFU and take advantage of the abject failure of the FAI to provide its own stadium. Renting to the soccer authorities for major internationals would generate extra revenue for the GAA which could be reinvested into the association.

If Croke Park was made available to the FAI for soccer internationals it does not follow that every club in the country would be forced to share their ground with the local soccer team. This hasn't been the experience in rugby and the GAA could make it clear that any deal they enter into with the FAI relates only to Croke Park.

Knowing the GAA, the 'soccer barrier' will be the last bastion to be breached. It will be over the dead bodies of many of the association's leading officials that soccer will be played at Croke Park. I do foresee international rugby being played there within the next five years. The Irish Rugby Football Union is a 32-county organisation which makes it more acceptable in the eyes of the GAA than the 26-county FAI. Rugby is not perceived within the GAA to pose any threat to the Association. This could change if

GAA players decided to switch codes in order to avail of rugby's move into professionalism.

One of the problems which has consistently plagued the GAA is that too many officers at County Board level remain in their positions for far too long. They establish a sufficiently strong power base to ensure that nobody challenges them; while over the years they become stale, conservative and dictatorial.

Change signals regeneration and the easiest way to get around this problem is to introduce a mandatory five year rule. In other words no officer can serve longer than five years in a given position. In the last ten years there has been a significant growth in the number of full-time GAA officials. Obviously it's more difficult to make them accountable but it must be done nonetheless. There should be no such thing as a job for life - be it full-time or honorary - within the GAA.

My biggest concern about the GAA centres on the direction which Gaelic football has taken in the nineties. Inter-county football training is now virtually an all-year round activity. There is no closed season any more. Teams train at all hours of the day and night, five or six times a week. Unfortunately virtually all of this training is geared towards improving players' fitness levels. But skills levels have suffered as a result and the overall standard of football has dropped in the last ten years.

It could be argued there are more contenders for the big honours in football now, unlike in my era when ourselves, Dublin and to a much lesser extent Offaly dominated. The reason for this is that standards have levelled off while the majority of counties are now preparing in a more professional way for the championship than they did twenty years ago.

Perhaps I'm old fashioned but I believe at inter-county training sessions virtually all the emphasis should be on ball work, skills practice and tactics, not about getting guys as fit as Olympic steeplechasers.The training methods now being used are producing players who are are superbly fit and exceptionally strong.

In match situations, this means that space is at a

premium. There is more physical contact between players, more tackles and more fouling resulting in play breaking down more often. Needless to say, I would like to see team managers devoting less time to fitness training and more on developing individual and team skills.

Team managers ought to concentrate less on devising negative tactics. There is far too much emphasis in the modern game on watching the opposition and dreaming up ways of trying to stop them playing. With both teams trying to outwit each other in a negative fashion, we see a situation where the two teams crowd out midfield and then bring the majority of their players back into their own half when they are defending. The use of these kind of tactics produces very poor quality matches.

Maybe I'm a hopeless romantic but I would like to see a return to the days when teams concentrated on their own strengths and stopped worrying so much about the opposition like Galway did this year.

The GAA deserve to be congratulated on finally getting some of their referees to clamp down on niggling personal fouling during this summer's football championship. This approach worked reasonably well, but the cynical hard man is still alive and well in Gaelic football.

Having tackled the problem of the persistent fouler, the GAA now needs to reform its outdated suspension system and replace it with one where match bans replace length of time bans. There is simply no justification for the current ludicrous system where a player can receive a three-month ban and miss no match because he was suspended near the end of the year.

At the moment a player can get booked in every single game he plays in, yet never miss a match through suspension. As in soccer, GAA players should be 'awarded' disciplinary points every time they are booked and when they reach a certain total they should be automatically banned for the next match. With such a myriad of competitions within the GAA it would be more straightforward if a player who is sent off in a particular competition serves his ban in the same competition.

The GAA badly needs to streamline its disciplinary

bodies. At the moment there are five different disciplinary groups, the four Provincial Councils and the Games Administration Committee. As a result it is virtually impossible to achieve any consistency in suspension policy and other key areas. The creation of a single disciplinary body is a priority.

There is hypocrisy at all levels of the Association with regard to professionalism. At one level you have GAA officials criticising the practice of paying coaches. Yet it is their own colleagues within the organisation who are authorising illegal payments to coaches. Everybody knows what's going on but they just turn a blind eye to it. In fairness, the GAA has made a few efforts to find out exactly what's going on but, with none of its own members prepared to tell the truth, these investigations have got no where. There appears to be an unwritten policy of 'sham amateurism' being pursued within the association. It must be either stamped out, which is virtually impossible, or legalised in some way.

Dozens of team managers, both at county and club levels, are being paid at the moment. The money may be disguised in the form of expenses but in reality its a salary. In other cases, players are paid - or are receiving benefit in kind - in order to change clubs.

In its drift away from the amateur status, the GAA is at the stage rugby was ten years ago. Back then everybody in rugby knew what was going on. But at official level they just hid their heads in the sand until eventually the whole thing exploded in their faces. The GAA must be wary that it doesn't take the same disastrous path chosen by rugby and opt for fully fledged professionalism. This policy has left the bulk of rugby clubs on these islands on the verge of bankruptcy. Of course it's easy to make pious statements about this issue from the sideline. I would be the first to admit that if I was offered £50,000 to manage a team I would find it hard to turn down the offer and I certainly wouldn't tell the Croke Park authorities about it.

Over the years I had overtures from several counties wondering whether I would be interested in managing their county teams. The contact usually came from a third party.

Among the counties interested in acquiring my services as a manager were Mayo, Sligo, Kildare, Tipperary, Waterford and Kerry. I never got round to talking about money because I wasn't interested in any of the jobs.

The main reason I turned them down was that I was still playing at the time and I wanted to concentrate on that. The other reality is that it wouldn't be practical for me to manage any inter-county team other than Kerry or Cork. I'm a teacher, I run a bar which is open seven days a week and I have a young family. I simply wouldn't have the time to coach an inter-county team which is virtually a full-time, all the year round job. And I certainly wouldn't be interested in driving a couple of hundred miles every second evening to do the job.

Anyway I don't enjoy managing teams. Even with an under-age I side have a headache for several hours after a match because I coach on the sideline like I played. I'm totally involved, I kick every ball and, although I have thankfully dropped my habit of criticising my own players I find the whole job mentally exhausting.

What I enjoy best is doing a bit of coaching with clubs and leaving it at that. I did some coaching with O'Donovan Rossa from Skibbereen and helped them prepare tactics for their big matches when they won the All-Ireland club championship in 1993.

Perhaps sometime in the future I might like to manage Kerry, although it is one of the most difficult managerial jobs in inter-county football for a variety of reasons. The pressure is enormous. Unless you deliver an All-Ireland title you are deemed a failure. A Kerry manager could lead his side to five National League titles in a row but they wouldn't matter one iota if he failed to deliver Sam.

There is huge commitment involved. It's a twelve month of the year job. Apart from his direct duties with the team, a Kerry manager is expected to attend club matches on a regular basis to check the form of players. Finally, there is no money involved. The Kerry manager receives his expenses and that's it on the financial side. There are no under the table payments.

One of the less publicised facts about 'outside' football

coaches is that they have a poor track record. Until 1998, Eugene McGee was the only 'outside' manager to have guided a team to an All-Ireland title. His tenure with Offaly in the late seventies-early eighties was before the big money started to be spent on recruiting managers from outside the county. So the moral of the tale is that money doesn't always buy success.

The GAA's most important asset, their players, are the most neglected. Playing football at the highest level nowadays requires extraordinary dedication. There is certainly no time for any other part-time activities. Indeed, there is little time to do a full-time job. I can't envisage players continuing to give this kind of commitment over an indefinite period when the only reward at the end of the year is an All-Ireland medal.

We have arrived at a point where players should receive some form of financial reward, be it direct wages or compensation for money lost because of their involvement in the game.

I cannot see Gaelic Games becoming a full-time professional game. The history of professional sport in this country does not make happy reading and the GAA will do everything in its power not to follow that route. It must be frustrating for players to see certain managers getting £25-£30,000 a year while they get 15p a mile travelling expenses. We simply don't have a sufficient population base to finance 32 professional football GAA teams and maybe sixteen professional hurling teams.

Having said that I find it fascinating that a National League soccer club like St Patrick's Athletic can sustain at least half a dozen full time professional players on their books while their average gate every fortnight is around 5,000. At the very least GAA players should be allowed to train full-time in the run-up to big matches, such as provincial and All-Ireland finals, and be compensated for loss of wages. The way things are shaping up, young married men will soon not be able to afford to play inter-county football any longer. A man with a young family and a big mortgage to repay has a stark choice to make - he can either support his family or play inter-county football.

It is virtually impossible to do the two things properly.

There is simply not enough hours in the day to devote quality time to family, job and football career. As a result the majority of current inter-county players are either single or have no families. Fellows working in farming or the building industry are being forced out of inter-county Gaelic football because (a) they don't have the time to devote to the training and (b) having done a hard day's work they are physically unable to do the kind of training now required.

The era of the dual player at inter- county level is past and the the day is fast approaching when the top footballers and hurlers will no longer be able to serve two masters - their county and club - at least at the same time. I can foresee a time when each county will select a squad of players in the spring who will devote themselves exclusively to inter-county football as long as the season lasts. They will only return to play for their clubs when the inter- county season is over.

I doubt if we will see another team to dominate football as Kerry did between 1975 and 1986. Every GAA player would give his right arm to win one All-Ireland medal. Once they win their All-Ireland the players will begin to wonder whether it's worth going through all that torture again. For all their efforts they end up with a medal, numerous parties and a holiday they had to fund raise for themselves. Inevitably they will pose the question: Is it worth it?

Fans and officials still believe the pursuit of All-Ireland glory is a great and noble calling. I believe players have a different attitude and while they may be prepared to go through hell to win one, two or even three All-Ireland medals, I cannot see any team winning four All-Ireland titles in a row in the future.

The GAA badly needs an international outlet. I believe more could be done by the association to spread their wings, not just to places like New York and Boston where there is a strong Irish emigrant population but further afield. Gaelic football, in particular, is an easy game to learn and an excellent one to play or watch: I believe the

GAA should look to new markets in which to sell their product. I always supported the Compromise Rules series. It's an excellent idea but the fact that Australia is so far away creates obvious logistical difficulties and I'm not sure it has a big future.

21

ALL TIME TEAMS

I lost sleep agonising over this chapter. From talking to GAA people who published their biographies over the last few years I know the one sure way to lose friends is to leave them out of your best team. Like politics and religion there is no chance of achieving unanimity. In selecting my Greatest Team of All Time and the best Kerry team of my era I only considered players who performed in the last 25 years - in other words during my own career.

I used certain criteria when choosing the teams. Firstly, players had to be skilful performers. Secondly, I judged them on their ability as a team player. Had I a choice between a brilliant individualist or a very good team player I opted for the latter, and, finally, I looked for players who were born winners - the sort of guy who would rally the troops when things weren't going well.

GREATEST TEAM OF MY TIME:

GOALKEEPER:

Of the present day keepers, Tyrone's Finbar McConnell is the most impressive. He is a very strong and imposing player. John O'Leary of Dublin would also be a contender. Even though he didn't look spectacular, he came off his line well and acted as a seventh defender. From my own era Martin Furlong was a very good goalkeeper who struck terror in the hearts of opposing forwards when he came off his line and met them full force on. But the best goalkeeper I came across as a shot stopper, motivator and for his all-round ability was Cork's **Billy Morgan.**

RIGHT CORNER-BACK:

I am very impressed by two of the present day corner-backs, Mayo's Kenneth Mortimer and Cathal Daly from Offaly. The latter has consistently impressed me since he came to prominence two seasons ago. He is a sticky kind of marker who doesn't resort to fouling. Mortimer is probably the best marker in the game right now, although he got a rude awakening in this year's championship against Galway.

Dublin's Gay O'Driscoll, who marked me on a few occasions, was a good reader of the game but he was a bit slow. The best number 2 I have seen in the last quarter of a century was Meath's **Robbie O'Malley**. An astute reader of the game, he didn't foul but forwards got nothing off him.

FULL- BACK :

The best full-back around at present is Meath's Darren Fay. His absence from last year's Leinster final may have cost the team the title. From the older generation, Dublin's Sean Doherty was strong and reliable, although he lacked speed. Cork's Kevin Kehilly was an excellent player. He was tough , tenacious and a real hard man in the best sense of the term.

My vote, however, goes to Meath's **Mick Lyons**. I became friendly with Lyons during the 1986 Irish Compromise Rules tour to Australia. Two weeks afterwards he marked me in a challenge game between Meath and Kerry and he creased me as we went for the same ball. It was typical of the man. He wasn't a dirty player by any means, but if he got a chance he would let you know who was boss. A really inspirational figure, he was the kind of player you would love to have on your side.

LEFT CORNER- BACK:

I struggled to come up with credible candidates for this position. Of the older generation Dublin's Robbie Kelleher was an excellent reader of the game, a good defender and, of course, he will be fondly remembered in Kerry for handing the ball to Mike Sheehy just prior to the famous goal in the 1978 All-Ireland final. Derry's Tony Scullion is the best of the recent vintage. But the guy I have nominated for the position is Cork's **Niall Cahalane**, who played there in the 1990 All-Ireland final although his natural berth was right half back.

The pair of us had many battles over the years and Cork people would suggest he had the Indian sign over me having held me scoreless in three Munster finals. Cahalane was a dour, tough campaigner with a fondness for holding on to your jersey. I became friendly with him off the field. When we meet I always ask him to return the county jerseys he pulled off me! As a leader and motivator he was peerless.

RIGHT HALF-BACK:

Going back to my early playing days Cork's Kevin Ger O'Sullivan, who marked me a few times, was an excellent player. Brian Canavan from Armagh was a very stylish player who concentrated on playing football. Two current right half-backs stand out, Cork's Ciaran O'Sullivan and Paul Curran, Dublin's best player in the nineties.

My vote goes to another Dublin player, **Tommy Drumm**, who was easily the most difficult direct opponent I ever encountered. Standing at over six foot - which is tall for a wing back - he was an excellent reader of the game. He never resorted to negative tactics and was the real footballers' footballer.

CENTRE-BACK:

Of the present crop Mayo's James Nallen has impressed me, although at times his defensive capabilities have been found wanting. Kildare's Glen Ryan is a great leader and motivator and Henry Downey is in the same mould.

From an earlier generation Armagh's Paddy Moriarty was a whole hearted player and a great leader. But the best centre back I saw was Dublin's **Kevin Moran,** although he had a relatively short GAA career.

I'm always slagging him that the only highlight of his career featured on television is when he kicked a wide after his famous run at the start of the 1976 All-Ireland final. Certainly it's the most publicised wide in the history of Gaelic football. Having said all that, he was a fabulous player and leader.

LEFT HALF-BACK:

Sean Og de Paor from Galway is the best left half-back in the game at the moment. A great leader he is always threatening on his forward runs. Offaly's Pat Fitzgerald, who played on both flanks was a lovely footballing wing-back. DJ Kane, who I came across a few times, was a very tenacious back but for me the best number seven over the last 25 years was Meath's **Martin O'Connell.** A good reader of the game, he was an inspirational player and, when the chips were down, he was never found wanting.

MIDFIELD:

I could pick at least three different combinations all equally credible because of the high standard of centre field play since the early seventies.

Frank McGuigan of Tyrone, whom I played with on numerous occasions in New York, was a stylish footballer. I had many tussles with current Leitrim manager and ex-Fermanagh player Peter McGinnity when he was a student at St Joseph's Training College in Belfast. He was a really outstanding fielder who was well able to score. He would be a certain starter on any team of players who never won an All-Ireland medal. Dermot Earley would also be a strong contender for such a team. I rate the Roscommon man as one of the best midfielders of our generation.

Meath's John McDermott is the pick of the current crop. Brian McGilligan was one of the strongest players I ever came across on a GAA field. He gave great service to Derry. Meath's Gerry McEntee also came into the reckoning.

In the end I opted for one present day player **Anthony Tohill** and one former star, **Brian Mullins**. Tohill is a fabulous all round athlete who is blessed with tremendous physique and work rate. He's a magnificent fielder and an excellent free taker.

But the first man I would pick on any team would be Mullins, whom I played against on many occasions but also alongside at Thomond College. He wasn't the most skilful midfielder that ever graced the game and one could count the number of scores he got on one hand. However, he was an excellent fielder and, more importantly, a great competitor who possessed a never-say-die-spirit. He hated losing - particularly to Kerry. When the chips were down Mullins was always the guy to turn to for inspiration.

RIGHT HALF-FORWARD:

I only considered one player - **Matt Connor**. He was a class above anybody who wore the number 10 shirt in the last quarter of a century. Sadly he is now confined to a wheelchair after a car accident in the mid-eighties. As a footballer, he had everything. Unlike the majority of scoring forwards he could win a ball. He had lovely balance, was an accurate free taker with both feet and an excellent goal poacher. Indeed, he was one of the finest footballers I ever came across and a real gentleman as well.

CENTRE-FORWARD

Dublin's Tony Hanahoe would be a contender, although his expertise was his work off the ball and his ability to take the centre back out of position. Greg Blaney of Down was a excellent conductor of the forward division who could spray accurate passes to his inside forwards - but his own scoring rate was below average. Donegal's Martin McHugh was an elusive type of player whose jinking runs caused panic in opposing defences and he was also an excellent free taker.

My choice is **Larry Tompkins**. He was probably Ireland's first professional Gaelic player. Tompkins devoted a huge portion of his time to football and became a 'manufactured' player. He practised and trained so hard his stamina and fitness levels were unbelievable. This was underlined when he attended the FA treatment centre at Lilleshall. He was fitter than any of the English professional soccer players who were being treated there at the time. For his work rate, scoring rate and commitment he is a must for the number eleven shirt.

LEFT HALF-FORWARD:

David Hickey of Dublin was one of the strongest forwards in the game but his scoring ability didn't match his work rate. Laois' Tom Prendergast was very stylish and skilful, as was Mickey Martin from Leitrim who unfortunately had gone off the scene when they made the breakthrough in 1994. Derry's Dermot McNicholl was a powerfully built wing-forward who was an excellent ball carrier but didn't score much.

The best young footballer around at the moment is Meath's **Trevor Giles**, who gets the nod for this position. It's hard to believe he's only 22. He has added a hardness and toughness to his play in the last eighteen months.

His work rate is exemplary and, while his free taking might be inconsistent, it's his vision, distribution and coolness under pressure which marks him out as special. Indeed, any young player ought to observe Giles when he gets possession. His head is up, he slows the game to his own pace and he is always looking to unhinge the opposing defence with a long kicked pass. I reckon if any player is going to challenge my record of nine All Stars it will be Giles. I envisage him being at the top for many years to come provided he makes a full recovery from his recent serious knee injury.

RIGHT CORNER-FORWARD:

I did a bit of juggling in the full-forward line. There was an abundance of credible candidates but I selected what I considered the best full forward line. Down's Mickey Linden is still producing the goods at the highest level and remains one of the game's top forwards. Jimmy Barry Murphy had tremendous vision and pace and was a very intelligent player. Two to watch for in the future are Raymond Gallagher from Fermanagh and Tipperary's Declan Browne, one of the outstanding forwards in the 1998 championship. My vote, however, goes to Derry's **Joe Brolly**, scorer of the winning goal in the 1998 Ulster final. Despite his unorthodox kicking style, he is lethal when he gets the ball on his left foot and is an excellent goal poacher. A fantastic character on and off the pitch, he is the kind of guy who should feature in any campaign to market Gaelic football.

FULL-FORWARD:

At least half a dozen worthy contenders. Going back to my own playing days Cork's Dinny Allen was an intelligent and pacy footballer. Jimmy Keaveney would have struggled to pass the bleep test but he was deceptively quick over five yards and woefully difficult to dispossess. Better still, he knew where the posts were.

Two Ulster players who I admire are Donegal's Tony Boyle and Seamus Downey from Derry. The latter may not look spectacular but he converts more of the chances that come his way than virtually any other forward in the game. Boyle is not an all action type full-forward either. Indeed, he looks slow but he has great vision and has the ability to create space for himself.

Sean Boylan has managed to convert Brendan Reilly from being an average wing back into one of the best full forwards in the game. Few players have managed to make the move so successfully. Reilly is very strong on the ball, he is well able to kick points with both feet and is cool under pressure. After kicking the winning point in the All-Ireland final replay two years ago he didn't even break into a smile.I picked another Meath man on my 'dream' team **Colm O'Rourke**, who began his inter- county career at full forward. He blossomed in his latter years having added a touch of steel to his game post 1986. He was a great target man and lethal on his left foot.

LEFT CORNER-FORWARD:

Meath's Bernard Flynn could score with both feet. He had great balance and could create space for himself, but unfortunately injury brought a premature end to his career. Tony McManus from Roscommon was a beautiful footballer whose skill level deserved an All-Ireland medal. Wicklow's Kevin O'Brien would fall into the same category. Even though he has fallen on barren times in the last couple of years, **Peter Canavan** of Tyrone gets the number fifteen shirt. In 1995 he almost single-handedly brought Tyrone an All-Ireland title. Although he lacks height, he never backs away from a challenge and can score with both feet.

MANAGER:

Meath boss **Sean Boylan** would be my manager for three reasons. (a) His ability to win All-Irelands with teams made up of individuals who, in their own right, were not outstanding players. Whatever method of motivation he uses, he can transform ordinary players into men possessed, once they pull on a Meath jersey (b) The manner in which he can transplant players into different positions. As we mentioned earlier full forward Brendan Reilly is a former wing back. (c) His tactical awareness on the line which he used to telling effect against Mayo in their two All-Ireland finals in 1996.

The Pat Spillane Dream Team is:

Billy Morgan
(Cork)

Robbie O'Malley Mick Lyons Niall Cahalane
(Meath)   (Meath)   (Cork)

Tommy Drumm Kevin Moran Martin O'Connell
(Dublin)   (Dublin)   (Meath)

Brian Mullins Anthony Tohill
(Dublin)   (Derry)

Matt Connor Larry Tompkins Trevor Giles
(Offaly)   (Cork)   (Meath)

Joe Brolly Colm O'Rourke Peter Canavan
(Derry)   (Meath)   (Tyrone)

Manager: Sean Boylan (Meath)

Painful as it was to pick the best team of my era it was a cakewalk compared to selecting the best Kerry team of the last 25 years.

I consider the 1978-'81 Kerry side the best GAA team of all time. I already stated that Maurice Fitzgerald would not have made the four- in- a- row team because his style of football would not have suited us. It does not necessarily follow that Fitzgerald cannot make my 'dream team' because I am now selecting players on their individual excellence rather than their ability to fit into a particular team pattern.

To ensure I'm not accused of family bias I have left out my brothers, Mike and Tommy although I consider both of them to be worthy candidates. But, modest fellow, that I am I picked myself at left half forward - and didn't consider any other candidates!

During the very early days of my career I played alongside Mick O'Connell and Mick O'Dwyer, both of whom were in the twilight of their inter county careers. As I wasn't playing with either of them in their prime I didn't consider them.

GOALKEEPER:

Declan O'Keefe has come on in leaps and bounds in the last twelve months and if I was picking this team in five years' time he might be a contender. At present it's a two-horse race between Paudie O'Mahony and **Charlie Nelligan.** O'Mahony was unfortunate with injury. He wasn't a spectacular goalkeeper but in 1975 he went through the championship campaign without conceding a goal. Charlie gets my vote for his consistency over a long period and the quality of his kick-outs.

RIGHT CORNER- BACK:

Ger O'Keeffe distributed the ball well and played the game of his life in the 1977 All-Ireland semi final, but **Jimmy Deenihan** was the tightest marker I ever came across in Gaelic football and I'm convinced his absence cost us the five-in-a-row.

FULL-BACK:

Barry O'Shea is developing into an excellent full- back, while Sean Walsh filled the role with distinction when he moved back from midfield. However **John O'Keeffe** stands head and shoulders above anyone who wore the number three shirt in Kerry in the past 25 years. He was the most stylish full- back I ever saw playing. It was a master stroke on O'Dwyer's part to move him from midfield to full- back in 1975.

LEFT CORNER-BACK:

My vote goes to **Paudie Lynch**. He was an astute reader of the game and he distributed the ball better than any other Kerry defender.

RIGHT HALF-BACK:

Tommy Doyle is a contender, but the number five shirt

has to go to **Páidí Ó Sé**. He was the heart of the team for so long. A great warrior, his ability of make life miserable for his direct opponent in All-Ireland finals is legendary.

CENTRE-BACK

The current number six, Liam O'Flaherty deserves to be considered. He has been producing top level performances throughout the nineties and was one of the team's best performers during the lean years. My vote however, goes to **Tim Kennelly.** Known as the 'horse', he never wilted under pressure. Immensely strong, he blocked up the centre of our defence and hit tremendously long clearances.

LEFT HALF-BACK:

Ger Power was outstanding as a wing back before making the successful transfer to the forward line. Ger Lynch was an excellent player, even though we never saw the best of him because his career was cut short by injuries. Eamon Breen is a great rallying force in the present team and is very effective going forward. I have selected **Seamus Moynihan**, who is the most consistent player in both club and inter- county football in Kerry over the last five years.

MIDFIELD

Pat McCarthy used his physical strength to telling effect during the 1975 campaign, while Ambrose O'Donovan was an inspirational captain in 1984 who reserved his best performances for big matches against Cork. Even though he won three All-Ireland medals, Timmy Dowd never realised his full potential. Realistically, I couldn't look beyond the **Jack O'Shea-Sean Walsh** partnership - the former for his work rate and the latter for his fielding ability and strength.

RIGHT HALF-FORWARD:

No shortage of contenders. Even though he was coming near the end of his career, Brendan Lynch did an effective job for us in the 1975 campaign. Ger Power, Tommy Doyle and Pa Laide have all done excellent jobs for Kerry in the number ten shirt. But I picked **Maurice Fitzgerald** to fill the position. The biggest tribute I can pay to him is that Kerry would not have won last year's All-Ireland without him.

CENTRE-FORWARD:

Mickey O'Sullivan, a great captain in 1975, was an excellent ball carrier but his career has cut short by injury. **Ogie Moran** became our lucky mascot during the golden era - every time he was picked at centre forward in an All-Ireland final we won. What greater recommendation could you have?

LEFT HALF-FORWARD:

Pat Spillane

RIGHT CORNER-FORWARD:

The full-forward line picks itself. **Mike Sheehy** gets the number thirteen shirt for his skill, vision and free taking.

FULL-FORWARD

Eoin Liston's arrival on the scene in 1978 completed our team. He was the perfect target man. He absorbed plenty of physical punishment and   distributed the ball in an unselfish and effective manner - even if he didn't pass it to me all the time!.

LEFT CORNER-FORWARD:

John Egan had amazing strength on the ball and was well able to score as well.

Of course there could only be one manager -
Mick O'Dwyer.

My Kerry team is:

Charlie Nelligan

Jimmy Deenihan   John O'Keeffe   Paudie Lynch

Páidí Ó Sé   Tim Kennelly   Seamus Moynihan

Jack O'Shea   Sean Walsh

Maurice Fitzgerald   Ogie Moran   Pat Spillane

Mike Sheehy   Eoin Liston   John Egan

22

FOR THE RECORD

PAT SPILLANE'S CHAMPIONSHIP RECORD:
All-Ireland Medals: 8
Munster Championship Medals: 12
All Star Awards: 9

COMPLETE CHAMPIONSHIP RECORD:

1975
Munster SFC:
Clonmel, June 15
Kerry 3-13; Tipperary 0-9

Kerry: P O'Mahony; Páidí Ó Sé, G O'Keeffe, Pat O'Shea; M O'Sullivan,
T Kennelly, G Power; G O'Driscoll, D Moran; B Lynch (0-5), P McCarthy
P Spillane (0-3); J Egan(2-3), R Prenderville (1-0), M Sheehy (0-2).
Subs: J Bunyan for O'Driscoll; J Deenihan for Pat O'Shea.
Tipperary: J O'Donoghue; E O'Gorman, E Webster, N Byrne; S Kearney,
V O'Donnell, M McDermott; J Kehoe, P Fanning; J Treacy, G Stapleton,
C O'Flaherty (0-4); L Myles (0-3), M Keating (0-2), G McGrath. Subs: J Keane
for McGrath. T McGrath for Treacy.

Munster SFC Final:
Killarney, July 13
Kerry 1-14; Cork 0-7

Kerry: P O'Mahony; G O'Keeffe, J O'Keeffe, J Deenihan; P Ó Sé, T Kennelly,
G Power; P Lynch, P McCarthy (0-1); B Lynch (0-4), M Sheehy (0-4);
M O'Sullivan (0-1), J Egan (0-2), J Bunyan, P Spillane (1-1). Subs: D Moran (0-1)
for P Lynch; G O'Driscoll for B Lynch.
Cork: B Morgan; B Murphy, H Kelleher, M O'Doherty; K J O'Sullivan,
K Kehilly, C Hartnett; D Long, D McCarthy; D Allen (0-3), S Coughlan,
A Murphy (0-1); J Barry-Murphy, D Barron (0-1), R Cummins (0-2).
Subs: D Hunt for O'Doherty; J Coleman for O'Sullivan; J Barrett for A Murphy.

All-Ireland SFC Semi-final
Croke Park, August 10
Kerry 3-13; Sligo 0-5

Kerry: P O'Mahony; G O'Keeffe, J O'Keeffe, J Deenihan;
P Ó Sé, T Kennelly, G Power (0-1); P Lynch (0-4), P McCarthy; B Lynch (0-2),
M Sheehy ; M O'Sullivan (0-1), J Egan (2-2), J Bunyan, P Spillane (1-1).
Subs: G O'Driscoll (0-2) for Sheehy; D Moran for O'Driscoll.
Sligo: T Cummins; R Lipsett, J Brennan, A Caffrey; M Brennan, B Murphy,
P Henry; J Stenson, T Colleary; M Laffey, M Hoey (0-3), F Henry; D Kearins, M
Kearins (0-2), J Kearins. Subs: D Connolly for Laffey; B Wilkinson for J Kearins;
T Carroll for Lipsett.

All-Ireland SFC Final
Croke Park, September 28
Kerry 2-12; Dublin 0-11

Kerry: P O'Mahony; G O'Keeffe, J O'Keeffe, J Deenihan; P Ó Sé, T Kennelly,
G Power; P Lynch, P McCarthy; B Lynch (0-3), D Moran (0-2), M O'Sullivan;
J Egan (1-0), M Sheehy (0-4), P Spillane (0-3).
Subs: G O'Driscoll (1-0) for O'Sullivan.
Dublin: P Cullen; G O'Driscoll, S Doherty, R Kelleher; P Reilly, A Larkin,
G Wilson; B Mullins (0-1), B Brogan; A O'Toole, T Hanahoe, D Hickey;
J McCarthy, J Keaveney (0-6), P Gogarty (0-2). Subs: B Doyle (0-1) for Brogan;
P O'Neill for McCarthy, B Pocock (0-1) for Reilly.

1976
Munster SFC:
Dungarvan, June 20
Kerry 3-17; Waterford 0-6

Kerry: P O'Mahony; G O'Keeffe, J O'Keeffe, J Deenihan; P Ó Sé, T Kennelly, G Power; P Lynch, P McCarthy; B Lynch (1-2), D Moran (0-2), M O'Sullivan (0-2), J Egan (0-2), M Sheehy (1-4), P Spillane (1-5). Subs: S Walsh for Moran.
Waterford: T Fleming; N Hayes, R Ahearne, N Cashin; J Moloney, J Glavin (0-1), W Moore; T Moore (0-1), R Dunford; D Conway (0-1), J Hennessy (0-2), E O'Halloran (0-1); S Ahearne, P Clancy, V Kirwan.
Subs: K O'Connor for Moloney;M Power for Hayes; P Keating for O'Connor.

Munster SFC Final:
Pairc Ui Chaoimh, July 11
Kerry 0-10; Cork 0-10

Kerry: P O'Mahony; G O'Keeffe, J O'Keeffe, J Deenihan; P Ó Sé, T Kennelly, G Power; P Lynch, P McCarthy (0-2); B Lynch, D Moran, M O'Sullivan; J Egan, M Sheehy (0-5), P Spillane (0-2).
Subs: S Walsh (0-1) for B Lynch; J Walsh for O'Sullivan.
Cork: B Morgan; S O'Sullivan, B Murphy, D O'Driscoll; J Coleman, T Creedon, K Kehilly; D Long (0-2), D McCarthy; C O'Rourke, S Coughlan (0-1), B Field (0-2); J Barry-Murphy (0-1), D Barron (0-1), D Allen (0-2).
Subs: S Murphy(0-1) for Field; K Collins for McCarthy.

Munster SFC Final (replay):
Pairc Ui Chaoimh, July 25
Kerry 3-20; Cork 2-19
(After Extra Time)

Kerry: P O'Mahony; G O'Keeffe, J O'Keeffe, J Deenihan; P Ó Sé, T Kennelly, G Power; P Lynch, P McCarthy; D Moran, M O'Sullivan (1-2), P Spillane (1-3); B Lynch, M Sheehy (0-11), J Egan (0-1). Sub: S Walsh (1-3) for O'Sullivan.
Cork: B Morgan; S O'Sullivan, B Murphy, D O'Driscoll; J Coleman, T Creedon, K Kehilly; D Long (0-1), D McCarthy (0-1); C O'Rourke (0-4), D Allen (0-1), S Murphy (0-5); J Barry Murphy (1-3), D Barron (0-3), S Coughlan (1-0).
Subs: K Collins for O'Sullivan; B Fields (0-1) for O'Rourke. Extra Time: O'Rourke for Coughlan; C Murphy for Fields; K Murphy for Creedon.

All-Ireland SFC:
Croke Park, August 8
Kerry 5-14; Derry 1-10

Kerry: P O'Mahony; G O'Keeffe, J O'Keeffe, J Deenihan; P Ó Sé, T Kennelly (0-1), G Power; P Lynch, P McCarthy; M O'Sullivan (0-1), D Moran (0-1), P Spillane (0-2); B Lynch (0-3), M Sheehy (3-3), J Egan (0-2). Subs: S Walsh (1-1) for McCarthy; G O'Driscoll (1-0) for B Lynch.
Derry: J Somers; L Murphy, T Quinn, P Stevenson (1-0); G Bradley, A McGurk, M Moran; T McGuinness (0-1), G McElhinney; B Kelly (0-4), M Lynch (0-2), F McCluskey (0-1); A McGuckian, L Diamond (0-1), J O'Leary (0-1).
Subs: B Ward for McGuckian; M McAfee for Murphy; P Chivers for McElhinney.

All-Ireland SFC Final:
Croke Park, September 26
Dublin 3-8; Kerry 0-10

Dublin: P Cullen; G O'Driscoll, S Doherty, R Kelleher; T Drumm, K Moran,
P O'Neill; B Mullins (1-1), B Brogan (0-1); A O'Toole (0-1), T Hanahoe (0-1),
D Hickey (0-1); B Doyle, J Keaveney (1-2), J McCarthy (1-1).
Subs: F Ryder for Hanahoe; P Gogarty for Doyle.
Kerry: P O'Mahony; G O'Keeffe, J O'Keeffe, J Deenihan; P Ó Sé, T Kennelly,
G Power; P Lynch, P McCarthy; D Moran (0-2), M Sheehy (0-3), M O'Sullivan
(0-1); B Lynch, (0-1), J Egan (0-1), P Spillane (0-2). Subs: C Nelligan for
O'Mahony; S Walsh for McCarthy; G O'Driscoll for O'Sullivan.

1977
Munster SFC:
Tralee, July 3
Kerry 3-14; Tipperary 0-9

Kerry: P O'Mahony; J Deenihan, P Lynch, G O'Keeffe; D Moran, T Kennelly,
G Power (0-1); P Ó Sé (0-3), J O'Shea; S Walsh (0-3), J Long, P Spillane (1-0);
B Walsh (2-3), J O'Keeffe (0-1), J Egan (0-3). Sub: T O'Keeffe for Moran.
Tipperary: J O'Shea; A O'Mahony, E Webster, J Kane; M O'Riordan,
V O'Donnell, B O'Neill; A Cahill, G McGrath (0-5); P Morrissey, G Stapleton,
T McGrath (0-1); S Kearney (0-1), H Mulhare (0-1), D Ryan (0-1).
Subs: M McKeogh for Stapleton; D McGrath for Webster.

Munster SFC Final:
Killarney, July 24
Kerry 3-15; Cork 0-9

Kerry: P O'Mahony; J Deenihan, J O'Keeffe, G O'Keeffe; D Moran, T Kennelly,
G Power; P Ó Sé, J O'Shea(0-2); J Egan (1-0), P Lynch(0-1), P Spillane (1-3);
B Walsh (0-5), S Walsh (1-1), M Sheehy (0-3).
Cork: B Morgan; S Looney, T Creedon, B Murphy; D O'Grady, J Coleman,
K Kehilly; D Long (0-2) S Coughlan (0-3); M Mullins, D McCarthy, S Murphy;
D Allen (0-1), J Barry Murphy (0-1), S O'Shea (0-2). Sub: S O'Sullivan for Looney.

All-Ireland SFC:
Croke Park, August 21:
Dublin 3-12; Kerry 1-13

Dublin: P Cullen; G O'Driscoll, S Doherty, R Kelleher; T Drumm, K Moran,
P O'Neill; B Mullins, F Ryder; A O'Toole (0-4), T Hanahoe (0-3), D Hickey
(1-1); B Doyle (0-1), J Keaveney (0-3), J McCarthy (1-0).
Subs: B Brogan (1-0) for Ryder; P Gogarty for McCarthy.
Kerry: P O'Mahony; J Deenihan, J O'Keeffe, G O'Keeffe (0-1); D Moran,
T Kennelly, G Power; P Ó Sé, J O'Shea; J Egan (0-2), P Lynch (0-1), P Spillane;
B Walsh, S Walsh (1-2), M Sheehy (0-7). Subs: T Doyle for B Walsh;
P McCarthy for J O'Shea.

1978
Munster SFC:
Killarney, June 18
Kerry 4-27; Waterford 2-8

Kerry: C Nelligan; J Deenihan, J O'Keeffe, D Moran; P Ó Sé, T Kennelly,
P Lynch; J O'Shea, J Mulvihill (0-2); G Power (0-3), T Doyle (0-3), P Spillane
(2-5); J Egan (0-5), S Walsh, M Sheehy (2-8). Sub: M O'Sullivan for Walsh.
Waterford: T Hunt; S Flavin, M Coffey, N Hayes; D Conway, S Breen, J Walsh;
R Dunford (0-2), F Murphy; T Casey (0-2), B Fleming (2-0), J Hennessy;
T Keating (0-1), M Hackett (0-1), J McGrath (0-1). Sub: P Keating (0-1)
for Walsh.

Munster SFC Final:
Pairc Ui Chaoimh, July 16
Kerry 3-14; Cork 3-7

Kerry: C Nelligan; P Lynch, J O'Keeffe, J Deenihan; P Ó Sé (0-1), T Kennelly,
D Moran; J O'Shea, S Walsh; G Power (1-0), T Doyle (0-2), P Spillane (0-4);
J Egan (0-2), E Liston, M Sheehy (2-5). Sub: P McCarthy for J O'Shea.
Cork: B Morgan; B Murphy, G Desmond, K Murphy; J Coleman; T Creedon
(0-1), B McSweeney; D McCarthy, C Ryan; D Allen (2-2), D Barron, S Murphy;
J Barry Murphy (1-0), R Cummins (0-3), J Barrett. Subs: J Kerrigan for
K Murphy; D Linehan (0-1) for S Murphy; V Coakley for Coleman.

All-Ireland SFC
Croke Park, August 13
Kerry 3-11; Roscommon 0-8

Kerry: C Nelligan; P Lynch, J O'Keeffe, J Deenihan; P Ó Sé, T Kennelly,
D Moran; J O'Shea (0-1), S Walsh; G Power (1-2), T Doyle, P Spillane (1-2);
J Egan (0-1), E Liston (0-1), M Sheehy (0-4). Subs: P McCarthy for Doyle;
M O'Sullivan for McCarthy; P O'Mahony (1-0) for Moran.
Roscommon: G Sheerin; H Keegan, P Lindsay, T Heneghan; E McManus,
T Donnellan, D Murray; D Earley (0-1), J O'Gara (0-1); J O'Connor (0-4),
M Freyne, S Kilbride; L O'Gara, T McManus, M Finneran (0-2). Subs: P Cox
for L O'Gara; M McDermott for Kilbride.

All-Ireland SFC Final
Croke Park, September 24
Kerry 5-11; Dublin 0-9

Kerry: C Nelligan; J Deenihan, J O'Keeffe, M Spillane; P Ó Sé, T Kennelly,
P Lynch; J O'Shea (0-1), S Walsh; G Power (0-1), D Moran, P Spillane (0-1);
M Sheehy (1-4), E Liston (3-2), J Egan (1-2). Sub: P O'Mahony for Deenihan.
Dublin: P Cullen; G O'Driscoll, S Doherty, R Kelleher; T Drumm, K Moran,
P O'Neill; B Mullins, B Brogan (0-1); A O'Toole, T Hanahoe, D Hickey;
B Doyle, J Keaveney (0-8), J McCarthy.

1979
Munster SFC
Milltown- Malbay, July 1
Kerry 9-21; Clare 1-9

Kerry: C Nelligan; J Deenihan, J O'Keeffe, M Spillane; P Ó Sé, T Kennelly,
P Lynch; J O'Shea (0-2), V O'Connor (1-2), G Power (2-2), T Doyle (0-5),
P Spillane (3-3); M Sheehy (1-4), E Liston (2-2), J Egan (0-1).
Clare: A Burke; T Tubridy, P Begley, P Garry; N Roche, S O'Doherty, M Keigh;
P Nealon, N Normoyle (0-1); T Curtin, J McGrath (0-1), M Downes (0-3); S Moloney
(0-4), V Casey (1-0), D O'Shea. Subs: M Flynn for Burke; A Moloney for O'Shea.

Munster SFC Final:
Killarney, July 23
Kerry 2-14; Cork 2-4

Kerry: C Nelligan; J Deenihan, J O'Keeffe, M Spillane; P Ó Sé, T Kennelly,
P Lynch; J O'Shea, V O'Connor; G Power (2-4), T Doyle (0-1), P Spillane (0-5);
M Sheehy (0-3), E Liston, J Egan.
Subs: D Moran for Doyle; S Walsh (0-1) for Moran.
Cork: B Morgan; T Creedon, K Kehilly, B Murphy; J Crowley, C Ryan,
J Coleman; V Coakley, J Courtney (0-1); P Kavanagh, D Barron, D McCarthy;
J Barry-Murphy (1-0), D Allen (1-2), C Kearney (0-1). Subs: S Murphy for
Coakley; S O'Sullivan for Coleman; T OReilly for Kavanagh.

All-Ireland SFC:
Croke Park, August 12
Kerry 5-14; Monaghan 0-7

Kerry: C Nelligan; J Deenihan, J O'Keeffe, M Spillane; P Ó Sé, T Kennelly, P Lynch; J O'Shea, V O'Connor (0-1); G Power (1-0), S Walsh (0-2), P Spillane (0-1); M Sheehy (3-5), E Liston (1-1), J Egan (0-3). Subs: D Moran (0-1) for O Sé; G O'Keeffe for Deenihan; T Doyle for Liston.

Monaghan: P Linden; E Hughes (0-1), S Hughes, F Caulfield; P Kerr, S McCarville, E Tavey; G McCarville, H Clerkin (0-1); A McArdle, D Mulligan, K Treanor; K Finlay (0-4), T Moyna, B Brady (0-1), Subs: G Finnegan for McArdle & PJ Finlay for Moyna.

All-Ireland SFC Final:
Croke Park, September 16
Kerry 3-13; Dublin 1-8

Kerry: C Nelligan; J Deenihan, J O'Keeffe, M Spillane; P Ó Sé, T Kennelly, P Lynch; J O'Shea (0-1), S Walsh; T Doyle, D Moran, P Spillane (0-4); M Sheehy (2-6), E Liston (0-1), J Egan (1-1). Sub: V O'Connor for O'Keeffe.

Dublin: P Cullen; M Kennedy, M Holden, D Foran; T Drumm, F Ryder, P O'Neill; B Mullins, B Brogan ; A O'Toole (0-1), T Hanahoe (0-2), D Hickey (0-2); M Hickey, B Doyle (0-3), J McCarthy. Subs: J Ronayne (1-0) for M Hickey; G O'Driscoll for McCarthy; B Pocock for O'Toole.

1980
Munster SFC Final:
Pairc Ui Chaoimh, July 6
Kerry 3-13; Cork 0-12

Kerry: C Nelligan; T Kennelly (0-1op), J O'Keeffe, M Spillane; P Ó Sé, G O'Keeffe, D Moran; J O'Shea, S Walsh; G Power (1-2), T Doyle (0-1), P Spillane (0-5); M Sheehy (0-3), E Liston (2-1), J Egan (0-1). Sub: V O'Connor for J O'Shea.

Cork: B Morgan; S O'Sullivan, K Kehilly, J Evans; J O'Sullivan, T Creedon (0-2), J Kerrigan; C Ryan (0-1), C Collins; S Murphy, D Allen (0-5), T Dalton (0-1); J Barry-Murphy, J Allen, D Barry. Subs: T O'Reilly (0-2) for S Murphy; M Healy for S O'Sullivan & V Coakley for J O'Sullivan.

All-Ireland SFC:
Croke Park, August 24:
Kerry 4-15; Offaly 4-10

Kerry: C Nelligan; G O'Keeffe, J O'Keeffe, M Spillane; P Ó Sé, T Kennelly, D Moran(0-1); J O'Shea, S Walsh; G Power (0-2), T Doyle (0-2), P Spillane (2-2); M Sheehy (1-3), E Liston (0-1), J Egan (1-4). Sub: J Deenihan for Walsh.

Offaly: M Furlong; M Wright, S Lowry, E Mulligan; S Darby, R Connor, L Currams; T Connor, G Carroll (2-1); A O'Halloran, K Kilmurray, P Fenning; M Connor (2-9), V Henry, J Mooney. Subs: C Conroy for Henry; T Fitzpatrick for O'Halloran.

All-Ireland SFC Final:
Croke Park, September 21
Kerry 1-9; Roscommon 1-6

Kerry: C Nelligan; J Deenihan, J O'Keeffe, P Lynch; P Ó Sé, T Kennelly, G O'Keeffe; J O'Shea(0-1), S Walsh; G Power (0-1), D Moran, P Spillane (0-1); M Sheehy (1-6), T Doyle, J Egan . Sub: G O'Driscoll for Power.

Roscommon: G Sheerin; H Keegan, P Lindsay, G Connellan; G Fitzmaurice, T Donnellan, D Murray; D Earley (0-1), S Hayden (0-1); J O'Connor (1-2), J O'Gara (0-1), A Dooley; M Finneran (0-1), T McManus, E McManus. Subs: M Dolphin for Dooley; M McDermott for Hayden.

1981
Munster SFC:
Listowel, June 28
Kerry 4-17; Clare 0-6

Kerry: C Nelligan, J Deenihan, J O'Keeffe, P Lynch; P Ó Sé (0-1), T Doyle,
M Spillane; J O'Shea (0-1), T Spillane (0-1); G Power, D Moran (0-1), P Spillane
(0-3); M Sheehy (0-6), E Liston (3-3), J Egan (1-1). Subs B O'Sullivan for O'Keeffe.
Clare: A Burke; T Tubridy, D O'Doherty, M Keogh; P Garry, M Murray, N Roche
(0-1); N Normoyle, T Bonfil; P McNamara (0-2), J McGrath (0-1), M O'Reilly;
P Burke, G Fitzpatrick (0-2), T Killeen.
Subs: S Moloney for Killeen; S O'Doherty for Garry.

Munster SFC Final:
Killarney, July 19
Kerry 1-11; Cork 0-3

Kerry: C Nelligan, J Deenihan, J O'Keeffe, P Lynch; P Ó Sé, T Doyle, M Spillane;
J O'Shea (0-1), T Spillane; G Power, D Moran, P Spillane (0-3); M Sheehy (1-5),
E Liston (0-1), J Egan (0-1).
Cork: B Morgan; M Healy, K Kehilly, J Evans; M Moloney, C Ryan, J Kerrigan;
T Creedon (0-1), C Collins; D Barry (0-1), S Hayes, T Dalton; F O'Mahony, D Allen
(0-1), D Barron. Subs: M Creedon for Morgan; J Lynch for Hayes.

All-Ireland SFC:
Croke Park, August 9
Kerry 2-19; Mayo 1-6

Kerry: C Nelligan, J Deenihan, J O'Keeffe, P Lynch; P Ó Sé, S Walsh,
M Spillane; J O'Shea (0-1), T Doyle (0-1); G Power (1-0), D Moran(0-3),
P Spillane (0-3); M Sheehy (0-6), E Liston (1-2), J Egan (0-3).
Sub: T Kennelly for Power.
Mayo: M Webb; M Gavin, A Egan, A Garvey (0-1); H Gavin, T Kearney,
M O'Toole; J Lyons (0-1), W Nally; JP Kean, WJ Padden, M Carney (0-1);
E McHale (1-0), J Burke (0-1), J McGrath (0-2).
Subs G Feeney for Egan; J Maughan for Carney.

All-Ireland SFC Final:
Croke Park, September 20
Kerry 1-12; Offaly 0-8

Kerry: C Nelligan, J Deenihan, J O'Keeffe, P Lynch; P Ó Sé (0-1), T Kennelly,
M Spillane; J O'Shea (1-0), S Walsh (0-1); G Power (0-1), D Moran(0-2),
T Doyle (0-1); M Sheehy (0-5), E Liston, J Egan (0-1).
Subs: P Spillane for Egan (67 mins); G O'Keeffe for M Spillane.
Offaly: M Furlong; M Fitzgerald, L Connor, C Conroy; P Fitzgerald, R Connor,
L Currams; T Connor (0-1), P Dunne; V Henry, G Carroll, A O'Halloran;
M Connor (0-4), S Lowry (0-2), B Lowry (0-1).
Subs: J Mooney for T Connor; J Moran for Henry.

1982
Munster SFC:
Ennis, June 6
Kerry 1-15; Clare 0-7

Kerry: C Nelligan, G O'Keeffe, J O'Keeffe, P Lynch; P Ó Sé, T Kennelly;
G Lynch, T Doyle (0-1), V O'Connor (0-1); G Power (0-2), D Moran (0-1),
P Spillane (0-2); M Sheehy (0-6), E Liston (1-1), J Egan.
Sub: J L McElligott for Power.
Clare: M Flynn; G Curtin, P Garry, M Keogh; N Roche (0-1), M Murray,
T Tubridy; G Fitzpatrick (0-1), N Normoyle; P McNamara (0-2) D O'Loughlin,
T Bonfil (0-1); S Maloney (0-1), M Brew, A Maloney (0-1).
Sub: G Killeen for Brew.

All-Ireland SFC:
Croke Park, August 15
Kerry 3-15; Armagh 1-11

Kerry: C Nelligan; G O'Keeffe, J O'Keeffe, P Lynch; P Ó Sé, T Kennelly,
T Doyle; J O'Shea, S Walsh (0-1); G Power (0-2), T Spillane (0-2), D Moran
(0-2); M Sheehy (1-4), E Liston (1-3), J Egan (1-1).
Sub: M Spillane for Moran; P Spillane for Doyle.
Armagh: B McAlinden; D Stevenson, J McKerr, J Donnelly; N Marley (0-1),
P Moriarty, P Rafferty; F McMahon (0-2), C McKinstry; D Dowling, J Kernan
(1-3), B Canavan; J Corvan (0-3), B Hughes (0-1), S Devlin.
Subs: A Shortt for Dowling; K McNally for Canavan;
B McGeown (0-1) for Devlin.

All-Ireland SFC Final
Croke Park, September 19
Offaly 1-15; Kerry 0-17

Offaly: M Furlong; M Lowry, L Connor, M Fitzgerald; P Fitzgerald (0-1),
S Lowry (0-1) , L Currams (0-1); T Connor , P Dunne; J Guinan, R Connor,
G Carroll; J Mooney (0-2), M Connor (0-7), B Lowry (0-3). Subs: Stephen Darby
for M Lowry; Seamus Darby (1-0) for Guinan.
Kerry: C Nelligan, G O'Keeffe, J O'Keeffe, P Lynch; P Ó Sé (0-2), T Kennelly,
T Doyle; J O'Shea (0-1), S Walsh (0-2); G Power, T Spillane (0-3), D Moran;
M Sheehy (0-3), E Liston (0-2), J Egan (0-3).
Sub: P Spillane (0-1) for Moran (HT) .

1983
(Missed entire championship through injury)

1984
Munster SFC:
Tralee, June 10
Kerry 0-23; Tipperary 0-6

Kerry: C Nelligan; P Ó Sé, J O'Keeffe, M Spillane; T Doyle, T Spillane, G Lynch;
T O'Dowd (0-4), J O'Shea (0-1); J Kennedy (0-6), S Walsh, P Spillane (0-3);
D O'Donoghue (0-1), E Liston (0-4), M Sheehy (0-4).
Tipperary: A Colville; J Lyons, G Kirwan, M Maher; P Morrissey, D Foley,
S O'Neill; R Flanagan, T Carr; B Conway, O Maher, E O'Dwyer; F Kelly (0-3),
J O'Donnell (0-3), K Barron.
Subs: A Healy for O'Dwyer; S Hennessy for Foley; D O'Keeffe for Conway.

Munster SFC Final:
Killarney, July 1
Kerry 3-14; Cork 2-10

Kerry: C Nelligan; P Ó Sé, S Walsh, M Spillane; T Doyle, T Spillane (0-1),
G Lynch; J O'Shea (0-1), A O'Donovan; J Kennedy (0-4), G Power, P Spillane
(2-0); M Sheehy (0-3), E Liston (0-1), W Maher (1-0).
Subs: D Moran (0-2) for Power(0-2); J Egan for Maher
Cork: J Kerins; M Lynch, M Healy, J Evans; N Cahalane, C Ryan, J Kerrigan
(0-1); D Creedon, C Corrigan (0-1); T Nation, M Burns (0-2), D Barry (1-4);
D Allen (0-1), J Allen (0-1), T Murphy.
Subs: K Kehilly for Healy, B Coffey (1-0) for Corrigan; C O'Neill for Burns.

All-Ireland SFC:
Croke Park, August 12
Kerry 2-17; Galway 0-11

Kerry: C Nelligan; P Ó Sé, S Walsh, M Spillane; T Doyle, T Spillane (0-1),
G Lynch; J O'Shea (0-5), A O'Donovan (0-1); J Kennedy (0-1), D Moran,
P Spillane (0-3); M Sheehy (1-4), E Liston, J Egan (1-2).
Sub: V O'Connor for Walsh.
Galway: P Comer; J Kelly, S McHugh, P Moran; P O'Neill, T Tierney(0-3),
M Coleman; R Lee, P Kelly (0-2); B O'Donnell (0-1), G McManus (0-1),
M Brennan (0-1); S Joyce, V Daly (0-2), P Conroy (0-1).
Subs K Clancy for McManus; E Guerin for McHugh, P Connolly for M Brennan.

All-Ireland SFC Final
Croke Park, September 23
Kerry 0-14; Dublin 1-6

Kerry: C Nelligan, P Ó Sé, S Walsh, M Spillane; T Doyle, T Spillane, G Lynch;
J O'Shea (0-1), A O'Donovan; J Kennedy (0-5), D Moran (0-1), P Spillane (0-4);
G Power, E Liston (0-3), J Egan. Sub: T O'Dowd for Egan.
Dublin: J O'Leary; M Holden, G Hargan, M Kennedy; P Canavan, T Drumm,
PJ Buckley; J Ronayne, B Mullins; B Rock (1-5), T Conroy (0-1), C Duff;
J Kearns, A O'Toole, J McNally.
Subs: M O'Callaghan for McNally, K Sutton for Ronayne.

1985
Munster SFC
Listowel, June 23
Kerry 2-18; Limerick 0-9

Kerry: C Nelligan; P Ó Sé, S Walsh, M Spillane; T Doyle(0-1), T Spillane,
G Lynch; J O'Shea (2-0), A O'Donovan; J Kennedy (0-2), D Moran (0-3),
P Spillane (0-4); M Sheehy (0-7), T Dowd (0-1), G Power.
Sub: J Higgins for Walsh.
Limerick: J Scully; D Barron, P Ives, J Reddington; E Leonard, D Fitzgerald,
J Collins; P Barrett, T Quaid; D Kielty, D Fitzgibbon, F Ryan; A Shanahan (0-2),
M Quish (0-5), J Keane. Subs: T Cummins (0-1) for Shanahan; T Browne(0-1)
for Fitzgerald, M O'Shea for Ryan.

Pairc Ui Chaoimh, July 21
Kerry 2-11; Cork 0-11

Kerry: C Nelligan; P Ó Sé, T Spillane, M Spillane;
J Higgins, T Doyle, G Lynch; J O'Shea (0-1), A O'Donovan; J Kennedy (0-1),
O Moran (0-1), P Spillane (0-2); M Sheehy (1-3), E Liston (1-2), G Power.
Subs: T O'Dowd (0-1) for O'Donovan.
Cork: J Kerins, N Cahalane, C Corrigan, J Evans; T Mannix, C Counihan,
J Kerrigan (0-2); B Coffey (0-2), M McCarthy (0-1); P Harrington, T McCarthy
(0-1) T Nation (0-1); T O'Sullivan, C O'Neill (0-1), D Barry (0-2).
Subs: M Beston(0-1) for Harrington; J Boylan for Coffey and C Ryan for Nation.

All-Ireland SFC:
Croke Park, August 11
Kerry 1-12; Monaghan 2-9

Kerry: C. Nelligan; P Ó Sé, T Spillane, M Spillane; J Higgins, T Doyle, G Lynch;
J O'Shea (0-2), A O'Donovan (0-1); J Kennedy, D Moran, P Spillane (0-3); M Sheehy
(0-4), E Liston (0-1), G Power (1-0).
Subs: T Dowd (0-1) for Moran; S Walsh for J Kennedy.
Monaghan: P Linden; E Sherry, G McCarville, F Caulfield; B Murray, C Murray,
D Flanagan; H Clerkin, D Byrne; R McCarron (0-3), E McEneaney (0-5), M O'Dowd
(1-0); E Hughes(0-1), E Murphy (1-0), E O'Hanlon. Subs: P Curran for Byrne;
Byrne for Curran; G Carragher for Byrne.

For the Record

All-Ireland SFC: (Replay)
Croke Park, August 25
Kerry 2-9; Monaghan 0-10

Kerry: C Nelligan, P Ó Sé, S Walsh, M Spillane; T Doyle, T Spillane, G Lynch; J O'Shea (0-1), A O'Donovan; T Dowd, D Moran, P Spillane (0-3); M Sheehy (0-4), E Liston (1-0), G Power (1-1).

Subs: J Higgins for Doyle; D Hanafin for Walsh; J Kennedy for Moran.

Monaghan: P Linden; B Sherry, G McCarville, F Caulfield; B Murray (0-1), C Murray, D Flanagan; H Clerkin; D Byrne (0-1); R McCarron (0-2), K Carragher, M O'Dowd (0-1); E McEneaney (0-5), E Murphy, E Hughes. Subs K Finlay for Carragher; P Curran for Flanagan

All-Ireland SFC Final
Croke Park, September 22:
Kerry 2-12; Dublin 2-8

Kerry: C Nelligan; P Ó Sé, S Walsh, M Spillane; T Doyle(0-1), T Spillane, G Lynch; J O'Shea (1-3), A O'Donovan; T O'Dowd (1-1),O Moran (0-1), P Spillane (0-2); M Sheehy (0-3), E Liston, G Power.

Subs: J Kennedy(0-1) for Power.

Dublin: J O'Leary; M Kennedy, G Hargan, R Hazley; P Canavan, N McCaffrey, D Synnott; J Ronayne (0-2), B Mullins; B Rock (0-3), T Conroy, C Redmond; J Kearns (0-2), J McNally (2-0), K Duff.

Subs: T Carr (0-1) for Redmond; PJ Buckley for Mullins.

1986
Munster SFC:
Clonmel, June 15
Kerry 5-9; Tipperary 0-12

Kerry: C Nelligan; P Ó Sé, S Walsh, J Higgins; S Stack, T Spillane, G Lynch (0-1); J O'Shea (1-1), T Dowd; J Kennedy (0-2), D Moran, P Spillane (1-2); M Sheehy (0-1), E Liston (2-2), G Power (1-0). Subs: D Hanafin for J O'Shea; W Maher for D Moran; D Lynch for J Kennedy.

Tipperary: T Toomey; M Fitzgerald, P McCormack, M O'Connell; D Foley(0-2), G Ryan, A Healy; G McGrath (0-1), M Leahy; J O'Meara (0-1), M Goonan, P McGrath; F Kelly (0-5), L Stokes (0-2), J Owens (0-1). Subs: F Howlin for M Fitzgerald; D Fogarty for J McGrath; P Dooley for L Stokes.

Munster SFC Final:
Killarney, July 7
Kerry 0-12; Cork 0-8

Kerry: C Nelligan; P Ó Sé, S Walsh, M Spillane; T Doyle (0-1), T Spillane, G Lynch; J O'Shea (0-2), A O'Donovan; J Kennedy (0-4), T Dowd (0-1), P Spillane; M Sheehy (0-4), E Liston, G Power. Subs W Maher for Pat Spillane.

Cork: J Kerins; T Nation, C Corrigan, J Evans; N Cahalane, C Counihan, D Walsh; J Kerrigan, M McCarthy; T McCarthy, B Coffey, D Barry (0-4); J O'Driscoll (0-1), C O'Neill (0-3), R Swain. Subs: P Hayes for Corrigan; T O'Sullivan for M McCarthy & T Mulcahy for Coffey.

All-Ireland SFC:
Croke Park August 24
Kerry 2-13; Meath 0-12

Kerry: C Nelligan; P Ó Sé, S Walsh, M Spillane; T Doyle(0-1), T Spillane, G Lynch; J O'Shea (0-1), A O'Donovan; J Kennedy, D Moran (0-1), P Spillane (0-2); M Sheehy (0-4), E Liston (0-3), G Power (1-0). Subs W Maher (1-1) for Kennedy; T O'Dowd for O'Donovan. M Galwey for Liston.

Meath: M McQuillan; J Cassells, M Lyons, P Lyons; C Coyle, L Harnan, T Ferguson (0-1); L Hayes (0-2), G McEntee; F Murtagh (0-1); B Stafford, D Beggy; C O'Rourke (0-2), M O'Connell (0-1), B Flynn (0-5).

Subs PJ Gillic for Beggy.

All-Ireland SFC Final:
Croke Park, September 21:
Kerry 2-15; Tyrone 1-10

Kerry: C Nelligan; P Ó Sé, S Walsh, M Spillane; T Doyle, T Spillane, G Lynch; J O'Shea, A O'Donovan; W Maher, D Moran (0-2), P Spillane (1-4); M Sheehy (1-4), E Liston (0-2), G Power (1-0). Subs T O'Dowd (0-2) for O'Donovan.

Tyrone: A Skelton; J Mallon, C McGarvey, J Lynch; K McCabe (0-1), N McGinn, P Ball; P Donaghy, H McClure; M McClure (0-1), E McKenna, S McNally (0-2); M Mallon (0-4), D O'Hagan (0-1), P Quinn (1-1).

Subs: S Conway for Lynch; S Rice for McKenna; A O'Hagan for M Mallon

1987
Munster SFC:
Dungarvan, June 21
Kerry 3-15; Waterford 2-8

Kerry: C Nelligan; P Ó Sé, S Walsh, M Spillane; G Lynch, T Spillane, T Doyle; A O'Donovan, J O'Shea (2-1); J Kennedy, D Moran (0-4), P Spillane (0-3); G Power (1-1), E Liston (0-5), W Maher (0-1).
Subs T O'Dowd for Kennedy; J Higgins for Lynch.

Waterford: K Heffernan; D Kirwan, P Quinn, P Keating; P Hayes, E Rockett, D Casey (1-0); J McGrath (0-2), L O'Connor (1-0); E O'Brien (0-2), P Whyte (0-1), P Curran (0-1); C McCraith, D Burke, J Maher (0-2).
Subs: L Dalton for McGrath.

Munster SFC Final
Pairc Ui Chaoimh, July 26
Cork 1-10; Kerry 2-7

Cork: J Kerins; A Davis, C Corrigan, D Walsh, N Cahalane, C Counihan, T Nation; S Fahy, T McCarthy; P Hayes, L Tompkins (0-8), J Kerrigan; J O'Driscoll (1-1), C Ryan (0-1), J Cleary. Subs: B Coffey for Hayes

Kerry: C Nelligan; P Ó Sé, S Walsh, M Spillane; T Doyle, T Spillane, G Lynch; J O'Shea (0-2), A O'Donovan; T O'Dowd, D Moran (0-1), P Spillane; M Sheehy (1-4), E Liston (1-0), G Power. Subs D Hanafin for Moran; M McAuliffe for O'Dowd.

Munster SFC Final (Replay)
Killarney, August 2
Cork 0-13; Kerry 1-5

Cork: J Kerins; A Davis (0-2), C Corrigan, D Walsh; N Cahalane, C Counihan, T Nation (0-1); S Fahy (0-2), T McCarthy (0-1); P Hayes, L Tompkins (0-3), J Kerrigan; J O'Driscoll (0-1), C Ryan, J Cleary (0-2).
Subs: T Leahy (0-1) for Hayes; D Culloty for Kerrigan.

Kerry: C Nelligan; P Ó Sé, S Walsh, M Spillane; T Doyle (0-1), T Spillane, G Lynch; D Hanafin (1-0), A O'Donovan; J Kennedy, J O'Shea (0-2), P Spillane; M Sheehy (0-1), E Liston, G Power. Subs T O'Dowd for Kennedy. M McAuliffe for O'Dowd, V O'Connor (0-1) for O'Donovan.

1988
Munster SFC:
Tralee, May 29
Kerry 3-19; Waterford 1-7

Kerry: C Nelligan; P Ó Sé, T Spillane, M Spillane; T Doyle, A O'Donovan, G Lynch; J O'Shea, M Fitzgerald(0-6); D McEvoy (1-1), W Maher (1-1), M McAuliffe (0-4); G Power (0-1), P Spillane (1-6), G Murphy.

Waterford: K Heffernan; D Kirwan, D Casey, F O'Brien; L Dalton, E Phelan (0-1), E Rockett; P Whyte, L O'Connor (0-1); P Curran, J Maher (1-2), E O'Brien (0-1); N Weldon, J McGrath, D Wyse (0-1)
Subs: R Guiry for D Casey; L Daniels(0-1) for Guiry.

Munster SFC Final
Pairc Ui Chaoimh, July 3
Cork 1-14; Kerry 0-16

Kerry: C Nelligan; M Spillane, T Spillane, M Nix; T Doyle (0-1), A O'Donovan, G Lynch; J O'Shea (0-1), D Hanafin; M McAuliffe(0-1), C Murphy (0-1), M Fitzgerald (0-10); W Maher(0-1), P Spillane (0-1), G Murphy. Subs: G Power for Maher; E Liston for C Murphy; J Shannon for McAuliffe.

Cork: J Kerins; A Davis, N Cahalane, D Walsh; S O'Brien, C Counihan, T Nation; T McCarthy, S Fahy (0-1); P McGrath (0-1), L Tompkins (0-5), J O'Driscoll (0-1); D Allen (1-1), D Barry (0-2), M McCarthy (0-2).
Subs C O'Neill (0-1) for Barry; B Coffey for O'Driscoll.

1989
Munster SFC:
Askeaton, May 14
Kerry 6-7; Limerick 1-10

Kerry: C Nelligan; K Savage, L Hartnett, M Nix; T Spillane (1-0), A O'Donovan, C Murphy; J O'Shea, M Galwey; J Kennedy, M Fitzgerald (1-2), T Fleming (1-2); M McAuliffe (1-0), E Liston (1-1), P Spillane (0-2). Subs: T Doyle for Hartnett; W Maher (1-0) for Kennedy, P Dennehy for McAuliffe.

Limerick: M McLoughlin; E Leonard, P Ives, J Reddington; W Roche, T Browne, L Barrett; N Leonard, P Potter; T Kelly, P Barrett, E Sheehan (0-4); T Cummins (1-1), D Fitzgibbon (0-1), F Ryan.
Subs: S Gleeson (0-3) for Cummins, G Hamilton (0-1) for Potter, T Quaid for Kelly.

Munster SFC Final:
Killarney, July 23
Cork 1-12; Kerry 1-9

Cork: J Kerins; S O'Brien, D Walsh, J Kerrigan; T Davis, C Counihan, B Coffey; S Fahy, L Tompkins (0-7); T McCarthy, D Barry, J O'Driscoll (1-1); P McGrath (0-2), D Allen (0-1), J Cleary (0-1). Sub: M Slocum for Walsh.

Kerry: C Nelligan; K Savage, A O'Donovan (1-0), M Spillane; C Murphy, T Doyle, M Nix; J O'Shea, T Spillane; T Fleming, M Fitzgerald (0-6), J Shannon; W Maher, E Liston (0-1), P Spillane (0-2).
Subs: A Gleeson for M Spillane; M McAuliffe for Shannon; P Dennehy for Maher.

1990
Munster SFC
Listowel, May 27
Kerry 1-23; Clare 0-13

Kerry: C Nelligan; D McCarthy (0-1), K Culhane, C Murphy; P Slattery, A O'Donovan, T Spillane; M Fitzgerald (0-9), J Shannon (0-2); P Laide (0-2), P McKenna (0-2), J O'Shea (0-1); S McEligott (0-4), P Spillane, S Geaney (1-2). Sub: N O'Mahony for Fitzgerald.

Clare: J Hanrahan; M Rouine, A Moloney, JJ Rouine; M Roughan, F Griffin, N Roche; F McInerney (0-2), M Comyns, A O'Keefe (0-3), K Kelleher; F Carrig, T O'Neill (0-3), M Flynn (0-4).
Subs: M Guerin for Comyns; J Enright for Roughan; G O'Keefe (0-1) for Carrig.

Munster SFC Final
Pairc Ui Chaoimh, July 1
Cork 2-23; Kerry 1-11

Cork: J Kerins; D Walsh, N Cahalane, S O'Brien; M Slocum (0-1), C Counihan, T Nation; L Tompkins (0-5), D Culloty (1-0); P Hayes (0-1), D Barry (0-3), P McGrath; C O'Neill (0-11), S Fahy (0-2), M McCarthy (1-0).
Sub: M O'Connor for Counihan.
Kerry: C Nelligan; S Stack, M Nix, C Murphy; P Slattery, A O'Donovan, T Spillane (0-1); M Fitzgerald (1-5), J Shannon; P Laide (0-1), E Breen, J O'Shea (0-1); S McEliggott (0-1), E Liston, S Geaney. Subs: P Spillane (0-2) for Shannon, D Farrell for Liston; S Burke for Slattery.

1991
Munster SFC
Ennis, May 26:
Kerry 5-16; Clare 2-12

Kerry: C Nelligan; J O'Connell, K Culhane, N Savage; L Flaherty, C Murphy (1-0), S Burke; N O'Mahony, T Fleming (0-1); J O'Shea (0-4), W Maher (0-3), M Fitzgerald (0-7); P Dennehy (1-0), D Farrell (2-1), P Spillane. Subs: E Breen for O'Connell; M Moriarty (1-0) for O'Mahony; M Nix for Savage.

Clare: J Hanrahan; S Clancy, A Moloney, M Rouine; C O'Neill, F Griffin, M Roughan; F McInerney (0-3), P Blake; P Vaughan (0-1), N Roche, G Killeen (1-1); M Burke, M Flynn (0-4), D Keane (1-1).
Subs: P Hickey (0-2) for Rouine; C Clancy for Burke; O Downes for Blake.

Killarney, June 16
Kerry 1-10; Cork 0-11

Kerry: C Nelligan; L Flaherty, K Culhane, S Stack; S Burke, C Murphy, M Nix; A O'Donovan (0-1), N O'Mahony; J Cronin (1-1); P Spillane, J O'Shea (0-1); P Dennehy (0-1); M Fitzgerald (0-5), T Fleming (0-1) .
Subs: M Moriarty for Cronin; D Farrell for Fleming.
Cork: J Kerins; T Nation, N Cahalane, A Davis; M Slocum (0-1), C Counihan, B Coffey; S Fahy (0-1), D Culloty (0-2); D Barry (0-1), L Tompkins (0-2), J O'Driscoll (0-2); P McGrath (0-1), C O'Neill, M McCarthy (0-1).
Subs: P Hayes for O'Neill; T McCarthy for M McCarthy.

Munster SFC Final
Killarney, July 21
Kerry 0-23; Limerick 3-12

Kerry: C Nelligan; J B O'Brien, K Culhane, S Stack; S Burke, C Murphy, M Nix; N O'Mahony, A O'Donovan (0-1); J Cronin (0-2), P Spillane (0-2), M Fitzgerald (0-12); P Dennehy (0-2), J O'Shea (0-4), T Fleming.
Subs: S Geaney for Fleming; W Maher for Nix; D Farrell for O'Mahony.
Limerick: R Bowles; E Leonard, P Ives, J Reddington; P Barrett, T Browne (0-1), L Barrett; J Quane (0-1), D Fitzgibbon; S Kelly (2-1), P Danaher, PJ Garvey (0-1); T Cummins, D Fitzgerald (0-4), J O'Donovan (1-2). Subs: F Ryan (0-2) for Garvey; L Long for Danaher; N Leonard for Quane.

All-Ireland SFC
Croke Park, August 12
Down 2-9; Kerry 0-8

Down: N Collins; B McKernan, C Deegan, P Higgins; J Kelly, DJ Kane, P O'Rourke; B Breen, E Burns; R Carr (0-4), G Blaney, G Mason (0-2); M Linden (0-2), P Withnell (2-1), J McCartan.
Subs: L Austin for Burns; A Rodgers for Withnell.
Kerry: C Nelligan; S Stack, T Spillane, K Culhane; S Burke, C Murphy, M Nix; N O'Mahony, A O'Donovan (0-1); J Cronin, P Spillane (0-2), J O'Shea; P Dennehy, M Fitzgerald (0-5), T Fleming. Sub: D Lyne for Murphy.

For the Record

Year	Played	Scored
1975	4	2-8
1976	5	2-14
1977	3	2-3
1978	4	3-12
1979	4	3-13
1980	3	2-8
1981	4*	0-9
1982	3**	0-3
1984	4	2-10
1985	5	0-14
1986	4	2-8
1987	3	0-3
1988	2	1-7
1989	2	0-4
1990	2*	0-2
1991	4	0-4
Total:	56	19-122 (179pts)

Average 3.197 points per game.

(* One appearance as substitute. ** two appearances as sub) .

Pat Spillane was only held scoreless in seven of the 56 championship games he played. In three of those he was marked by Cork's Niall Cahalane.

NATIONAL FOOTBALL LEAGUE MEDALS : 4

NFL Final (Replay)
Croke Park, May 26, 1974:
Kerry 0-14; Roscommon 0-8

Kerry: P O'Mahony; D O'Sullivan, P O'Donoghue, D Crowley; P Ó Sé, P Lynch, G O'Keeffe; J O'Keeffe , J Long; E O'Donoghue, M O'Sullivan, G Power; J Egan, S Fitzgerald, M Sheehy.

Roscommon: J McDermott, H Keegan, P Lindsay, G Mannion; T Regan, D Watson, J Kerrane; M Freyne, J O'Gara; J Kelly, D Earley, J Mannion; J Finnegan, T Heneghan, T Donnellan.

Subs: G Beirne for Watson; H Griffin for Mannion.

(Spillane played in drawn game but was dropped for replay)

NFL Final
Croke Park, April 17, 1977
Kerry 1-8; Dublin 1-6

Kerry: C Nelligan, J Deenihan, P Lynch, G O'Keeffe; P Ó Sé, T Kennelly, G Power; J O'Keeffe, J O'Shea; S Walsh, D Moran, M Sheehy; B Walsh, P Spillane, J Egan.

Dublin: P Cullen; G O'Driscoll, S Doherty, R Kelliher; T Drumm, K Moran, P O'Neill; B Brogan, A Larkin; A O'Toole, T Hanahoe, D Hickey; B Doyle, J Keaveney, J McCarthy. Subs: M Hickey for Brogan; F Ryder for Larkin.

NFL Final Replay
Pairc Ui Chaoimh, May 23 1982
Kerry 1-9; Cork 0-5

Kerry: C Nelligan, J Deenihan, J O'Keeffe, G O'Keeffe; P Ó Sé, T Kennelly, G Lynch; J O'Shea, S Walsh; J L McEligott, D Moran, T Doyle; G Power, E Liston, J Egan.

(Pat Spillane came on as a substitute in the drawn game)

Cork: M Creedon; M Healy, K Kehilly, J Evans; M Moloney, T Creedon, J Kerrigan; D Creedon, M Burns; D Barry, D Allen, T O'Reilly; D McCarthy, C Ryan, E Fitzgerald. Sub T Murphy for Fitzgerald.

NFL Final
Gaelic Grounds, Limerick, April 29, 1984
Kerry 1-11; Galway 0-11

Kerry: C Nelligan; P Ó Sé, V O'Connor, M Spillane; T Doyle, J Higgins, G Power; J O'Shea, S Walsh; T O'Dowd, D Moran, P Spillane; D O'Donoghue, T Spillane, M Sheehy. Subs E Liston for O'Dowd; W Maher for O'Donoghue.
\Galway: P Coyne; S McHugh, S Kinneavy, P Lee; P O'Neill, T Tierney, M Coleman; B Talty, R Lee; B O'Donnell, G McManus, S Joyce; V Daly, M Brennan, K Clancy. Subs: H Bleahen for R Lee; L Higgins for McManus.

Railway Cup Medals: 4

Croke Park, March 17, 1976
Munster 2-15; Leinster 2-8

Munster: P O'Mahony (Kerry); E Webster (Tipperary), B Murphy (Cork), J Deenihan; P Ó Sé (Kerry); K Kehilly (Cork), G Power (Kerry); D Long (Cork), D Moran (Kerry); D Allen (Cork), M Sheehy, M O'Sullivan; J Egan (Kerry), J Barry-Murphy (Cork), P Spillane (Kerry). Sub: G O'Keeffe for Webster.

Croke Park, March 17, 1977
Munster 1-14; Connacht 1-9

Munster: B Morgan; K Kehilly (Cork), J O'Keeffe (Kerry), B Murphy (Cork); D Moran, T Kennelly, G Power (Kerry); D Long, D McCarthy; S O'Shea (Cork), M Sheehy, P Spillane (Kerry); J Barry-Murphy (Cork), S Walsh, J Egan (Kerry). Subs: J O'Shea (Kerry) for McCarthy; D Allen (Cork) for O'Shea.

Croke Park, April 6, 1978 (Replay)
Munster 4-12; Ulster 0-19 (after extra time)

Munster: B Morgan; B Murphy (Cork), J O'Keeffe, J Deenihan; P Ó Sé, T Kennelly (Kerry), M Murphy (Clare); G McGrath (Tipperary), M Quish (Limerick); P Spillane, M Sheehy, G Power (Kerry); J Barry-Murphy (Cork), S Walsh (Kerry), J Hennessy (Waterford) Subs: J O'Shea (Kerry) for Quish; G O'Driscoll (Kerry) for Spillane; D Moran (Kerry) for Hennessy.

Ennis, March 17, 1981
Munster 3-10; Connacht 1-9

Munster: C Nelligan; J Deenihan, J O'Keeffe (Kerry), K Kehilly (Cork), P O Se, T Kennelly, D Moran; S Walsh, J O'Shea; G Power (Kerry), D Allen (Cork), P Spillane, M Sheehy, E Liston, J Egan (Kerry).

All-Ireland Club Championship Medals: 1
Croke Park, March 26 1978

Thomond College (Limerick) 2-14; St John's (Antrim) 1-3
Thomond College: L Murphy; M Heuston, S O'Shea, E Mahon; M Spillane, B McSweeney, M Connolly; T Harkin, B Talty; J Dunne, R Bell, D Smyth; M Kilcoyne, P Spillane (capt), J O'Connell.